BusinessObjects™ XI Release 2 For Dummies®

Cheat Sheet

SO-ARK-571

InfoView Toolbar

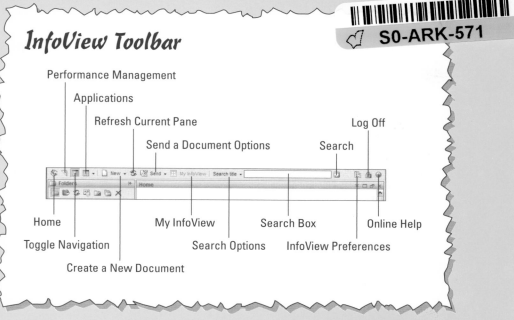

- Performance Management
- Applications
- Refresh Current Pane
- Send a Document Options
- Log Off
- Search
- Home
- My InfoView
- Search Box
- Online Help
- Toggle Navigation
- Search Options
- InfoView Preferences
- Create a New Document

Java Report Panel Toolbar — Web1

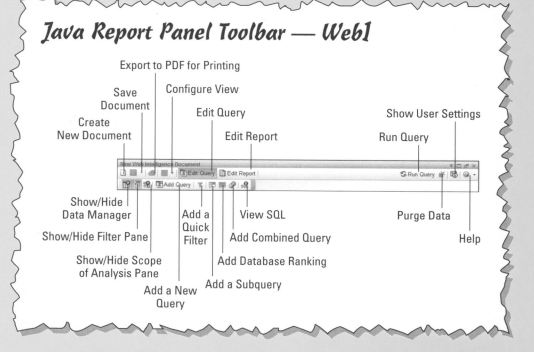

- Export to PDF for Printing
- Save Document
- Configure View
- Create New Document
- Edit Query
- Edit Report
- Show User Settings
- Run Query
- Show/Hide Data Manager
- View SQL
- Purge Data
- Show/Hide Filter Pane
- Add a Quick Filter
- Add Combined Query
- Help
- Show/Hide Scope of Analysis Pane
- Add Database Ranking
- Add a New Query
- Add a Subquery

BusinessObjects™ XI Release 2 For Dummies®

Desktop Intelligence Standard Toolbar

Find Again Reports Manager

Print Paste Edit Data Provider

Open Cut Delete Redo Slice and Dice

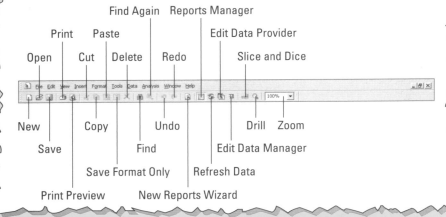

New Copy Undo Drill Zoom

Save Find Edit Data Manager

Save Format Only Refresh Data

Print Preview New Reports Wizard

Query Report Panel — Desk1

Default Scope of Analysis

Show/Hide Object Pane Manage Sorts

Wrap Result Objects User Objects

Sort Online Help

Simple Quick Filter Combine Queries

Show/Hide Description Pane View SQL

Scope of Analysis

Wiley, the Wiley Publishing logo, For Dummies, the Dummies Man logo, the For Dummies Bestselling Book Series logo and all related trade dress are trademarks or registered trademarks of John Wiley & Sons, Inc. and/or its affiliates. All other trademarks are property of their respective owners. Copyright © 2008 Wiley Publishing, Inc. All rights reserved. Item 8112-6. For more information about Wiley Publishing, call 1-800-762-2974.

For Dummies: Bestselling Book Series for Beginners

BusinessObjects™ XI Release 2

FOR DUMMIES®

by Derek Torres,
Stuart Mudie,
and Julie Albaret

WILEY

Wiley Publishing, Inc.

BusinessObjects™ XI Release 2 For Dummies®

Published by
Wiley Publishing, Inc.
111 River Street
Hoboken, NJ 07030-5774

www.wiley.com

Copyright © 2008 by Wiley Publishing, Inc., Indianapolis, Indiana

Published by Wiley Publishing, Inc., Indianapolis, Indiana

Published simultaneously in Canada

No part of this publication may be reproduced, stored in a retrieval system or transmitted in any form or by any means, electronic, mechanical, photocopying, recording, scanning or otherwise, except as permitted under Sections 107 or 108 of the 1976 United States Copyright Act, without either the prior written permission of the Publisher, or authorization through payment of the appropriate per-copy fee to the Copyright Clearance Center, 222 Rosewood Drive, Danvers, MA 01923, (978) 750-8400, fax (978) 646-8600. Requests to the Publisher for permission should be addressed to the Legal Department, Wiley Publishing, Inc., 10475 Crosspoint Blvd., Indianapolis, IN 46256, (317) 572-3447, fax (317) 572-4355, or online at http://www.wiley.com/go/permissions.

Trademarks: Wiley, the Wiley Publishing logo, For Dummies, the Dummies Man logo, A Reference for the Rest of Us!, The Dummies Way, Dummies Daily, The Fun and Easy Way, Dummies.com, and related trade dress are trademarks or registered trademarks of John Wiley & Sons, Inc. and/or its affiliates in the United States and other countries, and may not be used without written permission. BusinessObjects is a trademark of Business Objects SA. All other trademarks are the property of their respective owners. Wiley Publishing, Inc., is not associated with any product or vendor mentioned in this book.

For general information on our other products and services, please contact our Customer Care Department within the U.S. at 800-762-2974, outside the U.S. at 317-572-3993, or fax 317-572-4002.

For technical support, please visit www.wiley.com/techsupport.

Wiley also publishes its books in a variety of electronic formats. Some content that appears in print may not be available in electronic books.

Library of Congress Control Number: 2008925779

ISBN: 978-0-470-18112-6

Manufactured in the United States of America

10 9 8 7 6 5 4 3 2 1

WILEY

About the Authors

Derek Torres is a technical communicator and author. He spent several years writing documentation for Business Objects at its headquarters in Paris, France. He has also authored or coauthored several titles, including *The Unofficial Guide to Windows XP*, *The Unofficial Guide to Windows Vista*, and *The Windows Vista Ultimate Bible* (Wiley Publishing, Inc). He is currently working on his first novel. He can be reached at www.bofordummies.com.

Stuart Mudie is a Scot living in Paris, France. A professional communicator since 1995, he has worked with numerous companies in the IT and Telecommunications sectors, including three years at Business Objects headquarters in Paris. He is coauthor of *The Unofficial Guide to Windows Vista* (Wiley Publishing), a part-time lyricist, and can be found on the Web at www.stuartmudie.com.

Julie Albaret is a Business Intelligence consultant. She has worked in the BI field for over ten years, taking part in BI projects and studies for many companies. She spent six years working for Business Objects, including three years as a Performance Management specialist. She worked first as a sales consultant in Paris, then in Bangalore (India) as a software testing project manager, before returning to the company's Paris headquarters to work for two years as a Program Manager for Web Intelligence.

Dedications

To my late father

I regret that you didn't make it to see the book come out.

Derek Torres

To Ellie and Justine, with love

Stuart Mudie

Authors' Acknowledgments

Derek Torres: I want to thank my partners in crime, Stuart Mudie, Julie Albaret, and Patrick Albaret. It was a great team effort to pull this one together. I'd also like to thank our Executive Editor, Greg Croy, for his patience — we probably made him endure far more than he anticipated when he signed on for this project! I'd also like to thank our agent Lynn Haller for her hard work in selling this title. Thanks to everyone at Wiley past and present, including our Project Editor, Rebecca Senninger, and Jody Lefevere. Thanks to my friends and associates, past and present, at Business Objects. Thanks finally to my family for lending me to my laptop and publisher.

Stuart Mudie: Thanks to Justine and Ellie, for everything; my parents Marion and Bill Mudie, for encouraging me to dream, and then — most importantly — to follow those dreams; my brother Craig and his wife Leona, for giving me an excuse to break off from the writing of this book to be best man at their wedding; my co-authors Derek Torres and Julie Albaret, for their friendship over the years, and for joining me on this journey; Alan Daifuku, for hiring me to work at Business Objects in the first place, and for bringing me to live in France; my agent, Lynn Haller, for her hard work and dedication; our outstanding technical editor Patrick Albaret, for making everything clear; our Acquisitions Editor Greg Croy and our Project Editor Rebecca Senninger, for keeping us on the right track; and all the other fine folks at Wiley.

Julie Albaret: Thanks to Patrick, Stuart, and Derek for bringing me on this rich adventure; my family for their support and encouragement; my school EISTI friends and my coworkers at SQLI, Business Objects and Advanced-Schema, with whom I share the same passion and from whom I learnt and am still learning so much.

Publisher's Acknowledgments

We're proud of this book; please send us your comments through our online registration form located at www.dummies.com/register/.

Some of the people who helped bring this book to market include the following:

Acquisitions and Editorial

Project Editor: Rebecca Senninger

Executive Editor: Greg Croy

Senior Copy Editor: Barry Childs-Helton

Technical Editor: Patrick Albaret

Editorial Manager: Leah Cameron

Editorial Assistant: Amanda Foxworth

Sr. Editorial Assistant: Cherie Case

Cartoons: Rich Tennant
   (www.the5thwave.com)

Composition Services

Project Coordinator: Kristie Rees

Layout and Graphics: Stacie Brooks, Reuben W. Davis, Alissa D. Ellet, Brooke Graczyk, Melissa K. Jester

Proofreaders: Jessica Kramer, Christine Sabooni

Indexer: Lynnzee Elze

Special Help

Teresa Artman

Publishing and Editorial for Technology Dummies

Richard Swadley, Vice President and Executive Group Publisher

Andy Cummings, Vice President and Publisher

Mary Bednarek, Executive Acquisitions Director

Mary C. Corder, Editorial Director

Publishing for Consumer Dummies

Diane Graves Steele, Vice President and Publisher

Joyce Pepple, Acquisitions Director

Composition Services

Gerry Fahey, Vice President of Production Services

Debbie Stailey, Director of Composition Services

Contents at a Glance

Table of Contents

Introduction

*B*usinessObjects XI Release 2 is an industry-leading suite of tools for reporting, query-and-analysis, performance management, and information management. The tools that make up the suite allow you to access, format, and share data, as well as analyze the information this data contains and measure your organization's performance.

About This Book

For new users, business intelligence can seem dauntingly complex. *BusinessObjects XI Release 2 For Dummies* is an introductory-level book that helps you get started viewing and creating reports, building powerful queries on your organization's database, and measuring your company's performance — all without bombarding you with industry jargon and overly complex technical explanations.

The authors of this book have a combined experience of over 15 years of working with BusinessObjects tools; many of those years were spent working for the Business Objects company at its Paris headquarters. We combine and simplify — in a single book — what the official user documentation spreads across a large number of electronic manuals.

Foolish Assumptions

We wrote this book with certain assumptions in mind:

- ✔ You've recently encountered the BusinessObjects suite for the first time and are trying to get to grips with it, or that you want to take your knowledge of the system to the next level.

- ✔ You have a general familiarity with the personal computer, and you know your way around a basic user interface such as the one found in Microsoft Word — but at no time do we take it for granted that you are a technical expert.

✔ We also suspect that you probably won't read this book from cover to cover, at least not in one sitting (although there's nothing to stop you from doing so if you feel the urge). Rather, we expect you're more likely to jump from chapter to chapter, to dig around, and to use it as a quick reference when performing a task you haven't done in a while.

How This Book Is Organized

This book contains eight major parts. Each part consists of several chapters.

Part 1: Getting Started with BusinessObjects

Part I introduces you to some key Business Intelligence concepts. It goes on to look at the tools that make up the core of the BusinessObjects suite, and then walks you through installing them — both on a single computer and on a server — to the point where you're ready to roll your sleeves up, get stuck in, and use them. Finally, it takes a look at the Central Management Console (CMC), the Web-based administration tool you use to manage your BusinessObjects installation once everything is in place.

Part II: Universes

Universes are at the heart of any BusinessObjects system. Part II tells you what they are (hint: they're made of numbers, not stars), how to create one, and how to work with its different dimensions. Don't worry; it's less metaphysical than it sounds!

Part III: Using Your Desktop for Reporting

Part III explains how you can use the BusinessObjects desktop reporting tool to query, analyze data, and build reports. The desktop reporting tool is the actual BusinessObjects software installed on your computer, affectionately known to many users as *DeskI*. Think of it as the non-Web-based BusinessObjects.

Part IV: Making Web Intelligence Work for You

In Part IV, you find out all about InfoView, the Web-based portal that lets you work with your reports and access your organization's data online. For most users, InfoView is the "public face" of BusinessObjects — offering all the desktop reporting features over a Web browser and allowing you to create reports from anywhere with an Internet connection. If you're using BusinessObjects, you're more likely to work with InfoView than any other tool.

Part V: Keeping Track of How Your Organization Is Doing

In Part V, we cover how to use dashboards, analytics, and other tools and methodologies to measure your organization's performance against strategy.

Part VI: Getting the Best Possible Data with Data Marts

In Part VI, you discover what data marts are and how they fit into your BusinessObjects system.

Part VII: The Part of Tens

Part VII contains several short lists of useful information — including tips on how to prepare for a successful Business Objects integration, and a list of helpful resources beyond the pages of this book.

Part VIII: Appendixes

We close the book with our appendixes, which include an overview of Crystal Reports, BusinessObjects' companion reporting tool, and a glossary.

Icons Used in This Book

The Remember icon highlights useful information that you may want to come back to at a later point.

Technical Stuff delves a little further into the topic being discussed without necessarily being essential for your overall understanding. Think of it as an aside, something that we find interesting and hope you do too.

A tip is a simple word of wisdom, something useful that we've learned over our many years of working with Business Objects products.

The advice this icon designates can often save you from some serious headaches.

Where to Go from Here

Are you ready? Turn to Chapter 1 to get started creating and viewing both simple and complex reports — and making sense of the information hidden away in your organization's databases — using BusinessObjects XI Release 2.

Part I

Getting Started with BusinessObjects

The 5th Wave · By Rich Tennant

"They're pushing the company into a new, hip direction and asked if we would pimp the storage system."

In this part. . .

Undoubtedly, you're itching to get started. But as you probably know if you've taken the trouble to pick up this book in the first place, business intelligence can be a complex subject and it's worth taking the time to find your bearings a little before getting started with BusinessObjects

With this in mind, Chapter 1 gives you a general introduction to the world of business intelligence and some of its key concepts, before going on to look at how you can use BI applications and technologies to help you and your organization make better business decisions, and provides a brief overview of all the different products that make up the BusinessObjects XI Release 2 Enterprise product suite.

Part I then walks you through the steps involved in installing BusinessObjects, both on your local machine (Chapter 2) and, as is more typically the case, on a server (Chapter 3).

Chapter 4 introduces you to the workings of the Central Management Console (CMC), a Web-based system administration tool that lets you manage user profiles, security and access rights once your system is up and running.

Chapter 1

Business Intelligence and BusinessObjects XI Release 2: Working Hand in Hand

. . . .

In This Chapter

▶ Discovering how business intelligence can help your business

▶ Delving into BusinessObjects XI Release 2

. . . .

*B*efore you roll your sleeves up and get running with BusinessObjects XI Release 2, it's worth taking a moment to consider the bigger picture. At the beginning of this chapter, we give you an overview of business intelligence, and show how you can use business intelligence applications and technologies to help you make better business decisions.

If your business has been running Crystal Enterprise or BusinessObjects, you're probably faced with having to upgrade — specifically, to BusinessObjects XI. If so, welcome to some enhanced capabilities. If not — if you're just starting out with Business Objects XI — welcome to a whole new business universe. The last half of this chapter provides an overview of the different components that make up the BusinessObjects XI Release 2 Enterprise product suite — and offers some pointers on finding the right tools for the job — both for the migration and the projects to follow.

Fitting Business Intelligence into Your Business

Business intelligence (BI) is a business management term for the tools and methodologies used to collect, provide access to, and analyze data (which, in a typical organization, usually means information about a firm's operations such as details of sales, production, or human resources).

Life before business intelligence

In the beginning was the data, and the data was hidden away somewhere deep in the bowels of the corporate databases where only an elite of highly trained users were able to reach it.

If you needed access to any of this data to do your job effectively, the only way to get at it was to beg one of those highly trained elite users for help. But when your query finally made its way to the top of Mr. Elite User's in-tray, often several months later, the information that trickled down to you in the form of a spreadsheet or even a printed report would be horrendously out-of-date. As for whether Mr. Elite User was likely to understand your business requirements in the first place and so avoid supplying you with wrong (or at best irrelevant) information. . . well, you're better off not even going there.

"Timely? Pertinent? I'm sorry, we don't do those. Can I interest you in these global sales figures from the first quarter of last year instead?"

Business intelligence lets you keep track of what's going on in your company. It provides you with timely and pertinent insight so you can measure your performance against your company's established goals, and take action at a time when it is still possible for you to influence the outcome. Best of all, it lets you do it all yourself, rather than having to depend on IT professionals to provide you with the data you need at a time that suits their schedule.

Put simply, BI lets you make better business decisions because it gives you access to the right information at the right time.

BusinessObjects XI Release 2 has four main functional areas, which allow you to track, understand, and manage your business:

- ✔ **Reporting:** Reporting, as its name suggests, enables you to format and deliver information to large audiences both inside and outside your organization in the form of reports.

- ✔ **Query and analysis:** Query and analysis tools provide you with a means of interacting with business information (by performing your own ad hoc queries) without having to understand the often complex data that lies underneath this information.

- ✔ **Performance management:** Performance management tools let you keep track of and analyze key performance indicators and goals using Dashboards, Scorecards, and Analytics.

- ✔ **Data integration:** Data integration lets you extract information from a range of sources and transform it so that it becomes usable by your other BI tools, data marts, and data warehouses.

A tale of two products

BusinessObjects XI has illustrious ancestors: Both Crystal Enterprise and Business Objects products brought efficient, interactive reporting to databases — and a host of other tools that helped lay the foundation for what we now call business intelligence. Then their powers combined: Business Objects and Crystal Enterprise merged in late 2003 — and BusinessObjects XI fully integrated the features of *both* companies' products.

BusinessObjects XI Release 2 has been around since 2005; about a year and a half later, an update appeared: BusinessObjects XI Release 2 Productivity Pack. That's the subject of this book. And a formidable — though sometimes confusing — toolbox it is.

Taking a Closer Look at BusinessObjects XI Release 2 Enterprise

In this section, we take a look at some of the different members of the BusinessObjects XI Release 2 Enterprise family.

At first glance, BusinessObjects seems to offer a confusing range of tools that do the same job. But at least for the immediate future, there's a good reason for the overlap in product functionality: Crystal Enterprise and BusinessObjects were originally different products. Check out the sidebar "A tale of two products" to find out more.

Tools for migrating from previous installations

Which tools you'll need for the migration depends mainly on whether you're coming from a BusinessObjects or Crystal environment. Be patient, and follow the ancient wisdom that says *Get the right tool (or, in this case, wizard) for the job.*

Import Wizard

The Import Wizard (see Figure 1-1) is a locally installed Windows application used by administrators to import user accounts, groups, reports, and folders from Crystal Enterprise, BusinessObjects, or Crystal Info into BusinessObjects XI Release 2 Enterprise. You can also use the wizard to move a test deployment of BusinessObjects XI to a production environment.

In BusinessObjects XI Release 2, the Import Wizard supports upgrades from these existing implementations:

- ✓ BusinessObjects 5.1.4 and above
- ✓ BusinessObjects 6.0, 6.1, and 6.5
- ✓ Crystal Enterprise 8.5, 9, and 10
- ✓ Application Foundation 6.1.b, 6.1.3, and 6.5.1
- ✓ BusinessObjects XI (if you haven't installed the Productivity Pack until now)

You can also administrate remote servers from the Import Wizard.

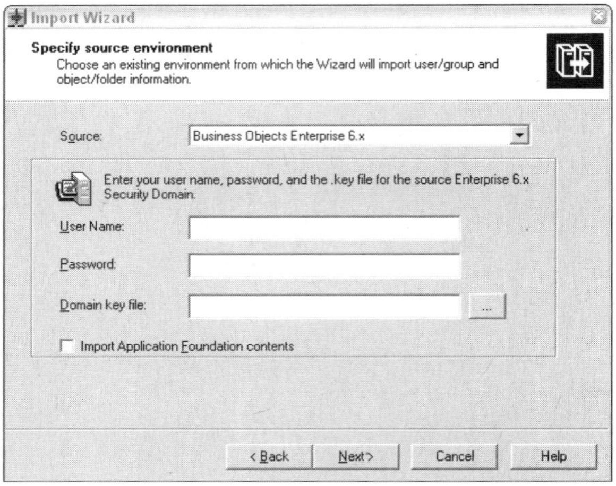

Figure 1-1:
Importing user/group and object/folder information from a previous version of Business-Objects using the Import Wizard.

Repository Migration Wizard

The Repository Migration Wizard has a much more specific use than the Import Wizard: It's used solely to migrate a Report Design Repository from previous versions of Crystal Enterprise Server into the BusinessObjects XI Release 2 repository.

The *repository* is the database server that stores all the information about your BusinessObjects system and its users.

Data Source Migration Wizard

The Data Source Migration Wizard lets you migrate reports based on Crystal queries, dictionaries, and InfoViews to BusinessObjects Enterprise XI.

The Data Source Migration Wizard has a slightly misleading name, because you can use it to migrate *two* types of objects: data sources and reports. It works by converting the data source for each report into an object that can be used in BusinessObjects Enterprise, and then resetting the report's data-source location so it points to the new object.

Report Conversion Tool

Okay, the Report Conversion Tool is not (strictly speaking) a migration tool — but you can use it to convert Desktop Intelligence reports to the Web Intelligence format — and then publish the converted reports — so it does serve as a bridge between technologies. It can convert the following types of report to the Web Intelligence XI Release 2 (.wid) format:

- **Legacy BusinessObjects reports** (.rep) previously migrated to the Desktop Intelligence (.rep) format using the Import Wizard.

- **Desktop Intelligence reports** created directly in the Desktop Intelligence tool.

The Report Conversion Tool isn't a panacea. It can't convert all Desktop Intelligence reports, nor all Desktop Intelligence features. Exactly what gets converted depends on the features of the original report; some features prevent the report from being converted at all; other features may be modified or removed during the conversion process.

You can also use the Report Conversion Tool to open reports from previous versions of the BusinessObjects desktop-reporting tool directly in Desktop Intelligence. However, to be sure that you take full advantage of the product's security features, you're better off using the Import Wizard to import your legacy reports.

All it takes to design a universe

As we explain in Part III, the concept of a *universe* (in effect, a collection of business objects) lies at the heart of any BusinessObjects XI Release 2 installation. When it comes to building and managing these universes, you have a couple of different tools at your disposal.

Designer

Business Objects Designer is the tool that enables BusinessObjects XI users to create universes (see Figure 1-2).

The person who creates business universes is called (believe it or not) a *universe designer*. Depending on the situation at your company, this person may be the database administrator, a programmer, a project manager, or even a report creator who has sufficient technical skills to create universes for other users.

Whatever the purpose of the larger universe may be, the purpose of a business universe is to let nontechnical users run queries against a database in order to create reports and analyze data. Its simple interface is designed to provide a business-focused front end to make the SQL structures in the database more easily understandable, using vocabulary that's familiar to business users.

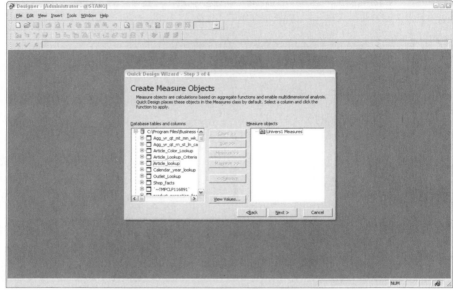

Figure 1-2:
Using the Quick Design Wizard in Designer to create a universe.

Universe Builder

Universe Builder is another tool that you use for — you guessed it — building business universes. How it differs from Designer mainly concerns whether or not your metadata source was compatible with BusinessObjects XI Release 2 at the time it was released. If it was, you're probably better off building your Universes with Designer. If not, use Universe Builder instead.

For more information on the specifics of Universe Designer, see Chapter 5.

BusinessObjects Desktop Intelligence

BusinessObjects Desktop Intelligence is a desktop reporting tool that allows you to analyze data, perform ad-hoc queries to fetch new data, and create new reports of your own. Now a feature of BusinessObjects XI, it was previously known as BusinessObjects — a stand-alone flagship product. It makes a seriously powerful desktop tool.

Using a desktop tool instead of a permanent network connection gives you a handy advantage by freeing up your IT resources as you use less bandwidth.

Part III explains the workings of BusinessObjects Desktop Intelligence in more detail.

BusinessObjects Web Intelligence

Sometimes, having to open a full-client application just isn't the most convenient way of working, especially if your machine isn't powerful enough for the job.

Fortunately, BusinessObjects also features a tool that makes it possible for you to perform a range of query and reporting tasks directly from a browser-based interface: BusinessObjects Web Intelligence.

Part IV looks in more detail at how Web Intelligence works.

Enterprise Performance Management

Although Desktop Intelligence and Web Intelligence are powerful tools in their own right, there may still come a time when you want to move on from the reports they let you build and take your use of the BusinessObjects XI suite to the next level.

Part V describes how you can use the suite's Performance Management tools to create more complex dashboards, metrics, and analytics that allow you to keep track of how your organization is doing.

Publishing Wizard

The Publishing Wizard lets you add new documents to BusinessObjects XI Release 2 Enterprise. You can assign object rights to specific BusinessObjects Enterprise folders — allowing you to control who publishes what, and where (within the company, anyway).

Although the Publishing Wizard is a Windows application, you can use it to publish reports to servers running on both Windows or Unix.

InfoView

Consider InfoView your company's business intelligence portal. As a browser-based tool, InfoView is the main interface for most users who work with objects in BusinessObjects XI Release 2. You can use InfoView to view, manage, and work with your organization's different business-intelligence objects — including Crystal reports, Web Intelligence documents, and Desktop Intelligence documents, as well as the suite's Enterprise Performance Management tools.

Part IV looks at InfoView in more detail.

Central Management Console

The Central Management Console (CMC), shown in Figure 1-3, is the Web interface that lets you or your administrator control and make best use of your BusinessObjects deployment. It enables you to carry out such tasks as setting up user roles, server administration, managing passwords, and more.

Chapter 4 examines this tool more closely.

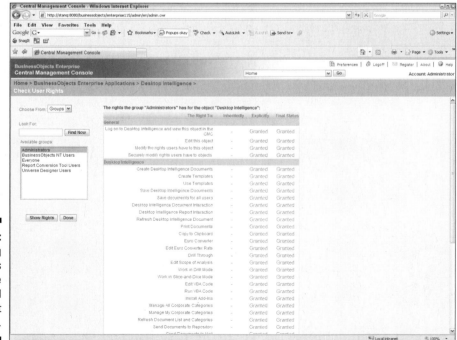

Figure 1-3: Managing user rights with the Central Management Console.

Chapter 2

Deploying on a Single Computer

● ●

In This Chapter

▶ Checking the minimum requirements

▶ Installing BusinessObjects Enterprise on your computer

● ●

*T*ypically (as you might suspect), BusinessObjects XI Release 2 Enterprise is not to be found on just any old home computer. Most end users interact with the tools that make up this product suite over the Web, using InfoView. However, the following client tools are also available as stand-alone applications you can install on your local PC:

- **BusinessObjects Designer:** Enables you to create Universes (which requires fewer superpowers than you may think).

- **Desktop Intelligence:** Allows you to analyze data, perform ad-hoc queries to fetch new data, and create reports. Often referred to as *DeskI*.

- **Publishing Wizard:** Makes it easier for you to add new documents to BusinessObjects XI Release 2 Enterprise.

- **Business Views Manager:** A tool from the Crystal Reports world that lets you build *Business Views* — objects that give report designers and end users access to specific types of business information.

- **Import Wizard:** Used by administrators to import user accounts, groups, reports, and folders from Crystal Enterprise, BusinessObjects, or Crystal Info into BusinessObjects XI Release 2 Enterprise.

- **Report Conversion Tool:** Lets you convert Deski reports to the Web Intelligence (WebI) format, and then publish them.

- **SDKs:** Used by developers to integrate Business Objects products into other applications.

In this chapter, we show you how to install these applications locally if you're responsible for developing applications or migrating data, or if you manage BusinessObjects Enterprise content.

Making Sure You're Ready

To run BusinessObjects XI R2 — even if all you want to do is install the client software on your local PC — you need a pretty decent (and recent) machine.

Forget about trying to put BusinessObjects XI R2 on that old laptop that the IT department has had hanging around for the last five years; it just won't be powerful enough.

To run BusinessObjects Enterprise XI R2 effectively, your computer must meet the following minimum hardware requirements:

- ✔ Pentium III 700 MHz
- ✔ 1GB of RAM
- ✔ 5GB hard-drive space
- ✔ CD-ROM drive (unless you are installing directly from a network)

In addition, you must be running one of the following operating systems:

Windows 2000 SP4 Professional	Windows XP SP1 Professional
Windows XP SP2 Professional	Windows 2000 SP4 Advanced Server
Windows 2000 SP4 Datacenter Server	Windows 2000 SP4 Server
Windows Server 2003 Datacenter Edition	Windows Server 2003 Enterprise Edition
Windows Server 2003 Standard Edition	Windows Server 2003 Web Edition
Windows Server 2003 SP1 Datacenter Edition	Windows Server 2003 SP1 Enterprise Edition
Windows Server 2003 SP1 Standard Edition	Windows Server 2003 SP1 Web Edition

We recommend not running BusinessObjects XI R2 with Windows Vista. You might get BusinessObjects XI R2 to run on Vista, but Business Objects won't give you any help if you run into problems.

Installing BusinessObjects Enterprise on Your Computer

After you determine that your computer is up to the task, you are ready to get down to the nitty-gritty of actually installing the product. Sit back, hold tight, and follow these steps:

1. **Insert the installation CD (or DVD) in your CD-ROM drive (or browse to the location on your network where the installation files are stored, and then click the** Setup.exe **file).**

   The Installation Wizard runs automatically; you're given a choice of languages (a quite impressive 12 at the time of writing) in which to install the product, and links to other relevant reading material (as shown in Figure 2-1).

2. **(Optional) Choose a language from the menu on the left.**

   You are then presented with links to a whole host of reading material, including the Installation Guide and the Release Notes, the Education and Consulting pages on the Business Objects Web site, and the Technical Support Web site.

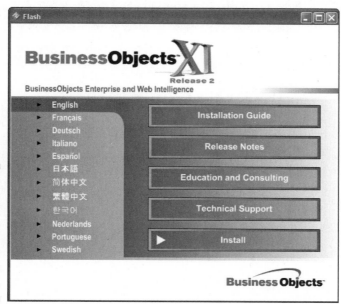

Figure 2-1:
Installation
Wizard
launch
screen, with
a choice of
languages
and links.

3. **Click Install.**

   You are greeted with a Welcome Screen that invites you to exit all Windows programs you may have running before continuing with Setup.

4. **When you've closed all Windows programs, click Next.**

   The License Agreement appears.

5. **Read the License Agreement (you *do* read those things, don't you?), select the I Accept the License Agreement option button, and then click Next.**

   On the following screen, you're presented with a choice between performing a Client Installation and a Server Installation, as shown in Figure 2-2.

   Because you're installing BusinessObjects on your computer, the Client Installation, which installs Designer, Desktop Intelligence, Publishing Wizard, Business Views Manager, Import Wizard, Report Conversation Tools, and SDKs, is what you're interested in.

6. **Select the Perform Client Installation option button, and then click Next.**

   The next screen invites you to specify the folder where you want to install the software, as shown in Figure 2-3.

7. **Choose to accept the default option (**`C:\Program Files\Business Objects\`**) or click the Browse button to select an existing directory or create a new one. In either case, click Next when you're done.**

Figure 2-2:
Make your choice between a Client Installation and a Server Installation.

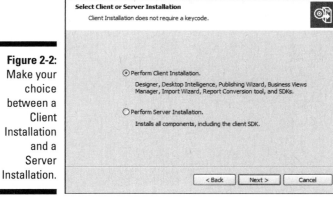

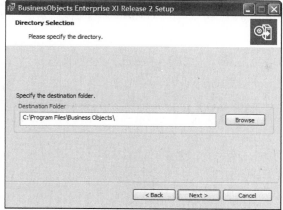

Figure 2-3:
Specify the destination folder where you want to install the software.

The final screen offers you one last chance to go back and change any of the details, as shown in Figure 2-4; or, more precisely, a chance to click the Cancel button and start over from scratch! (If you're a Business Objects User Interface designer, a summary of what those details are would have been nice to see at this point!)

8. **If you can remember what options you selected and you're completely certain they correspond to what you want to do, click Next.**

Now you can sit back while the software is installed. When everything is ready, the final screen of the installation wizard informs you that the installation is complete. You're good to go!

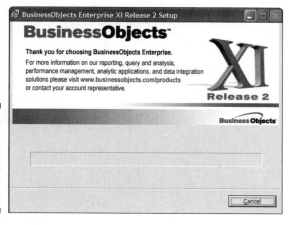

Figure 2-4:
A Business-Objects XI R2 installation in progress.

Chapter 3

Performing a Server Installation

- -

In This Chapter

▶ Making sure you're ready

▶ Installing BusinessObjects Enterprise on your server

- -

Although (as Chapter 2 describes) you *can* install some of the client tools that make up the BusinessObjects XI Release 2 Enterprise product suite on your local PC, the fact is, you're far more likely to install the suite on a server. Then you can allow several, several dozen, or several hundred users to connect to these tools remotely over the Web.

This chapter describes how you perform such an installation — first by ensuring that you have everything in place before you start, and then by taking you through each of the steps involved.

Making Sure You're Ready

Before you go anywhere near that shiny installation DVD, you must first examine the system you already have in place: Ensure that it meets the minimum requirements for running a server-based installation of the BusinessObects XI R2 product suite.

Minimum requirements

To run BusinessObjects Enterprise XI R2 effectively, your server must meet the following minimum hardware requirements:

- ✔ Pentium III 700 MHz

- ✔ 1GB of RAM

- ✔ 5GB hard-drive space (plus 1.5GB for the Performance Management feature)

- ✔ CD-ROM drive (unless you're installing directly from a network)

You must also be running one of the following operating systems.

Windows 2000 SP4 Advanced Server	Windows 2000 SP4 Datacenter Server
Windows 2000 SP4 Server	Windows Server 2003 Datacenter Edition
Windows Server 2003 Enterprise Edition	Windows Server 2003 Standard Edition
Windows Server 2003 Web Edition	Windows Server 2003 SP1 Datacenter Edition
Windows Server 2003 SP1 Enterprise Edition	Windows Server 2003 SP1 Standard Edition
Windows Server 2003 SP1 Web Edition	AIX 5.2
AIX 5.3	HP-UX 11.11 (PA-RISC)
HP-UX 11.23 (PA-RISC)	Solaris 8 for SPARC
Solaris 9 for SPARC	Solaris 10 for SPARC
Red Hat 4.0 Advanced Server for x86	Red Hat 4.0 Enterprise Server for x86
SuSE Linux 9.0 Enterprise Server for x86	

The computer you're setting up as your server needs to have both an application-server program and compatible database software that can store information about the system and its users. Ideally, these should be in place *before* you start installing the BusinessObjects software, but you can always install them as part of the BusinessObjects installation process. The upcoming sections describe these two requirements in more detail.

Choosing an application server

The machine on which you plan to install and run BusinessObjects XI R2 must have an application-server program up and running before you do the installation. Fortunately, BusinessObjects supports a range of application servers; while you're deciding which one to use, take a good look at your current environment:

- Note which application servers you currently have in place.
- If you intend to develop custom applications, decide which Web-development environment you want to use.

If you don't have an application server already in place on your server computer, BusinessObjects comes with one on your installation CD: Tomcat, which you can install along with BusinessObjects. Indeed, when we walk you through the installation process later in this chapter, we assume you're doing just that.

The first question you need to address is which *development environment* — the programming language or languages you intend to use to develop your custom Web applications — you want to work in.

As it happens, the choice is pretty simple: Active Server Pages (ASP) or its more recent successor ASP.NET or JavaServer Pages (JSP). Be aware that whichever option you go for also affects, or is influenced by, your choice of application servers (the machine hosting your Web applications):

✔ If you want to develop your custom applications using ASP or ASP.NET, you must use Microsoft Internet Information Server (IIS).

✔ If you want to develop your custom applications using JSP, you can choose any of the supported application servers shown in Table 3-1. (Tomcat is one of those.)

Examining the relative merits of the ASP and JSP environments is beyond the scope of this book. A simple Web search will reveal scores of sites that debate the benefits of one or the other; if you don't have your own opinion on the matter already, we're pretty sure you will before long. Nonetheless, it's worth noting that certain features — including support for DHTML in Web Intelligence, and Enterprise Performance Management capabilities — are only available in the JSP version.

Table 3-1	Supported JSP Application Servers
Application Server	*Java Development Kit (JDK)*
OAS 10G Rel.2 (10.1.2)	1.4.2_x
SAP WAS 6.40 SP11	1.4.2_x
Tomcat 5.0.27	1.4.2_08+
WebLogic 8.1 SP4	1.4.2_x
WebSphere 5.1.0.4	1.4.1_x
WebSphere 5.1.1.0	1.4.2_x
WebSphere 6.0.0.1	1.4.2_x

> ## What's in a name?
>
> In prior releases of BusinessObjects (before BusinessObjects XI), the database at the heart of the system was called the repository, and when Crystal Enterprise was a stand-alone product, the Central Management Server used to be known as the Crystal Management Server or Automated Process Scheduler (APS).

Database software: Repository of all knowledge . . .

. . . at least that's the way BusinessObjects XI R2 sees the database software it uses to store information about the system and its users. You have to have a database program installed on your computer before you install BusinessObjects. The Central Management Server (CMS) feature of BusinessObjects interacts with this database program, which serves as the CMS database; Chapter 4 details how you can access and manage it.

BusinessObjects also includes Enterprise Auditor, a tool that enables you to monitor and record key information about the usage of your BusinessObjects deployment. If you want to use it, however, you need to have yet another database — this one specifically dedicated to Auditor — in place.

BusinessObjects XI R2 supports a range of databases, including Microsoft SQL Server 2000 SP3, Microsoft SQL Server 7.0 SP4, Oracle9.2, Oracle10.1, IBM DB2, Sybase ASE, Sybase AS IQ, and NCR Teradata. For details of exactly what is currently supported, we suggest you consult the Business Objects Web site: `www.businessobjects.com/pdf/products/xi/boe_xi_supported_platforms.pdf`. Be warned: It's a pretty long and complicated list!

If you don't have a database-server program already in place on your server computer, Business Objects helps you out: You can install MySQL as part of the BusinessObjects XI R2 installation process.

Installing BusinessObjects XI R2 on Your Server

After you have all the prerequisites in place for installing BusinessObjects XI R2, you're ready to get down to the installation process proper. Follow these steps to do so:

1. **Insert the installation CD (or DVD) in your CD-ROM drive or browse to the location on your network where the installation files are stored; then click** Setup.exe.

   The Installation Wizard runs automatically; you're given a choice of languages in which to install the product (a quite impressive 12 at the time of writing), as shown in Figure 3-1.

2. **(Optional) Choose a language from the menu on the left.**

   You're presented with links to a whole host of reading material, including the Installation Guide and the Release Notes, the Education and Consulting pages on the Business Objects Web site, and the Technical Support Web site.

3. **Click Install to get the installation process under way.**

   A Welcome Screen appears, inviting you to exit all Windows programs you may have running before continuing with Setup.

4. **Close all Windows programs, and then click Next.**

5. **Read the License Agreement, click the I Accept the License Agreement option button, and then click Next.**

   You're presented with a choice between performing a Client Installation and a Server Installation, as shown in Figure 3-2.

   Because you're installing BusinessObjects on a server, what you want is (unsurprisingly) the Server Installation. It installs all components, including the client SDK.

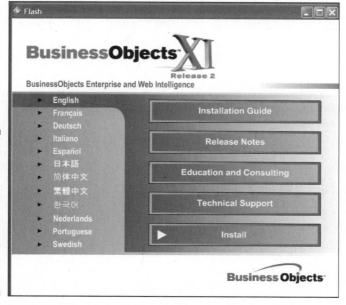

Figure 3-1:
The Installation Wizard launch screen offers a choice of languages and links.

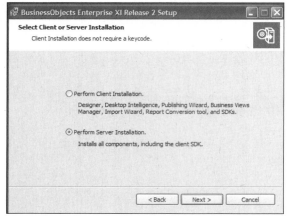

Figure 3-2:
Choose
Server
Installation.

6. **Select the Perform Server Installation option button, and then click Next.**

   You're asked to enter your user information (full name and organization) and the product keycode, as shown in Figure 3-3.

7. **Enter your full name, organization, and product keycode. Choose whether to install Performance Management. Click Next.**

   Performance Management is a series of more advanced tools, which we examine more closely in Part V, that you can use to create dashboards, metrics, and analytics to track how your organization is performing.

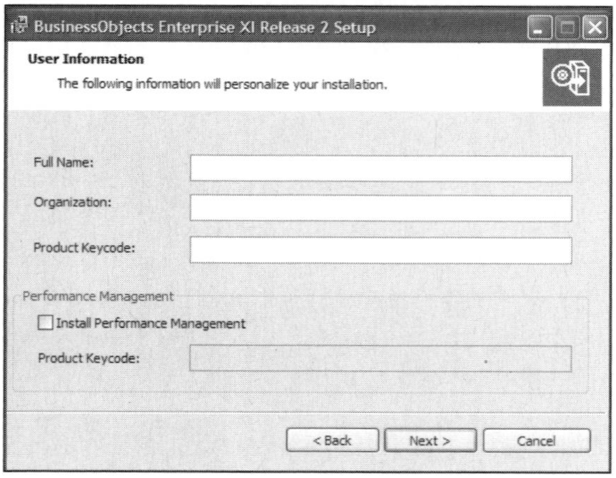

Figure 3-3:
Personalize
your
installation
on the User
Information
screen.

Only the product keycode is mandatory. Ask your BusinessObjects administrator for it if you don't know what your keycode is.

Now you're ready to specify the folder into which you want to install the software, as shown in Figure 3-4.

Figure 3-4: Specify the destination folder where you want to install the software.

8. **Choose to accept the default option (**`C:\Program Files\Business Objects\`**); click Browse if you want to select an existing directory (or you can create a new one). Click Next when you're done.**

9. **Choose the type of installation you want to perform by checking the appropriate check box, and then click Next.**

   Figure 3-5 shows these available options:

   - *New:* Installs a standard set of both client and server components from the BusinessObjects XI R2 suite.

     If you choose this option, you must also specify whether you intend to use an existing database server, or install a MySQL database server as part of the installation process.

   - *Expand:* Lets you add additional components to an existing installation.

   - *Custom:* Lets you specify exactly which components you want to install, as shown in Figure 3-6.

   For the purposes of these steps, choose to perform a New installation, and to install MySQL as your database server at the same time.

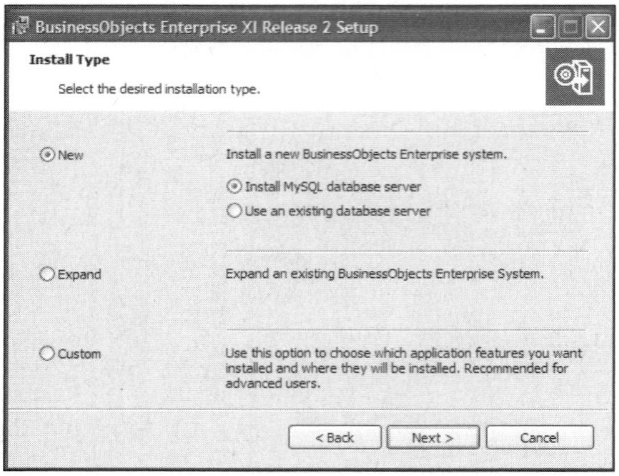

Figure 3-5:
Choose which type of installation you want to perform: New, Expand, or Custom.

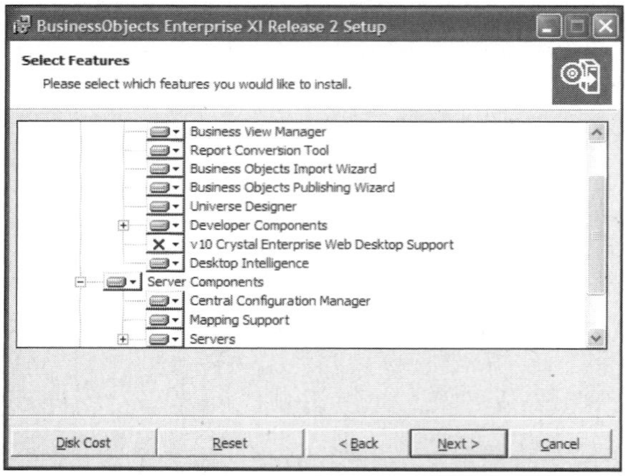

Figure 3-6:
In a Custom installation, specify exactly which components you want to install.

If you install MySQL as your database server, the next screen asks you to configure the MySQL installation, as shown in Figure 3-7.

10. Enter the port number, and then enter your choice of passwords for the root account and CMS user account. Click Next.

Enter the port number either by selecting the number suggested by default, or by entering whichever port number your organization has configured for the MySQL installation.

At this point, you're ready to install the Java and/or .NET Web *component adaptors*; these programs connect your BusinessObjects installation to your application server (see Figure 3-8). See the section "Choosing an application server," earlier in this chapter, for more information.

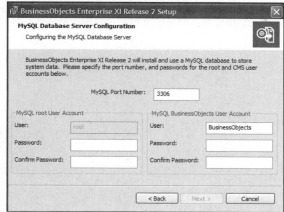

Figure 3-7:
Configure
your MySQL
installation.

11. **Choose an application server to install: Check the appropriate check box and/or option button. Then click Next.**

You have these possible choices:

- A preinstalled Java application server

  This choice requires manual configuration outside the BusinessObjects installer.

- Tomcat

- Microsoft IIS ASP.NET

For the purposes of these steps, choose to install and configure Tomcat as part of the BusinessObjects installation process.

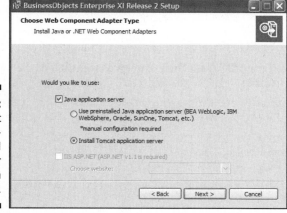

Figure 3-8:
Connect
Business-
Objects XI
R2 to your
application
server.

If you install the Tomcat application server, the next screen asks you to configure its installation, as shown in Figure 3-9.

12. **Enter the installation directory and the appropriate port numbers, then click Next.**

The general process looks like this:

a. *Specify the Tomcat installation directory.*

By default, this is `C:\Program Files\Business Objects\Tomcat`, but you can change the installation directory by clicking Browse and then browsing to a new location.

b. *Type the Connection, Shutdown, and Redirect port numbers.*

We recommend accepting the default port numbers proposed by the installer; for more information about what these ports do, consult the Tomcat documentation.

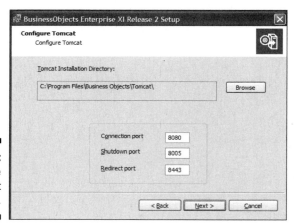

Figure 3-9:
Configure your Tomcat installation.

The final screen gives you one last opportunity to go back and change any of the details (or rather, to cancel the installation and start over); unfortunately, the installer doesn't provide you with a summary of just what those details are.

13. **If you're completely certain you've entered the correct information, click Next and sit back and wait while the software is installed.**

The final screen of the installation wizard (eventually) informs you once the installation is complete.

Chapter 4

Taking Control with the Central Management Console

*B*usinessObjects XI Release 2, as you may have noticed, provides a pretty complex suite of reporting, query and analysis, and performance-management tools. Such a broad range of products clearly has to cater to the needs of a variety of different user profiles, while at the same time handling security and access rights that become ever more complex as your system grows.

Fortunately, the suite comes with a tool designed to help you (or your system administrator) face up to all this complexity — straight from an easy-to-use Web interface. That tool is the Central Management Console (CMC), and this chapter takes a look at how it works.

Knowing Your Rights: The BusinessObjects Security Model

Before you dive straight in to the workings of the Central Management Console (CMC), you need a clear understanding of the BusinessObjects XI R2 security model and how it lets you manage what users can and cannot do.

Objects, groups, and users

Three key concepts you need to retain when thinking about the BusinessObjects security model are objects, groups, and users. Sure, these names may be familiar to you from other contexts, but it's still worth reviewing their usage in the BusinessObjects system:

- ✔ **Objects:** Objects lie at the heart of the BusinessObjects system. They gave their name not only to the product, but to the company itself.

    In BusinessObjects XI R2, objects can include reports, Web Intelligence documents, Microsoft Office files (Word, Excel, or PowerPoint), Adobe Acrobat PDFs, text files, hyperlinks, folders, and more.

    In the CMC, you manage objects in (surprise!) the Objects Management area.

- ✔ **Groups:** A *group* is a logical grouping of individuals who all require similar rights and permissions. Combining them in this way allows you to make any changes to their rights and permissions in one place instead of having to modify each user's account individually.

    Examples of groups could include specific roles (such as the group of people responsible for designing BusinessObjects universes) or particular departments or teams (such as managers in the Accounts Department).

- ✔ **Users:** A *user* is each individual person who needs to interact with the BusinessObjects system in some way.

How it all hangs together

How do these different elements combine in the BusinessObjects security model? It's quite simple. You assign rights to each item in the system — objects, users, and other features — which determine the individual actions that users can perform on each particular item. And that's it!

For example, if you want to allow managers in a certain team to access all the reports stored in a particular folder, you browse to the Rights tab for the folder in question, and then add the group to which these managers belong to the list of those who are allowed to access the folder.

Of course, it isn't *quite* as simple as that — there are different kinds of rights you can assign to items, for instance — but that's the basic idea.

Rights are set on objects and folders, not on the people who will access them. If you set the rights on the Rights tab of a specific group of managers, for example, then you are determining which groups can access *this group of managers* (taken as an object), not what this group of managers can access. This is an important distinction.

Discovering the Central Management Console

Okay, you know the theory (or at least some of it) and you're ready to get started and do some real work with the CMC. We show you how to launch the Central Management Console and give you a tour of the home page.

Launching the CMC

To launch the CMC, do the following:

1. **Choose All Programs➪BusinessObjects XI Release 2➪ BusinessObjects Enterprise➪BusinessObjects Enterprise Java Administration Launchpad.**

    We assume you're using the JSP version of BusinessObjects. If you're using ASP, replace BusinessObjects Enterprise Java Administration Launchpad with BusinessObjects Enterprise .NET Administration Launchpad.

    You can also access the CMC directly from your Web browser. If you're using the JSP version, simply type `http://Webserver:8080/ businessobjects/enterprise115/adminlaunch/launchpad.html` in the address bar of your browser, where *Webserver* is the name of the Web server machine. For the ASP version, type `http://Webserver/ businessobjects/Enterprise115/WebTools/adminlaunch/ default.aspx`.

    A new browser window opens (see Figure 4-1).

2. **Click the Launch the Central Management Console link.**

3. **Enter your User Name and Password, and then click Log On.**

    Provided your account has sufficient rights to access the Central Management Console (basically, if you have at least some administration rights), the CMC home page opens, and you're good to go.

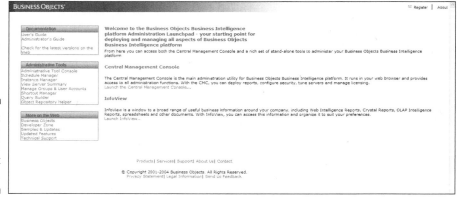

Figure 4-1:
Launching
the Central
Management
Console.

The CMC Home Page

Figure 4-2 shows the CMC Home Page. Take a good look. If you're going to be carrying out administration tasks in BusinessObjects — creating, organizing and removing folders, managing users and user groups, scheduling events, and more — this is where it all happens. As likely as not, you'll be seeing quite a bit of this page.

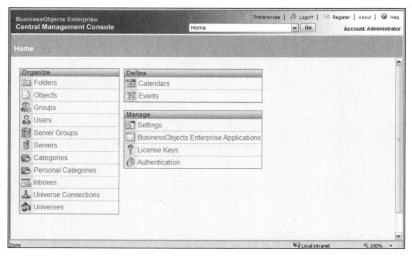

Figure 4-2:
The CMC
Home Page.

The CMC Home Page is broken down into three main areas:

✔ **Organize:** This area is where you interact with folders, objects, groups, users, servers, and so on, in a brave attempt to keep everything in order.

✔ **Define:** The Define area is where you set up scheduled events.

✔ **Manage:** The Manage area is where you handle the settings for the different BusinessObjects applications, license keys, and enable *trusted authentication* (users can log on once per session, rather than repeatedly whenever they open a new application).

The tasks you can perform from the CMC Home Page are legion, and we could fill this book on just that topic. Rather, we prefer to concentrate on managing users, and assigning them rights to the different objects that make up the whole system. Rest assured, that in itself is complex enough.

Managing Users

This section looks at some of the tasks involved in creating, managing, and deleting user accounts, and shows you how to access the tools that make up BusinessObjects XI Release 2 suite.

When you install the BusinessObjects system, the install process creates two user accounts by default:

✔ **Administrator:** The Administrator account belongs to two groups: Administrators and Everyone. An administrator can perform all tasks in each BusinessObjects application installed. By default, the Administrator account is not assigned a password, but quite clearly you should assign one straight away.

✔ **Guest:** The Guest account belongs to one group: Everyone. By default, the Guest account is not assigned a password.

Adding a new user account

When it comes to managing users, one of the most common tasks you may be required to carry out is to create a new user account — for example, when a new employee joins your organization.

To add a new account, follow these steps:

1. **Click the Users button on the CMC Home Page.**
2. **Click New User.**
3. **When asked to specify the authentication type, select Enterprise.**

   The New User page appears, as shown in Figure 4-3.
4. **Fill out all the relevant information for this account, including account name, full name, e-mail address, and description.**

   Note that only the account name is mandatory; all the other fields are optional.

When filling out the user details, you can also use the description area to include any extra information about the user or account you are creating.

5. Enter the password for the account and check the relevant password options:

- *Password never expires*: The password you set remains valid for as long as the account exists.

- *User must change password at next logon*: You set a password, which may well be the standard password used across your company for first-time access to all applications, and the user then changes this password to one of her own choice the first time she logs on.

- *User cannot change password*: You set the password, and that's it — the user doesn't get any say in the matter!

6. Select the connection type.

The type of BusinessObjects XI Release 2 license your organization has dictates which connection type you should use:

- *Concurrent User:* Choose this type if your license specifies a certain number of users who can connect at the same time.

- *Named User:* Choose this type if the user has an individual license in her own name.

7. Click OK.

The new user is added to the system, by default in the Everyone group.

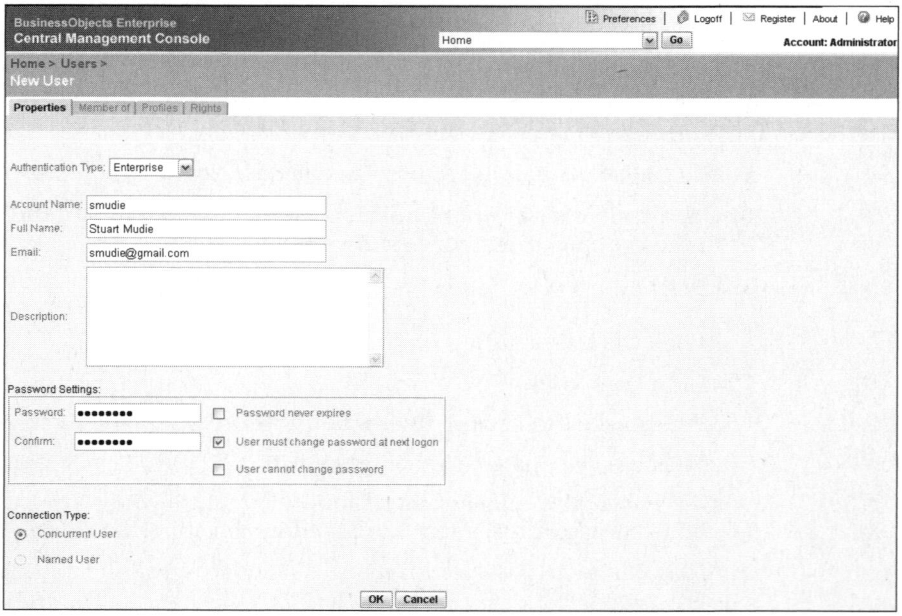

BusinessObjects Enterprise
Central Management Console

Preferences | Logoff | Register | About | Help

Home [ ] Go   Account: Administrator

Home > Users >
New User

Properties | Member of | Profiles | Rights |

Authentication Type: Enterprise [ ]

Account Name: smudie

Full Name: Stuart Mudie

Email: smudie@gmail.com

Description:

Password Settings:

Password: ●●●●●●●●   ☐ Password never expires

Confirm: ●●●●●●●●   ☑ User must change password at next logon

☐ User cannot change password

Connection Type:

⊙ Concurrent User

○ Named User

OK   Cancel

Figure 4-3:
Creating a
new user
account.

Adding users to groups

A user that does not belong to any groups, and therefore does not have any access rights, is not going to be very productive. This section describes how to add a user to one or more groups.

You can add users to groups when the user is first created, or at any other time as your needs evolve.

The CMC lets you add users to groups in one of two ways, each with a slight difference in focus:

- ✔ In the Users management area of the CMC, you can add one user to one or more groups.
- ✔ In the Groups management area of the CMC, you can add one or more users to one group.

Adding one user to one or more groups

To add one user to one or more groups, for instance when a new employee joins your company, follow these steps:

1. **Click the Users button on the CMC Home Page.**

2. **Under Account Name, click the name of the user whose group membership you want to change.**

3. **Click the Member Of tab.**

4. **Click the Member Of button to view the groups available for this user to join.**

5. **Select the group or groups you want the user to become a member of in the Available groups area.**

   You can select multiple groups by Ctrl+clicking.

6. **Once you've made your choice, click the > arrow to add the user to the group(s) selected, as shown in Figure 4-4.**

7. **Click OK.**

   On the Member Of tab, you see a list of all the groups the user is a member of.

All users in the system are members of the Everyone group by default.

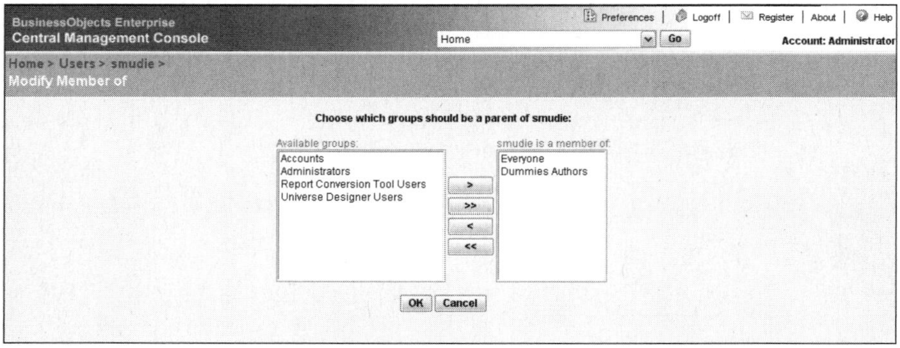

Figure 4-4:
Adding a
new user
account to
several
groups.

Adding several users to one group

To add one or more users to one group, for instance if you create a brand-new group and don't want to have to go through the tiresome task of adding each user individually, follow these steps:

1. **Click the Groups button on the CMC Home Page.**

2. **Click the name of the group you want to assign the user(s) to.**

3. **Click the Users tab.**

4. **Click Add Users.**

5. **Select the user(s) you want to add to the group.**

   You can select multiple users by Ctrl+clicking.

6. **Once you've made your choice, click the > arrow to add the user(s) to the group.**

7. **Click OK.**

   On the Users tab, you see a list of all the users who are members of this group, as shown in Figure 4-5.

When adding users to a group, you can search for a specific user by entering the user's name in the Look For field.

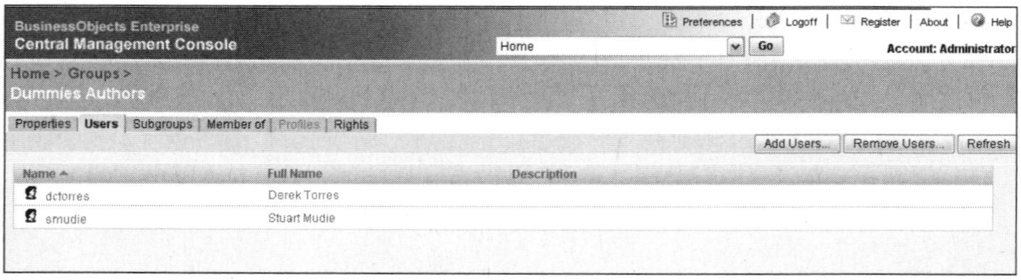

Figure 4-5:
Adding
users to a
group.

Deleting a user account

All good things must come to an end. On that sad day when a user no longer needs to access the BusinessObjects system, you can delete his or her account as follows.

To delete a user account, follow these steps:

1. **Click the Users button on the CMC Home Page.**
2. **Select the check box for the user you want to delete.**
3. **Click Delete.**
4. **When asked to confirm that you want to delete the account, click OK.**

   The account is deleted.

When you delete an account, it's gone forever. If the user might need to access the account again in the future, select the Account Is Disabled checkbox in the user's Properties page instead.

Setting passwords

You can also use the CMC to manage password settings, both for an individual user and for all the users in the system. Note that any changes made apply only to Enterprise accounts (that is, accounts managed from directly within the BusinessObjects system). Nonetheless, if you are working with accounts mapped to an external user database, such as Windows NT, LDAP, or Windows AD, your external system should allow you to put similar restrictions in place.

Changing password or password settings for a single user

To change the password or password settings for one user at a time, for instance if a user can't remember his password, follow these steps:

1. **Click the Users button on the CMC Home Page.**
2. **Click the name of the user whose password settings you want to change.**
3. **On the Properties tab, in the Enterprise Password Settings area, type and confirm the new password.**
4. **Select or clear the check box f   .ny other password settings you want to change:**
   - Password never expires
   - User must change password at next logon
   - User cannot change password
5. **Click Update to apply your changes.**

Changing password settings for every user

To change password settings for all users, for instance if your organization changes its security policy to require user passwords to adhere to certain characteristics, follow these steps

1. **Click the Authentication button on the CMC Home Page.**

2. **Click the Enterprise tab.**

3. **Select the check box for each password setting that you want to use, providing a value where required, as shown in Figure 4-6.**

   - *Password Restrictions:* Require users to have passwords of a certain length, and/or containing both uppercase and lowercase characters.

   - *User Restrictions:* Oblige users to change at regular intervals, and prevent them from using the same one or two passwords over and over again.

   - *Logon Restrictions:* Disable a user's account after a certain number of failed logon attempts, and decide under what circumstances it may subsequently be re-enabled.

   - *Trusted Authentication:* Enable or disable the Trusted Authentication feature, and decide its settings.

4. **Click Update to apply your changes.**

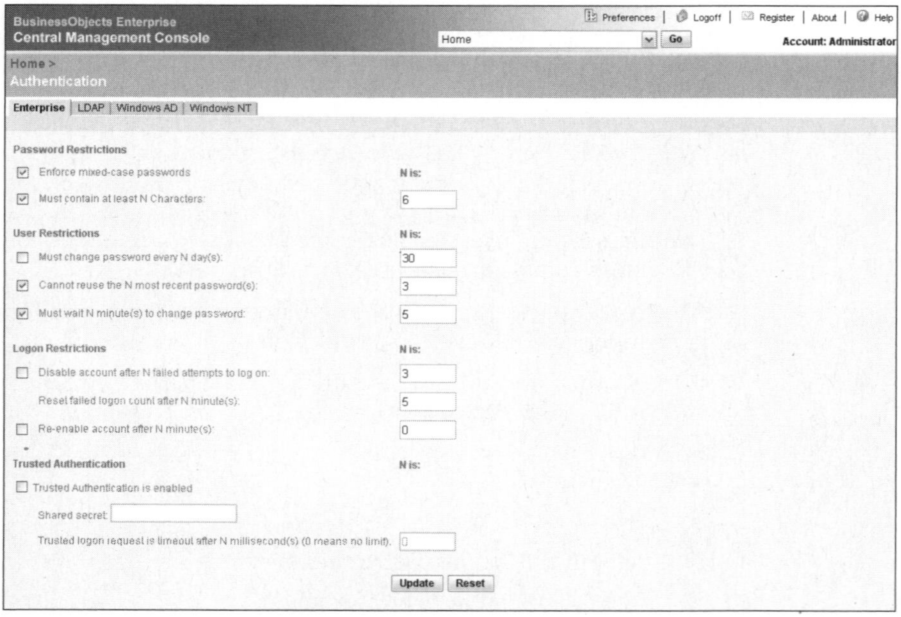

Figure 4-6: Changing password settings for all users in the Authentication area of the CMC.

Using Groups (To Make Your Life Easier)

Whenever you create a new user account, do you really want to have to go through the whole rigmarole of assigning all the relevant rights to the account *every single time*? No, we didn't think you would. Fortunately, that's where groups come in.

Groups are collections of users who all share the same rights and permissions. You can create a group, for example, for a particular department (such as the Accounts department), for a specific role (such as Report Writers), or for a geographic location (such as Europe). Bundling users together in groups allows you to change rights and permissions in one centralized location rather than having to modify them for each account individually — which, we're sure you'll agree, is a pretty nice idea.

When you install the BusinessObjects system, some groups are already created by default:

- ✔ **Administrators:** Members of the Administrators group can perform all tasks in each BusinessObjects application installed. By default, the Administrator group contains only the Administrator user.

- ✔ **Everyone:** Each user in the system is a member of the Everyone group. By default, the Everyone group grants members access to all reports in the Report Samples folder.

- ✔ **NT Users:** When you install the BusinessObjects system on Windows, the installation process creates a BusinessObjects NT Users Group. By default, members of this group can view folders and reports.

  This group is added to Windows on the local machine, and the user who carried out the installation is automatically added to this group (under his or her Windows logon). Consequently, if you enable NT authentication, users can user the Windows accounts to log on to the BusinessObjects system.

- ✔ **Universe Designer Users:** Members of this group can access the Universe Designer folder and the Connections folder. By default, this group has no users. You must add users as required.

  Members of the Universe Designer Users group can also control which users have access rights to Designer.

Creating a new group

To create a new group, do the following:

1. **Click the Groups button on the CMC Home Page.**

2. **Click New Group.**

3. **Click the Properties tab, and then enter a Name and Description for the new group, as shown in Figure 4-7.**

4. **Click OK.**

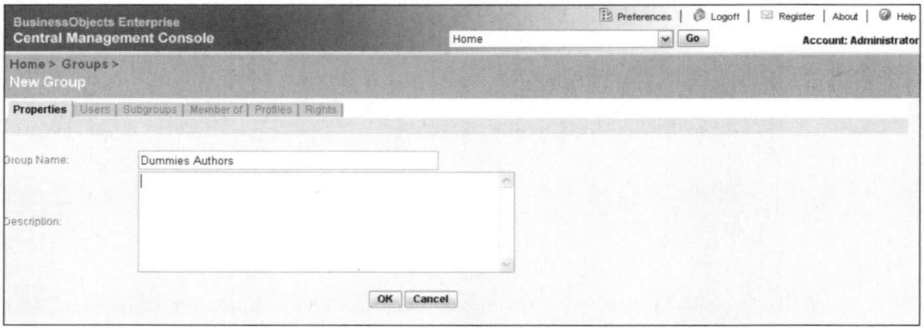

Figure 4-7:
Creating a
new group.

Adding subgroups

Groups can exist independently, or they can be subgroups of another group at a higher hierarchical level. Creating a subgroup makes managing access rights that are common across multiple groups even easier, because subgroups inherit the rights of their parent group.

There are two ways of adding subgroups: You can add one or more groups to a parent group (working from the point of view of the parent group), or you can make a group a member of a parent group (working from the point of view of the subgroup).

To add a subgroup, follow these steps:

1. **Click the Groups button on the CMC Home Page.**

2. **Click the name of the group you want to add a subgroup to.**

3. **Click the Subgroups tab.**

4. **Click Add/Remove Subgroups.**

5. **Select the group or groups you want to add as subgroups of this group.**

   You can select multiple groups by Ctrl+clicking.

6. **Once you've made your choice, click the > arrow.**

The subgroup(s) are added to the group, as shown in Figure 4-8.

7. Click OK.

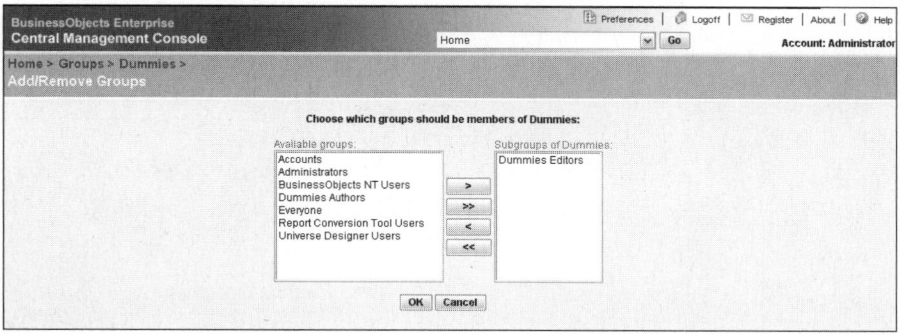

Figure 4-8:
Adding a
subgroup.

To make a group a member of a parent group, follow these steps:

1. Click the Groups button on the CMC Home Page.

2. Click the name of the group you want to make a member of a parent group.

3. Click the Member Of tab.

4. Click the Member Of button.

5. Select the parent group or groups you want to make this group a member of.

You can select multiple groups by Ctrl+clicking.

6. Once you've made your choices, click the > arrow.

The subgroups are added to the group, as shown in Figure 4-9.

7. Click OK.

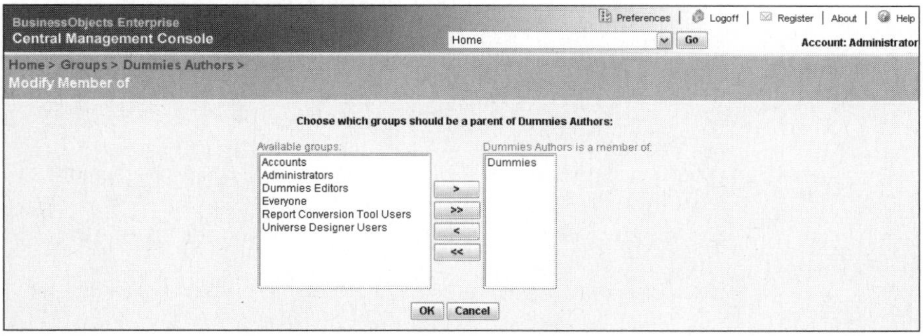

Figure 4-9:
Making a
group a
member
of a parent
group.

Deleting a group

Sometimes, you may discover that a group is no longer required. In that case, you can delete the group.

You cannot delete the default Administrator or Everyone groups.

To delete a group, follow these steps:

1. **Click the Groups button on the CMC Home Page.**
2. **Select the check box for the group you want to delete.**
3. **Click Delete.**
4. **When asked to confirm that you want to delete the account, click OK and the group is then deleted.**

Take special care when deleting a group, as you cannot recover a group you delete by mistake.

Exploring the Rights Tab

As an administrator, you can view and change the rights principals have to any object within the system — folders, reports, or whatever — from the Rights tab of the object in question.

Displaying the Rights tab

To display the Rights tab, do the following:

1. **Click the Folders button on the CMC Home Page, and then browse through your folder hierarchy until you find the object you're looking for.**

   Alternatively, you can click the Objects button to view a list of all the objects in the system.
2. **Click the name of the folder or other object whose rights you want to manage.**
3. **Click the Rights tab.**

   A page showing the Rights currently assigned to the object in question appears, as shown in Figure 4-10.

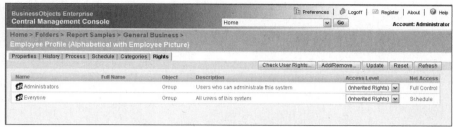

Figure 4-10:
Assign user
rights and
permissions
from the
Rights tab.

Reading the Rights tab

The columns of the Rights tab provide information on who has access to the object, and what type of access they have:

✔ **Name:** Lists each of the principals granted access to the object. Typically, access is granted to groups rather than individual users, but specific users can also be included in this list. To add or remove a group or user for this object, click Add/Remove.

✔ **Object:** States whether the principal is a group or user.

✔ **Description:** Provides more detailed information on who the principals are than may be understood by a simple name.

✔ **Access Level:** Shows the level of rights assigned to the principal for this object. You can choose a predefined access level or select Advanced to define more rights yourself. For more information on access levels, see the upcoming "Understanding access levels" section.

✔ **Net Access:** Shows the net (or *aggregate*) total of the rights assigned in the Access Level column, together with any rights inherited by the principal.

Understanding access levels

Think of access levels as being like "packages" of rights that principals might commonly need. For an administrator, they speed up the process of assigning user rights by avoiding the need to assign individual rights one at a time.

The predefined access levels are

✔ **No Access:** The principal cannot access the object.

✔ **View**

• *If set at the folder level,* the principal can view the folder, all objects within the folder, and the generated instances of each object.

- *If set at the object level,* the principal can view the object, its history, and its generated instances.

Rights include viewing objects and viewing document instances.

✔ **Schedule**

- *The principal can generate new instances* by scheduling an object to run against a specified data source, either once or on a recurring basis.

- *The principal can view, delete, and pause* the scheduling of instances that they own.

- *The principal can also schedule* to different formats and destinations, set parameters and database logon information, and carry out a range of scheduling related tasks.

Rights include All View Access Level rights, plus

- Schedule the document to run

- Define server groups to process jobs

- Copy objects to another folder

- Schedule to destinations

- Print the report's data

- Export the report's data

- Edit objects that the user owns

- Delete instances that the user owns

- Pause and resume document instances that the user owns

✔ **View On Demand:** The principal can refresh data against a data source, as and when required.

Rights include All Schedule Access Level rights, plus being able to refresh the report's data.

✔ **Full Control:** The principal has full administrative control of the object.

The Full Control Access Level enables principals who are not members of the Administrators group to add, edit, and delete other principals' content through the CMC. Assign it with caution!

Rights include all available advanced rights, including these:

- Add objects to the folder

- Edit objects

- Modify rights users have to objects

- Delete objects

- Delete instances

Understanding inheritance

An important concept to bear in mind when considering rights in BusinessObjects is the concept of *inheritance*. Basically, to avoid the administrator having to set rights on every single object — which would quickly become a Herculean task — the rights a user has with regard to any object in the system come from a combination of the different groups and subgroups the user belongs to, and the rights the objects have *inherited* from the parent folders they are contained in.

For example, a user who is Canadian Sales Director may belong to two groups: *Canada* and *Senior Managers*. For a specific object, such as the folder *Sales Reports*, the Canada group may have the *View Objects* permission denied and the Senior Managers group may have the same permission granted. In this case, the Canadian Sales Director would not be able to view any objects in the folder in question — which may surprise her!

The BusinessObjects rights system is quite restrictive, and a single inherited "denied" for any permission is enough for the permission to be, well, denied.

Managing Applications

You may not want all your users to have access to the same applications, in part because they simply don't need them — in the same way that a plumber and an electrician don't carry around the same toolkit — or, more likely, because you want retain a certain level of control over some tools (such as Designer, for instance).

With this in mind, you can specify which groups (or even which individual users) can access several of the applications in the BusinessObjects XI Release 2 suite, and exactly what rights they have in each case. You can also use the BusinessObjects Applications area of the CMC to change the appearance and even the functionality of some applications.

The applications you can manage from the CMC are:

- ✔ The CMC itself
- ✔ Crystal Reports Explorer
- ✔ Designer
- ✔ Desktop Intelligence
- ✔ Discussions
- ✔ InfoView
- ✔ Web Intelligence

For example, you may want a group of users to be able to view Web Intelligence documents but not create new ones, and for this same group not to have access to the Desktop Intelligence tool.

To set rights for specific Web Intelligence features, follow these steps:

1. **In the Manage area of the CMC Home Page, click BusinessObjects Enterprise Applications.**

2. **Click Web Intelligence.**

3. **Click the Rights tab, and then click Web Intelligence in order to expand the list of rights you can grant or deny.**

4. **Select the options you want, and then click Apply.**

   In our example, we would explicitly deny the Create Document right for this group. We would also set Log On to Desktop Intelligence and view this object in the CMC to denied, so that no users in this group could log on to DeskI.

Part II
Universes

"Somehow I always thought creating a universe from my desktop was a figurative idea."

In this part. . .

Did you think that installing BusinessObjects was all you needed to do to get the ball rolling? If so, you'd better think again! At this point, you basically have a car without an engine. Now it's time for you to start putting together the engine *(universe)* that will run Business-Objects. Without a BusinessObjects universe, there's no way that you can prepare the data for the folks in Sales to use to query and build reports in time for next week's department meeting.

If you're the person who is responsible for putting together the universes for your BusinessObjects environment, you're in the right place. The chapters in this part give you the rundown on how to create a basic universe to get you going. Chapter 6 shows you how to define a universe, while Chapter 7 shows you how to use joins between your tables. The part wraps up with Chapter 8, where you take a closer look at dimensions.

Admittedly, you won't be a master of the universe after this part, but you'll be able to get things going and help those folks in Sales get ready for the big meeting.

Chapter 5

Creating a Universe from the Safety of Your Desk

*W*hen you think of BusinessObjects or any other business-intelligence tool, the first thing that probably comes to mind is reports. Why not? Reports are the rock stars of BusinessObjects; they are what most users ultimately work with.

Of course, before you can use reports, you need a universe in place. No, not the big one (that one's already in place), but a specific body of metadata:

✔ In business intelligence, *metadata* is information that describes your data and the way it's structured; don't confuse it with actual data!

✔ A *universe* is a set of metadata that describes what's in a relational database that's dedicated to a specific group of users.

For example, say that you own a boutique. You may have a partial or entire database dedicated solely to `Customers`. The metadata that describes that data makes up the `Customers` universe.

BusinessObjects lets you create the universe you need (what a concept), so that later on you can create the reports you want. There's no shortage of ways to create a universe in BusinessObjects:

✔ **BusinessObjects Designer:** The easiest way to go about creating a universe with Designer is to use the Quick Design Wizard (see the section "Working with BusinessObjects Designer" for details).

✔ **Designer via the Universe Parameters window:** You can put together your universe manually. Just flip ahead to the "Building a Universe the Old-School Way" section.

✔ **BusinessObjects Universe Builder:** In certain conditions, you can automatically generate universes using a catchy, convivial wizard. For example, if Universe Builder supports your metadata or if you need to have backward compatibility with BusinessObjects 6.5, you should use this option. See the section "Becoming Master of the Universe (Builder)."

In this chapter, we show you how to create a universe using all three of these methods. Which one you choose depends on many factors.

BusinessObjects lets you create a universe by first selecting a source of metadata — whether that source is OLAP, ODBC, SAP, Oracle, or whatever. With your metadata source in place, you pick bits and pieces of the data to include in your universe, so users can work with this data in their own terms. Think of it as an all-you-can-eat data buffet.

Depending on your organization, you may never actually be called upon to create a universe. Creating universes can be somewhat tricky at times; most companies tend to leave that chore to BusinessObjects consultants or experienced professionals. But if you're using BusinessObjects as an extension to another product that you already use at the office, you may need to know how to create your own universes.

Working with BusinessObjects Designer

BusinessObjects Designer (or *Designer* for short) is one of the applications that BusinessObjects XI Release 2 Enterprise makes available while you're installing the client software. (We discuss the purpose of Designer in greater detail in Chapter 1.) When you build a universe with Designer, you have access to the Quick Design Wizard the very moment the application opens; if you are new to creating universes, the Quick Design Wizard is the best way for you to get started because it figuratively holds your hand and walks you step by step through the process

The most important thing to keep in mind about Designer is that it employs the semantic layer to help users understand the data they're working with.

The *semantic layer* (a patented Business Objects technology) maps the data in your database — in effect, translates it into commonly used business terms. The idea is to make complex data easier to understand. As shown in Figure 5-1, for example, data could be mapped to terms such as `Purchase Order`, `Inventory`, and so on. In the figure, data is displayed in the red cylinder while `Purchase Order`, `Inventory`, and `Materials` appear in front of the user.

Designer has always been the traditional way of creating universes in BusinessObjects; up until this release, it was the *only* way. If you're using a SQL or ODBC connection to your data, Designer is the way to go for you.

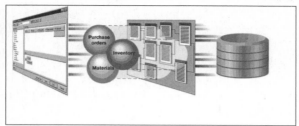

Figure 5-1:
The
semantic
layer in
Designer.

Starting BusinessObjects Designer

To start building a universe in Designer, follow these steps:

1. **Choose Start➪All Programs➪BusinessObjects XI Release 2➪ BusinessObjects Enterprise➪Designer.**

   The User Identification dialog box appears, as shown in Figure 5-2.

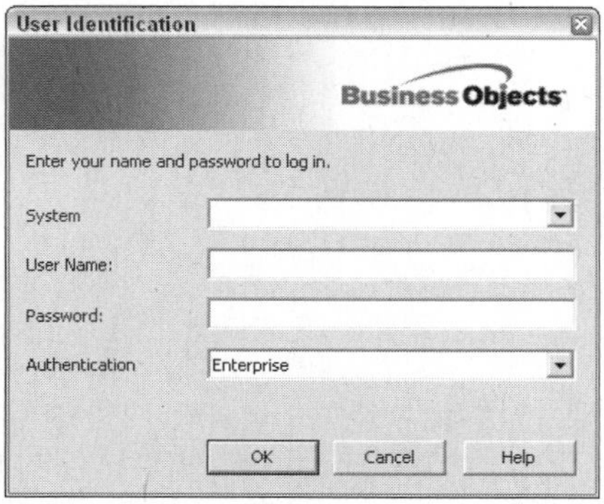

Figure 5-2:
The User
Identification
dialog box.

2. **Select the BusinessObjects XI Release 2 Enterprise installation that's on your computer or network from the System drop-down list.**

   If you have more than one installation on your network, you may have several options available. Otherwise, there is but a single system.

3. **Select one of the five authentication methods available in the Authentication drop-down menu.**

   Ask your BusinessObjects administrators which authentication method to use. If this is your first time using the software, the drop-down list is empty. Either manually enter your BusinessObjects XI Release 2 server details (which you can get from your BusinessObjects administrator) or select Standalone (No CMS).

4. **Enter your user name and password in the User Name and Password text boxes and click OK.**

Contact your BusinessObjects administrator if you do not know your user name/password.

The Designer application appears if you logged in properly; the Quick Design Wizard opens immediately so you can start building your universe (see the next section).

Creating a universe with the Quick Design Wizard

After you start Designer, Quick Design Wizard opens automatically (see Figure 5-3); there are four screens to creating your universe.

Set aside 15–20 minutes to create your universe.

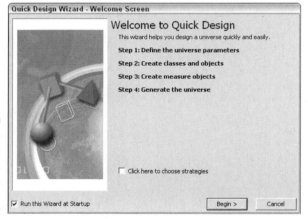

Figure 5-3:
The Quick
Design
Welcome
screen.

Quick Design Wizard - Welcome Screen

Welcome to Quick Design

This wizard helps you design a universe quickly and easily.

Step 1: Define the universe parameters

Step 2: Create classes and objects

Step 3: Create measure objects

Step 4: Generate the universe

☐ Click here to choose strategies

☑ Run this Wizard at Startup   Begin >   Cancel

Follow these step to create a universe:

1. **On the Quick Designer Wizard Welcome screen, click Next.**

   The Step 1 — Define the Universe Parameters screen appears, as shown in Figure 5-4.

2. **Enter a name for your universe and select a database connection:**

   • *If this is the first time you're using Designer to create a universe*: Create a database connection by clicking the New button. The New Connection Wizard appears. Or, you can also use an existing connection stored in the CMS. Go to Step 3.

- *If you don't need to create a database connection*: Skip to Step 9.

You can also choose whether your universe has strategies. In a BusinessObjects universe, a *strategy* is an automated, built-in routine. Check the Click Here to Choose Strategies box if you want strategies. (You actually choose your strategies in Step 10.)

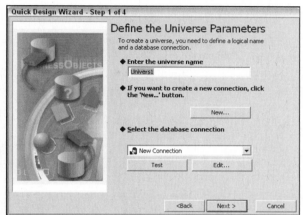

Figure 5-4:
The Step 1
window.

3. **Click Next in the New Connection Wizard.**

   The Database Middleware Selection page appears; it's a data-access driver that connects to the database. You might use, for example, Microsoft ODBC driver, or the IBM DB2 client. If you're not sure which node to use, contact your BusinessObjects administrator. Should this button not appear, it is because you do not have the proper rights. Contact your BusinessObjects administrator to obtain them.

4. **Select the database node from the collapsible/expandable menu and click Next.**

   The Login Parameters page appears. This is where you decide what to call your new connection and determine whether it's just for you or whether other users can use the connection.

5. **On the Login Parameters screen, set the following options:**

   a. *Set the database connection name and type with the Type drop-down list.*

   b. *Enter your user name and password in the User Name and Password text boxes, respectively. Remember that this is the database user name and password, which are different from the BusinessObjects user name and password. Questions? Ask your Database Administrator.*

c. This step varies depending on your selected database connection type in Step A. For example, if you're using an ODBC driver, select the data source name from the Data Source Name drop-down list. On the other hand, if you're using an OLEDB driver, set the server name and database name.

d. Click Next.

The *data source* isn't a file, but rather the connection parameter to your database.

6. **Click the Test Connection button; the results appear at the bottom left of the window. Click Next.**

   If your connection failed, click the Back button and check your selected settings. You may have selected a database node that is not available on your computer.

   When in doubt about your database node, choose ODBC.

   If you are using ODBC and the connection doesn't respond, check your data-source properties by choosing Control Panel⇨Administrative Tools⇨Data Sources (ODBC).

7. **Select the advanced settings for your database connection settings in the Advanced Settings screen, and then click Next.**

   This page offers advanced settings depending on the selected database node. For example, you can tell BusinessObjects how to handle connections by using the radio boxes providing three distinct options:

   • *Disconnect after each transaction:* This option lets you disconnect from the server after you finish whatever it is you are trying to do. If you don't like the default, we recommending choosing this option.

   • *Keep the connection active for X minutes:* This option lets you set an amount of time (the default selection is 10 minutes) to keep a connection alive. Once that period expires, the connection is dropped. We recommend maintaining this default value.

   • *Keep the connection active during the whole session (local mode only):* This option maintains a permanently open connection. For security and performance reasons, this isn't a good option to choose.

     You can also set array fetch and bind sizes, as well as the login timeout. You're well enough to leave alone these advanced features and keep the default values. There is no compelling reason for you to change these default values.

8. **Set any customized settings on the Custom Parameters screen and then click Finish.**

   If there are any customized settings, you have two options: You can remove them or you can modify their value. By default, there is but a single option — Binary Slice Size — that you can modify by entering a number in the text box and clicking Set. You can also remove custom settings by clicking each parameter name and then clicking Remove.

   The New Connection Wizard finishes; you return to the first screen of the Quick Design Wizard, where your new database connection appears (see Figure 5-5).

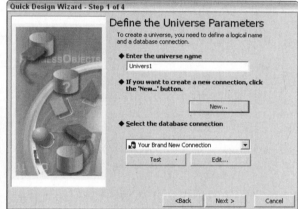

Figure 5-5:
The new database connection appears.

9. **Click Next.**

   The Choose the Strategies screen appears — if, in Step 2, you decided to include strategies (see Figure 5-6). In you didn't, skip to Step 11 to create classes and objects. This is primarily for advanced users; we recommend keeping the default values and going on to the next step.

   Don't forget to test your connection again!

10. **If you decided to select strategies in Step 2, select one of the three strategies in the Choose the Strategies screen and click Next.**

   In this window, you select a strategy for objects, joins, and tables by using the appropriate drop-down lists. If you select a strategy, a description appears below the drop-down menu. Again, this is really for advanced users, but you can find out more about objects, joins, and tables in Chapter 6.

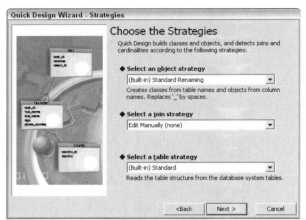

Figure 5-6:
The
Strategies
window.

11. **Create initial classes and objects from your list of database tables and columns by adding them to your universe; click Next.**

    • The information presented in the left column represents actual data that is in your database. Designer lets you transform your data into objects and classes, which makes comprehension easier for users.

    • You can select an individual column or table from the list or you can select multiple tables by Ctrl+clicking. Click the Add and Remove buttons to add these elements to your universe or remove them.

12. **Create measure objects from your list of database tables and columns by adding them to your universe in the Create Initial Classes and Objects; click Next.**

    You can manually add tables and columns to the measure objects in your universe by selecting the desired elements and clicking the Count, Sum, Minimum, Maximum, and Average buttons. These buttons make up an aggregate function that allows you to display values. Such additions make up a unique class called `Measures` that lets you define key indicators for your analysis, such as revenue or customer numbers.

    Press Ctrl to make multiple selections.

13. **Click Finish.**

    The final window displays a list of how many classes, objects, filters, and joins you created, as shown in Figure 5-7.

Now that you've created a universe, sit back and take a break! Of course, we've really just scratched the surface. In Chapter 6, we cover how to use filters and joins in your universes.

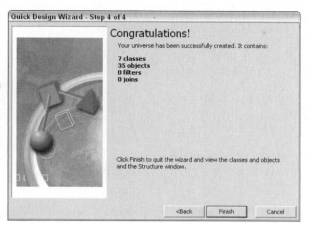

Figure 5-7:
This
window
summarizes
what's in the
universe
you've
created.

Before you take that break, be sure to save your universe in Designer by choosing File➪Save. (Who knew it was that easy to save the universe?)

Your new universe now appears as a schema in Designer, as shown in Figure 5-8. This schema lists the tables that are included in your universe, as well as any selected columns. You can also find the same information presented in the left panel of Designer. The tables are displayed in a hierarchical menu, which you can expand or collapse as necessary to see the available columns (objects).

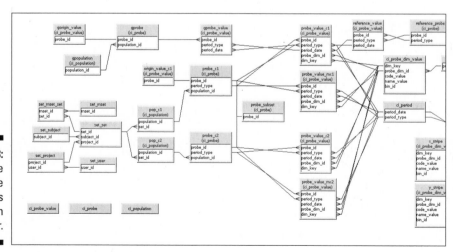

Figure 5-8:
The
universe
appears as
a schema in
Designer.

Building a Universe the Old-School Way

Some of us love a challenge, or at least insist on doing things the hard way! For those of you who are anti-wizard, or simply like to have more creative control, there is more than one way to build a universe. (For instance, you can start with a really big bang . . . just kidding.)

Using the Quick Designer Wizard, Designer lets you put together your universe à la carte via the Universe Parameters. This feature is similar to the Quick Designer Wizard; the primary difference is that you create your universe by working one tab at a time (with complete control over each step) instead of from wizard page to wizard page.

Lots of folks find this from-the-ground-up way of creating a universe easy enough to understand; if you're more comfortable using wizards, try Quick Design Wizard (see the preceding section). Avoiding the wizard doesn't offer a guaranteed advantage, but more advanced users tend to appreciate the non-wizard interface: You can go right in and set up your universe without explanations or multiple screens.

Here's how to do this:

1. **Start BusinessObject Designer.**

   Turn to the earlier section "Starting BusinessObjects Designer" if you need help starting BusinessObjects Designer.

   The Quick Design Wizard opens (refer to Figure 5-3).

2. **Click Cancel in the Quick Designer Wizard screen; in Designer, choose File⇨New.**

   The Universe Parameters window appears; it's similar in function to the Quick Design Wizard, just slightly less convivial.

3. **On the Definition tab (see Figure 5-9), enter a name in the Name text box and a description in the Description text box, and select a connection for your universe from the Connection drop-down menu.**

   If no existing connections are available, click New and go to Step 3 in the "Creating a Universe with the Quick Design Wizard" section. At this point, you can consider yourself done — everything that is mandatory is now complete. Of course, you can take the hard way out and carry on to Step 4.

   If you decide to carry on with the other tabs, save yourself some time and skip the Summary tab. It is a read-only tab that provides a summary of your universe; for example, it shows the number of objects, tables, etc. It's basically useless when you create a universe because everything equals to zero!

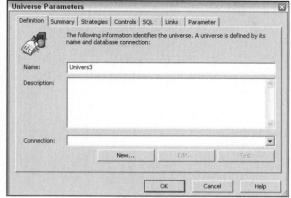

Figure 5-9:
The
Definition
tab in the
Universe
Parameters
window.

4 On the Strategies tab, set any desired strategies for your universe.

If you select one of the available strategies, its definition appears below the drop-down menu, as shown in Figure 5-10.

The drop-down menus you see change depending on your connection type. For example, you might have drop-down menus for objects, joins, and tables. Each one features a series of choices that are unique to that drop-down menu. For example, the Tables drop-down menu only has (Built-in) Standard, while the Joins drop-down menu has more options: Edit Manually and All Matching Column Names.

Steps 5 through 8 are more oriented toward modifying universe properties than of actual use when creating a universe. If you modify the Controls, SQL, and Parameters tabs without knowing what you are doing, you run the risk of impacting query generation later on and obtaining incorrect results. If you are not comfortable with that risk, go on to Step 9.

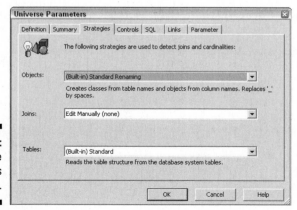

Figure 5-10:
The
Strategies
tab.

5. In the Controls tab, set any query result limits.

This tab lets you set maximum results for returned results or for the amount of time spent processing a query. The default results are largely sufficient for most users; however, feel free to change as necessary.

6. On the SQL tab, set query and generation options for your universe.

This tab has a number of options available for queries, multiple paths, or Cartesian products. By default, most options are selected, as shown in Figure 5-11. We recommend keeping these default settings unless compelled to do otherwise.

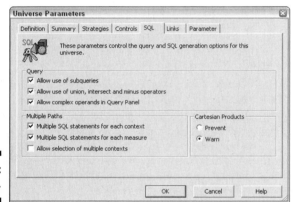

Figure 5-11:
The SQL tab.

7. On the Links tab, if you have any existing, exported universes, you may opt to dynamically link them.

If this is your first universe, you won't see any universes listed here yet. If you do have other universes, you can add or remove links between them.

You can only link exported universes; in other words, you or someone else had to create and export these universe to the CMS.

8. On the Parameter tab, add any properties as necessary.

This is an advanced feature; you could easily leave this tab as is and continue. Of course, you can use it by adding any SQL parameter that is available for a universe. These include, for example, AUTO_UPDATE_ QUERY, DISTINCT_VALUES, and END_SQL. Enter a property name and value, using the text boxes, as shown in Figure 5-12. After you enter this information, click Add. You can also replace an existing value, or even delete it.

9. Click OK.

Your new universe is now complete. At this point, you have an empty universe. It appears in BusinessObjects Designer's Universe and Structure pages that you can access by choosing File⇨Open.

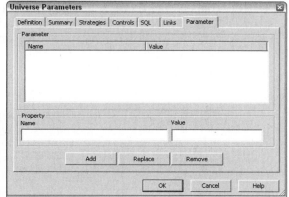

Figure 5-12:
The
Parameter
tab.

Becoming Master of the Universe (Builder)

The third way of building a universe involves an application called BusinessObjects Universe Builder. Universe Builder has one notable advantage: Although you have to install it on the same machine as BusinessObjects XI Release 2 Enterprise, it operates completely independently.

Over time, more users will probably use the Universe Builder over Designer simply because Designer doesn't allow the use of plug-ins that either didn't exist when it was released or have been updated since its release. Universe Builder uses Designer to create and manage some features, such as CMS login and reading connections; it also uses the Designer SDK (for developers). Nevertheless, Universe Builder shares some very basic purposes with Designer; for example, both allow you to connect to metadata sources and then map this metadata to more easily understood concepts — classes and objects, for example. A handy sidebar ("Universe Builder versus Designer") offers a look at how these two applications compare.

Universe Builder versus Designer

Understanding the difference between Universe Builder and Designer can be somewhat difficult; understanding when to use one or the other can be even more confusing! After all, both applications are designed to help you create your own universe. Basically, what it comes down to is this: Was your metadata source already compatible with BusinessObjects XI Release 2 *at the time of its release?* In other words, will your metadata play nicely with BusinessObjects XI Release 2? If there is no compatibility, you will need to use Universe Builder.

If your metadata was supported by BO XI R2, then you should use BusinessObjects Designer. On the other hand, if it wasn't supported, or if the metadata source uses a plug-in that was subsequently updated or was released since the release of BO XI R2, then you should use Universe Builder. Incidentally, SAP-BW users should also use Universe Builder because the application creates a universe automatically on the basis of data type. Universe Builder is the right tool not only because it supports your metadata type, but it also allows automatic universe creation.

Universe Builder also offers compatibility with BusinessObjects 6.5 As data-exchange plug-ins are updated over time, more and more Business-Objects users will move to Universe Builder to create their universes.

Starting Universe Builder

Like Designer, the Universe Builder is easy to find and easy to launch.

To open Universe Builder, follow these steps:

1. **Choose Start⇨All Programs⇨BusinessObjects XI Release 2⇨ BusinessObjects Enterprise⇨Universe Builder.**

   The Universe Builder application launches and the User Identification window appears.

2. **Select the installation that's on your computer or network from the System drop-down list.**

3. **Select an authentication method from the Authentication drop-down menu.**

4. **Enter your user name and password in the User Name and Password text boxes.**

   You can ask your BusinessObjects administrator for these details; if you have nothing, you can leave all fields blank, select Standalone (No CMS) from the Authentication drop-down list.

5. **Click OK.**

Did you know that you can also open the Universe Builder from Designer? To do that

1. **Close any open universes in Designer.**

2. **Choose File⇨Metadata Exchange.**

   The Metadata Exchange window opens, as shown in Figure 5-13.

3. **Select the desired metadata type from the Create a Universe From drop-down menu.**

4. **Click OK.**

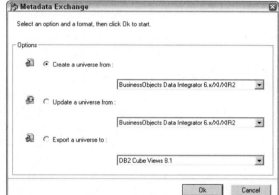

Figure 5-13:
The
Metadata
Exchange
window in
Designer.

The subsequent window that appears — the Universe Builder pane — makes up the actual Universe Builder interface (see Figure 5-14).

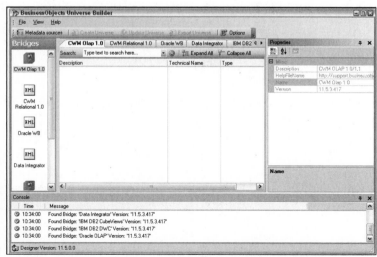

Figure 5-14:
The
Universe
Builder
pane.

Creating a universe with Universe Builder

Now you're ready to start creating a universe with Universe Builder. If you're already familiar with the Designer application, you will probably find that Universe Builder is equally intuitive and certainly more modern-looking!

To create a universe with Universe Builder, follow these steps:

1. **Select your metadata source, either by clicking icons under the Bridges menu or clicking the tabs across the top of the Universe Builder panel.**

   You can choose from seven different metadata sources. If you don't know which metadata source your company supports, ask your BusinessObjects administrator.

2. **Click the Metadata Sources button.**

   The Connection Wizard for your chosen metadata source appears. For example, if you chose the CWM OLAP metadata source in Step 1, the CWM OLAP Connection Wizard opens.

3. **Click Next.**

4. **Click the Browse File button and choose an XML source file.**

   Of course, the source file isn't always an XML file. It could also be, for example, an Oracle OLAP file. If you do use an Oracle OLAP file, things are done a little differently and we really recommend you check out the Universe Designer documentation from Business Objects.

5. **Click Finish.**

   The name of the source file appears; its corresponding database appears underneath the XML file as shown in Figure 5-15.

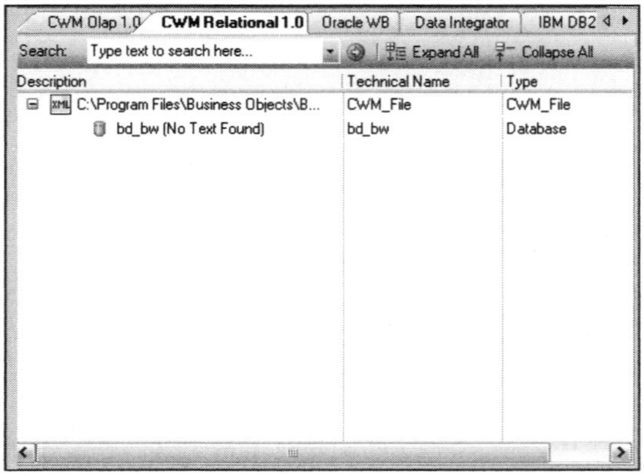

Figure 5-15:
The XML file and its database.

6. **Select the database name; then right-click it and select Create Universe.**

   Alternatively, select the database name and then choose File➪Create Universe.

   Be careful; if you click the XML metadata source name instead, the Create Universe command is dimmed.

   The Universe Builder Wizard for that particular metadata source appears.

7. **Click Next.**

8. **Select the data-source elements you want to include in your universe, using the arrow buttons.**

   The first arrow button adds a single element to your universe; you can add all elements by clicking the second arrow button.

   Pressing Ctrl while selecting multiple files doesn't work here.

9. **Select the metadata source connection.**

   This indicates which of the available connections to use when you open the universe. You can also set your universe name here. There are settings that allow saving the new universe automatically, as well as replacing an existing universe. We recommend saving the universe automatically.

   If no metadata source connection appears, you cannot use Universe Builder. Try creating your universe directly with Designer instead.

10. **Click Next.**

    Review the summary page that recapitulates the previous steps and your selections.

11. **Click Finish once you are satisfied and are ready to generate your universe.**

When you've completed the wizard, your new universe is complete. It now appears in BusinessObjects Designer's Universe and Structure pages (which are displayed when you open the universe in Designer).

Chapter 6

Defining a Universe

*Y*ou're now well on your way to setting up your universe in BusinessObjects. (Remember, in BusinessObjects-speak, a *universe* is the buffer between the user and data in a data warehouse containing objects and classes.) Oh, wait — you mean you thought that you were *done* in Chapter 5? Hardly! Up to this point, you've created a universe, but you've basically created just the shell of a universe. You're miles (hey, at least it isn't light-years) away from being able to create your first report or document.

Creating a BusinessObjects universe can be compared to a creating a house. In Chapter 5, you laid a foundation for your universe to fall back on. Before you get too deep into creating a universe, it may help you to work with other universes that other developers have already created. In fact, BusinessObjects provides (for example) a number of sample universes that can get you started. We go into what to expect before you start diving in and creating your own universes.

There's more to BusinessObjects universes than just creating them; you can open other universes in your BusinessObjects installation, or even import one, (which has far greater effects). After you create a universe, you might want to save it for future use or even export it to help train a colleague later on. Who knows — perhaps that colleague will also read this book and import your creation!

Planning for Your Universe

Most likely, you've already created the shell of your universe using BusinessObjects Designer. Now you have to start thinking about turning that shell into something useful — not just for you, but perhaps for an entire organization of people. This next step of planning is a costly event — not in money, but in hours.

Creating a universe can — and should — involve the participation of many people within your organization.

Your role as universe designer is important — it requires technical know-how, a good understanding of your organization, and strong analytical skills. You also need to know your limitations — and know when to turn to other team members' strengths. Even if you aren't the most technical person in your organization, you need a comfortable knowledge of your database system(s) within the organization; those are the data sources that feed your universe. No data equals no universe!

Not everyone within an organization can be a one-stop-shop for all information about the organization. Nor can a single person effectively deduce your organization's needs accurately; don't be surprised if you have to depend on the expertise of other members of your organization. You'll want to determine exactly what data BusinessObjects is going to hold before you build a universe to hold it. This kind of information may not necessarily be at your fingertips. For example, a project manager — or any of various people whose jobs are less technical but more intimately involved with "the big picture" of the organization — may well be able to help you here.

Analyzing your data

The first step is a thorough analysis of your organization and its needs. This can take a decent (or indecent) amount of time, depending on the size of your operations. In addition to determining (not alone!) what information your users will need to access and analyze, you also need to start creating business questions and/or scenarios that your users may face. The idea is to make your universe relevant to your organization and its users.

Project managers, business analysts, or other team members who work with your organization's customers are likely the people best equipped to help you create such questions and perform such analysis. Their input is crucial to determining what objects and classes you'll need to create for your universe to make it helpful.

Creating a structure for your universe

After you have an accurate sense of your organization's needs, the next step is to figure out what kind of structure your universe needs. As you see in later chapters, you can start by creating a universe schema with a number of tables. At this stage, you want to stop and think: Is a single universe enough for your organization? Or should you consider creating additional universes to adequately address your organization's requirements? The answers to these questions will have an impact on the structure you choose for your universe.

Importing Universes

Before you get busy planning and creating your own BusinessObjects universe, you may want to import an existing or sample universe to familiarize yourself with it first.

It's possible to both open and import a universe. What's the difference? There's a big one! *Opening a universe* in BusinessObjects Designer simply opens it and makes its features available to you. The universe is not included in your BusinessObjects installation. On the other hand, *importing a universe* brings it into your Central Management Console (CMC) — and, by extension, makes it part of your BusinessObjects installation. If you opened a universe in Designer and then opened your Web browser and logged into the CMC, the opened universe is not listed among the available universes.

When you open a universe, you have two choices:

✔ You can open a local universe that has never been exported. This means that it is a universe that can only be used on your machine.

✔ You can open a local copy of an imported universe. When you import a universe, you open the latest version of the universe stored on the CMS.

To import a universe, follow these steps:

1. **Open BusinessObjects Designer by choosing Start⇨All Programs⇨ BusinessObjects XI Release 2⇨BusinessObjects Enterprise⇨Designer.**

2. **Choose File⇨Import.**

3. **From the Folder drop-down menu, select the folder that contains the universe you want to import, as shown in Figure 6-1.**

4. **Select the universe you want from the list of available universes (or click the Browse button to find the universe manually).**

5. **Click OK in the Select a Universe Folder dialog box.**

6. **Click OK in the Import Universe dialog box.**

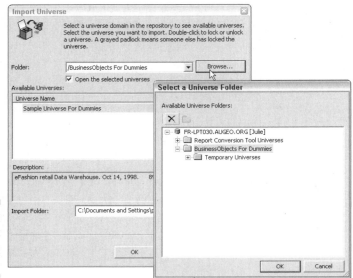

Figure 6-1:
The Import
Universe
window.

Your chosen universe opens in the Designer application, as shown in
Figure 6-2, and in the CMC of your server machine, using a Web browser.

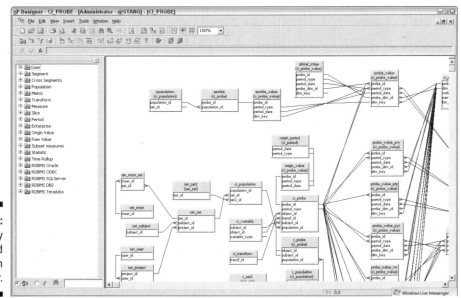

Figure 6-2:
The newly
imported
universe in
Designer.

Saving Universes

So you're working away with your universe, getting some great content. Sooner or later, you're going to want to save the universe. (We'd never dream of putting a cheap science-fiction joke here. Nope. Not us.) When you save your BusinessObjects universe, think of it as much the same thing as saving a Microsoft Word document: You're simply saving the current *state* of the universe so you can work on it later — or you're looking to avoid data loss in case the power goes out for some reason.

By saving a universe, you are saving the universe *file* on your local drive and not actually in your repository. The file isn't available in your installation's CMC.

To save your universe, follow these steps:

1. **Start creating your new universe using BusinessObjects Designer.**

2. **Click the Save icon or choose File⇨Save.**

   The Save As dialog box appears.

3. **Enter a valid name for your universe, as shown in Figure 6-3.**

   You're limited to 100 characters for the universe name.

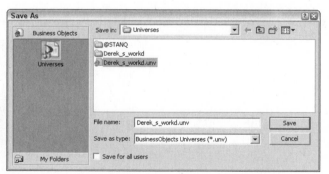

Figure 6-3:
The Save As
dialog box.

4. **Click Save.**

Saving a universe keeps the security (and the peace). If you are sharing your computer with someone else, another user without the rights to see the universe in the CMS isn't authorized to open your locally saved copy.

Alternatively, you may want to save your universe as a PDF. You're not exactly saving the whole BO universe as a PDF, but rather, the various bits of information that your universe contains (such as the components and the schema of your tables).

To save your universe details as a PDF, follow these steps:

1. **Start creating your new universe using BusinessObjects Designer.**

2. **Choose File⇨Save As.**

3. **Select a location for your file.**

4. **Enter a name for the universe.**

5. **Select Portable Document Format (*.PDF) From the Save As Type drop-down list.**

The PDF file of your universe details is stored in the location you selected.

You can configure the contents of the PDF file by selecting the different options in the Options dialog box (Tools⇨Options⇨Print/PDF), as shown in Figure 6-4. This tab allows you to specifically determine what features, if any, should be output to PDF format. The categories of printable features are in three sections: General, List Components, and Full Description. Each option represents a feature or item that is displayed in the PDF. We recommend selecting the items that satisfy the level of detail that you require. Just keep in mind that the more selections you make, the more crowded your PDF will be!

If you want to print the universe structure and want to display the full structure within a single page — a good thing when you have a large universe — choose View⇨Page Break. Figure 6-5 shows how the two tables `Outlet_lookup` and `shop_facts` are not displayed on the same page.

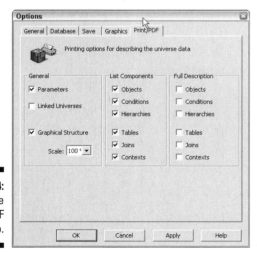

Figure 6-4:
The
Print/PDF
tab.

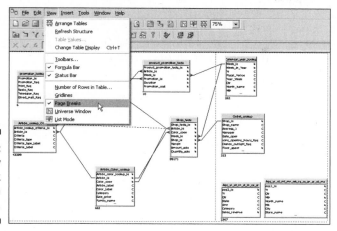

Figure 6-5:
The View
Page Break
feature in
action.

Exporting Universes

As a universe designer, you'll need to export your universe as soon as you're satisfied with it so you can make it available to everyone in your organization who's using BusinessObjects.

To make your universe available to BusinessObjects users throughout your organization, you export the universe so it appears in the CMC. Otherwise the universe is only available in your local repository, and only you will have access to it.

To export a universe, follow these steps:

1. **Launch BusinessObjects Designer.**

2. **Choose File➪Export.**

   The Export Universe dialog box opens, as shown in Figure 6-6.

3. **From the Domain drop-down menu, select the folder for the universe you want to export or locate it manually by clicking the Browse button.**

   Making no selection is the equivalent to selecting all groups displayed. If you select only a single group, the universe won't be available for people belonging to unselected groups.

4. **Select a universe from the list of available, active universes from the Universes box.**

5. **Click the Add button to add any inactive universes.**

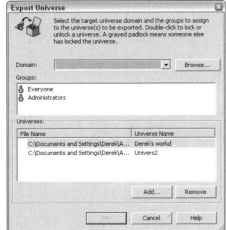

Figure 6-6:
The Export
Universe
dialog box.

6. Select the inactive universes and click Open.

When exporting a universe, make sure that your universe has a secured connection, one that is stored in the CMS. If your universe doesn't have a secured connection, an alert occurs and you have to set a connection to your universe, as shown in Figure 6-7.

Figure 6-7:
Setting a
secured
connection.

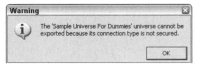

7. Click OK in the Export Universe dialog box.

The exported universe now appears in the CMC, as shown in Figure 6-8.

Exporting a universe is required if you plan on using it with Web Intelligence.

If you are still working on the universe and you don't want other people to access it, you can export it to a specific folder (for example, a Temporary Universe folder). After you export the universe, you can ask your administrator to allow only you to use this folder (see Chapter 4 on CMC rights). When you have finished development on it, you can make it available to all users and then export it to a different folder.

The system asks if you want to move or copy it to the new location. If you are completely finished with it, you can move the universe. Otherwise, copy it to continue working on it in your own development folder.

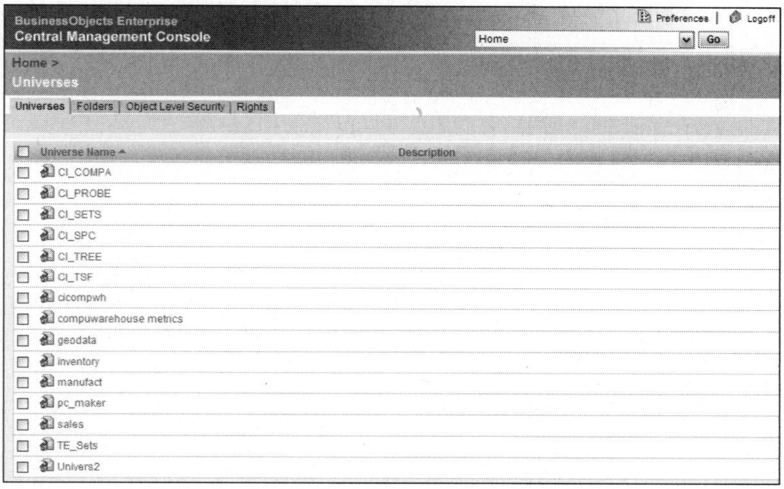

BusinessObjects Enterprise	Preferences | Logoff
Central Management Console	Home ▾ Go

Home >
Universes

Universes | Folders | Object Level Security | Rights

☐ Universe Name ▲	Description
☐ CI_COMPA	
☐ CI_PROBE	
☐ CI_SETS	
☐ CI_SPC	
☐ CI_TREE	
☐ CI_TSF	
☐ cicompwh	
☐ compuwarehouse metrics	
☐ geodata	
☐ inventory	
☐ manufact	
☐ pc_maker	
☐ sales	
☐ TE_Sets	
☐ Univers2	

Figure 6-8:
The CMC with a newly exported universe.

Chapter 7

Joining Your Universe

In This Chapter

▶ Adding tables to your universe

▶ Creating joins between your tables

▶ Detecting joins

▶ Using loops

*I*f you're reading this chapter, it's likely that you've already created your universe shell in Chapter 5. This means that you've created the schema that composes your universe and you've probably added a few tables. That's a great first step toward creating your first universe. As you probably have guessed by now, a BusinessObjects universe isn't something that you create overnight, or at least not in a few book pages!

Not every BusinessObjects user has to create a universe; this important task comes with a lot of responsibility that isn't necessarily for beginning users, especially in a corporate environment. An administrator-level user who has extensive BusinessObjects or business-intelligence experience is likeliest to be creating universes.

But even if you're just learning the ropes of BusinessObjects, it's worth having a go at creating a universe. So now it's time to tie together those tables you created in your schema. To do so, you use a *join* — the logical equivalent of a pipe or duct that connects two or more tables. It's sort of like the plumbing in your bathroom — imagine that the sink, the toilet, and the shower are each a database table. You use a join, or plumbing pipes, to connect the tables in a way that makes sense and serves a purpose for each of them (sink, toilet, and shower).

For example, say that you have a table for customers and a table for orders. Among the various columns available in the tables, both might have an account number field in both tables. You can create a join from the account number field in the Customer table to the account number in the Orders table.

Joins and *loops* (a collection of joins) are a major component of creating your universe. Therefore this entire chapter is dedicated to these two concepts; it's the next step in the long journey that is creating a universe. Rome wasn't built in a day; BusinessObjects universes aren't either.

Before You Join: Creating Tables

Before you get too carried away, you need to take a few preliminary steps before you can work with joins. For example, it won't hurt to actually have a table in your universe to which you can add a join! This is easily and quickly done in Designer.

To insert a table in your universe, follow these steps:

1. **Launch Designer; choose Start⇨All Programs⇨BusinessObjects XI Release 2⇨BusinessObjects Enterprise⇨Designer.**

2. **Log on to Designer.**

3. **Create or open an existing universe.**

   See Chapter 6 if you're not sure how to open a universe.

4. **Double-click anywhere in the open area in the Structure window.**

5. **Using the Table Browser, which displays all tables and databases views to which you have access, select a table and click Insert or drag and drop it onto the Structure window.**

You now have a universe with table(s). If you're looking to work with joins, you'll want to have at least two.

Creating a Join

Using a join in your universe schema helps ensure that correct data is returned when users perform a query using the data in your universe. Joins keep tables connected between appropriate columns so you only get the right query data — and not every possible combination that could be returned without the use of joins. The join is simply a condition that connects the data in the various tables that make up your universe.

You can create a join in BusinessObjects Designer in a number of ways, though you'll most likely end up creating joins either by hand or using a join that BusinessObjects automatically finds for you.

Creating joins manually

Manually creating a join in your BusinessObjects Designer database schema is just a matter of dragging and dropping.

To create a join, follow these steps:

1. **Place the mouse cursor at the spot where you want to create your join; this is a column.**

   You'll know that you're ready to create a join when the cursor changes form to resemble a hand, as shown in Figure 7-1.

Figure 7-1: The hand-shaped cursor.

2. **Click the left mouse button and drag the mouse to the corresponding column.**

   The column appears highlighted when you drag; the cursor turns into a pencil, as shown in Figure 7-2.

Figure 7-2: The selected column is highlighted; the cursor is now a pencil.

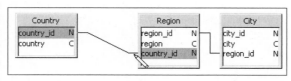

3. **Release the mouse.**

   If you don't want to set any properties, you can stop here.

4. **Double-click anywhere in the new join.**

   The Edit Join window appears, as shown in Figure 7-3. You can set important settings for your join, such as the type or its *cardinality* (the minimum and maximum number of instances between two entities). This window also lets you set information such as which two tables and columns to use for your join. (This window isn't critical if you're creating a join manually by using drag-and-drop.)

   If you want to create a join without using your mouse, you can use the Edit Join window to set the tables and columns manually.

5. **Click OK after you enter any properties.**

In general, a join links data from one table to data of a second table. The SQL generated, for example, is `Country.country_id=Region.country_id`, which appears in the Edit part of the Join Properties window or in the Formula bar. A query retrieves all counties and their associated regions.

But perhaps your database contains countries without any regions or even customers without orders. (This kind of information can be useful if you want to launch a marketing campaign for these customers.) In that case, define your join by checking the Outer Join checkbox (refer to Figure 7-3) and your query returns all countries or customers even if they don't have a region or orders.

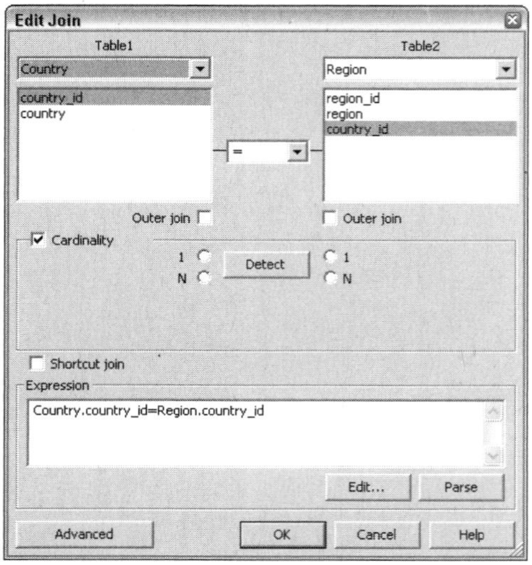

Figure 7-3:
Edit Join
window.

Using auto-detected joins

If you're not comfortable with the idea of locating and/or creating your own joins, you can always let BusinessObjects Designer earn its pay and do it for you. If your database schema features a large number of tables or columns in it, then we recommend letting Designer detect and suggest joins for you — to either the tables or columns.

Before you get too comfortable, you have some work to do! We don't really recommend working with a *strategy*, which is a file that uses information on the schema in your database. Strategies are a somewhat outdated concept that is really difficult for beginning users to follow. Instead, use the Universe Builder.

However, if you decide to go forward and select a strategy, you can create a strategy in one of two ways:

> ✔ Use one of the canned strategies that come with BusinessObjects. If you're not comfortable with writing your own script, you can select a pre-loaded strategy from the Parameters window. For example, an easy strategy is to select matching column names in the database schema.
>
> ✔ Write your own SQL strategy.

There's only one major drawback to using the auto-detection feature in BusinessObjects Designer. When your strategy creates a join between two columns with slightly different names, but that contain the same data, the auto-detection feature won't find them. For example, if you have an Account No. column and an Account Number column, Designer doesn't consider them to be the same thing, even if the data in the table indicates otherwise. Before you use this method to create your joins, be sure your tables all have matching column names.

To create an auto-detected join, follow these steps:

1. **Choose File⇨Parameters to open the Strategies tab in BusinessObjects Designer.**

   The Universe Parameters window opens with the Strategies tab showing, as shown in Figure 7-4.

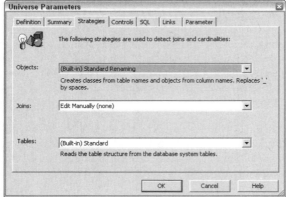

Figure 7-4:
The
Universe
Parameters
window.

2. Select a strategy from the Joins drop-down list.

Choose the strategy that makes the most sense in your situation.
If you're confused, each strategy provides a brief description of its
purpose below the drop-down list.

This strategy or rule is applied when searching for joins to create.

3. Click OK.

**4. Back in the Structure pane of BusinessObjects Designer, select the
area to "consider" when applying the strategy.**

You can either drag across a specific area to include (as shown in
Figure 7-5) or select tables individually by Shift-clicking.

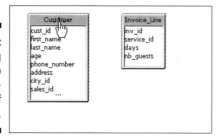

Figure 7-5:
Selecting
the area to
apply auto-
detection of
joins.

5. Choose Tools⇨Automated Detection⇨Detect Joins.

The Candidate Joins dialog box opens, as shown in Figure 7-6. The joins
that Designer detected are listed.

Figure 7-6:
Creating
detected
joins.

6. **Select a join and click Insert.**

   If only one join is available, it is selected. If no joins are available, the Insert button is grayed out.

7. **Click Close.**

Deleting a join

If you find that a particular join is no longer needed, select it and then press the Delete or the Backspace key.

Before deleting a join, think about any repercussions that this might have on your universe and other users in the future. You can't get your joins back.

Using Loops

After you get the hang of joins, you can take things even further by using loops. A *loop* is a collection of joins that create consistent paths between tables in your database schema.

Universe schemas need to be more flexible than database schemas because they often require the use of more than a single path to get the job done. You can ask BusinessObjects Designer to find and resolve loops within your universe schema.

We recommend revisiting the BusinessObjects documentation online when working with loops, as the technical level involved with SQL clauses goes beyond the scope of this book.

Before you start with loops, you need to make sure that cardinalities are set in your schema. Double-click your join, and choose the appropriate cardinality in the Edit Join window (as shown in Figure 7-7):

Figure 7-7:
Cardinalities
in the Edit
Join
window.

- ✔ **One-to-one:** A single row in a column has only a single row in the column of the other table.

- ✔ **One-to-many:** A single row in a column can have one or many rows in the column of the other table.

- ✔ **Many-to-one:** Many rows in the column can have a single row in the column of the other table.

We recommend clicking the Detect button, which checks all loops and proposes the cardinalities settings or an alias resolution (used by the Detect Alias tool) or a context resolution based on the Detect Context tool.

After you verify that you've set your cardinalities, you can see what (if any) aliases are needed to fix your loops.

Setting cardinalities is very important because all three algorithm tools are based on cardinalities. If cardinalities are missing, the result provided by these tools may be wrong. When you are using the detect loop tool, a warning message is displayed, as shown in Figure 7-8.

Figure 7-8:
The Detect
Loop tool
warning
message.

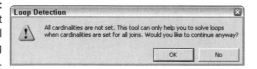

Chapter 8

Adding Dimensions to Your Universe

So you have yourself a brand-new universe — but now you need a dimension. Although that sounds like something straight out of science fiction, in this case a *dimension* is really just an object that you'll analyze. To make your BusinessObjects universe truly complete, your dimension needs one or more classes — and a few objects.

Classes and objects are the bread and butter of your universe. They are the data from your data source that you use to create your queries. But they're also much more than that. The *object* is really a SELECT statement that is mapped to one or more column in one or more tables in your universe schema. (Here's the English translation: When you build a query in WebI, the SELECT statement is referenced through the column that your object represents.) A working knowledge of SQL helps you with these tasks. If you're a bit rusty, check out *SQL For Dummies*, 4th Edition by Allen Taylor (Wiley Publishing).

In the bigger picture, you include your objects in a *class,* which is simply a logical container that works like a suitcase (it can hold objects or other classes). You can create a class that's no more than a single object — though you're likely to have considerably more objects than that in the class, depending on how much data you have that fits the class.

Classes don't have any technical mumbo-jumbo behind them, which makes them different from objects. In effect, classes keep your universe tidy. You can create as many as you need to make sense of your objects. It's important that classes be presented in a logical way that allows other users to find what they need with minimum hassle. That logical way is the dimension: a grouping of related classes.

BusinessObjects Designer is the right tool to help you create your dimensions, including your objects and classes.

Creating Objects

In the BusinessObjects suite and in Universe Designer, you will find three different kinds of objects, as shown in Figure 8-1. Each one has its own set of properties:

- **Dimensions:** Defined by their blue square icon, you use dimension objects for analyzing your data, or even creating hierarchies with them. These are the center of your analysis. Its value has a value for the report creator; for example, the dimension can be a product dimension (product line, product), time dimension (year, month), location dimension (country, region, city), people dimension (manager, employee).

- **Measures:** This object is symbolized by a pink bumble icon. A measure object is an indicator; it has a meaning associated with a dimension. "Number of employees" and "Sales Revenue" are measures. Not only are you interested in the sales revenue, but the sales revenue by country, for each product.

- **Detail:** This object is represented with a green pyramid. A detail object qualifies a dimension. For example, this could be the address of a person, or the description of a product. A detail object must be associated with its parent dimension.

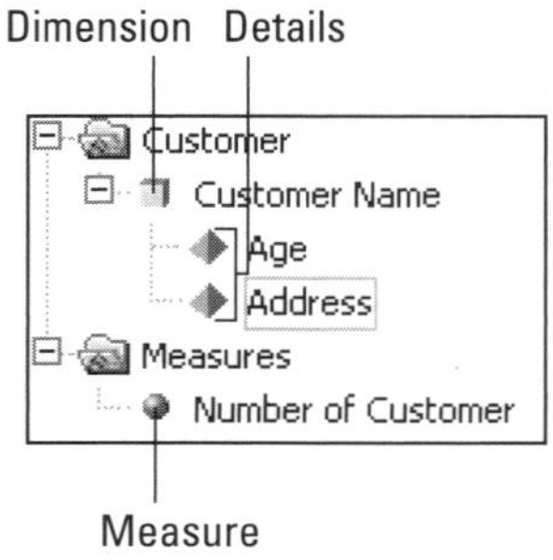

Dimension   Details

Figure 8-1:
The
different
kinds of
objects.

Measure

Even though creating an object isn't a hard task, you need one before you can use classes. As with most things in BusinessObjects, you can create an object in BusinessObjects Designer in two ways:

- ✔ Create an object manually using the Universe pane.

- ✔ Drag and drop objects from the Structure pane.

Taking the manual-y approach

If you like to dive right in and get your hands dirty, consider the manual approach to creating objects.

Creating an object manually in BusinessObjects Designer involves adding an object to a class in the Universe window (see Figure 8-2) and then setting properties for the object.

Figure 8-2: The Universe window and its classes.

You can add an object in just a few steps:

1. **Select the class in the Universe window where you will add your new object and click Insert Object.**

   You can also right-click the class and select Insert Object.

   The Edit Properties dialog box opens, as shown in Figure 8-3.

Figure 8-3:
The Edit
Properties
dialog box.

2. **Enter a name for your object in the Name text box.**

   We recommend carefully naming your object in a way that makes sense to other users. Don't use the column names that you find in the database schema; not everyone has access to the schema and they may be confused by unusual-looking object names.

3. **Click the >> button to the right of the Select area.**

   The Edit Select Statement window opens, as shown in Figure 8-4.

4. **Add a Select statement from the Tables and Columns, Classes and Objects, Operators and Functions areas or manually add it in the text box.**

   Some knowledge of SQL is helpful here. If you don't know SQL, ask your administrator. Otherwise, you can leave this blank for now.

5. **Back on the Definition tab, select Number from the Type drop-down list for all numeric formats, dates, and alphanumerics.**

6. **Add a brief description in the Description text box, which is available for users that use the object in the Query Panel.**

7. **Click OK.**

   The new object appears under the class in the Universe window.

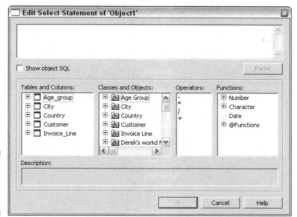

Figure 8-4:
The SQL
editor.

Doing things automatically

If you want to use the drag-and-drop approach, you can always add an object automatically in Designer. This involves dragging a table column from the Structure pane and dropping it into a class in the Universe pane.

You do have to pay attention if you use the automatic option. Make sure you drop the object exactly where you want it to appear. Designer takes the liberty of assigning the newly created object to the class closest to which you dragged the column. So, if you're not paying attention or aren't fully awake when creating an object, be sure to verify that your object is exactly where you expected it to be! Don't worry too much if you accidentally drop your object into the wrong place; you can always move it again via drag-and-drop!

Don't forget that by creating an object automatically, Designer also automatically names your object, using the column name. Keeping the column name as the object name might confuse users who aren't used to seeing the schema and column-name conventions. We recommend giving the object a more user-friendly name. You're simply creating a representation of the actual data-source data, which isn't always user-friendly.

The advantage of adding an object manually automatically sets the default object properties for you. In addition to naming the object, Designer also sets the default data type based on the column data type.

To create an object in Designer automatically, follow these steps:

1. **Select a column from a table in the Structure pane.**

2. **Drag the column under a class in the Universe pane.**

3. **(Optional) Double-click the class to open the Edit Properties dialog box and make any changes to the object name, data type, or strategy that you need.**

Creating a Measure

Creating a measure is really quite easy! Simply drag and drop a column from the table and your dimension is automatically created. Figure 8-5 shows a measure defined as `Number of Customers` and displayed by country.

Figure 8-5: Customers by country.

Country	Number of Customer
France	7,00
Germany	7,00
Japan	7,00
UK	7,00
US	7,00

Figure 8-6 shows the same measure `Number of Customers` displayed by region.

Figure 8-6: Customers by region.

Country	Region	Number of Customer
US	East Coast	2,00
US	Mid West	1,00
US	South	1,00
US	West	3,00
UK	England	3,00
UK	Northern Ireland	2,00

Depending on the associated dimension, the value of the measure is different. To implement this feature inside Designer, you have to use an SQL aggregation function in the `SELECT` clause of the object and set the Object type to `Measure`. Most common SQL aggregation functions are `Sum`, `Count`, `Count (Distinct)`, `Max`, `Min`. For more aggregation functions, see the documentation for your particular database.

Creating Classes

Your classes are essentially groups and subgroups into which your objects are organized. Just as with objects, you can create classes either manually or automatically in BusinessObjects Designer, using your table and Universe pane.

Before you start creating groups, spend some time organizing your data and thinking up logical categories that would make appropriate group names.

For simplicity and better organization, you can also create subclasses for your objects. This allows you to arrange objects into subsets for a specific class — another way to facilitate the user experience for your colleagues. When working with a large body of data, it's essential that you maintain as tidy a house as possible.

Creating a brand, spankin' new class manually

Is one way of creating a new class inherently better than another? That all depends! If you took our advice in the previous section and decided to think up a hierarchy of classes with user-friendly, appropriate names, then you are probably better off creating classes manually. You save the time and hassle of having to edit all the default properties. Instead, you can create and set the properties without having to backtrack.

To create a new class manually, follow these steps:

1. **In BusinessObjects Designer, verify that you are in the Universe pane and click Insert Class.**

   Alternatively, you choose Insert➪Class.

   The Edit Properties dialog box opens, as shown in Figure 8-7.

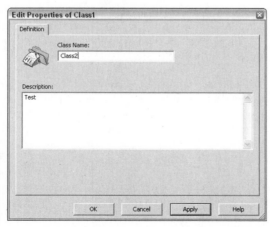

Figure 8-7: Adding classes.

2. **Enter the name of the class in the Class Name box.**

Class and subclass names should be unique in the universe. If you have a `Location` class for your Human Resources department, you cannot create another `Location` class for your product line. On the other hand, you can have multiple objects using the name in the universe; the uniqueness of an object name is only limited to the same class. Along those lines, the class name and object name pair should have unique names.

3. **(Optional) Add a description in the Description box.**

4. **Click OK if you are done.**

Clicking Apply saves your changes without closing the dialog box.

You cannot add multiple classes; you can only update the current class. To add multiple new classes, you must start over with Step 1.

The Universe pane displays your new class, ready for use (as shown in Figure 8-8).

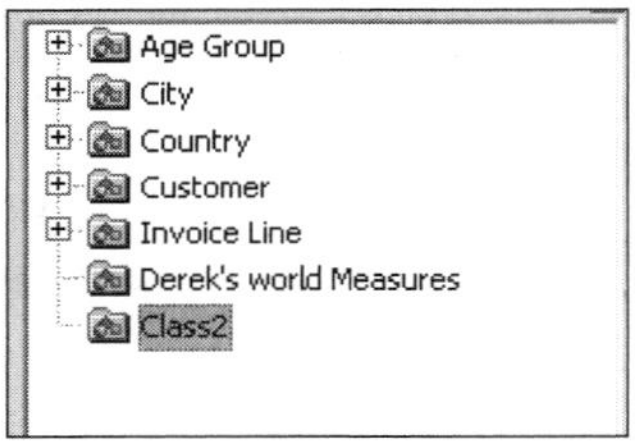

Figure 8-8:
The
Universe
pane shows
your new
class.

⊞ 📇 Age Group
⊞ 📇 City
⊞ 📇 Country
⊞ 📇 Customer
⊞ 📇 Invoice Line
📇 Derek's world Measures
📇 Class2

Creating a class automatically

Creating a new class automatically is very similar to creating a new object automatically. You simply select the table you want and drag it to your Universe pane in Designer.

This way of creating a class has the same drawbacks as creating an object automatically. Designer uses the table name as the default class name. It's possible that the table names in your table schema aren't very user-friendly and they're not readily understandable to all users. For that reason, you should make it a point to edit the new class name right away.

Creating a class automatically also does one other little thing: It creates new objects for the class. In addition to modifying the class name, you can also edit the newly created objects and their properties.

To create a new class automatically, follow these steps:

1. **Select a table in your table schema.**

2. **Drag the table to the Universe pane and drop it where you want it to appear in relation to the existing class hierarchy.**

   The new class appears in the Universe pane, within the hierarchy, using the default table name (as shown in Figure 8-9). It also contains an object for every table column included in the drag sequence; if you dragged a table and included five columns, the new class contains five objects.

You can always modify your class by double-clicking its corresponding folder or by right-clicking it and choosing Edit➪Class Properties.

Figure 8-9: The new class appears with default object(s).

Using subclasses

Earlier in this chapter, we mentioned that you can use subclasses to better organize your objects within a class. Why stop there? You can even plan on using subclasses within your subclasses if it's really necessary.

To create a subclass, follow these steps:

1. **Click an existing class folder or name in the Universe pane.**

2. **Choose Insert➪Subclass.**

3. **Add a name and a description for the subclass.**

4. **Click OK.**

   The subclass appears in the Universe pane under the selected class, as shown in Figure 8-10.

Figure 8-10: The subclass appears under the class in the hierarchy.

Searching for an object

You have two choices when searching for your object in all the classes and objects that you created. The first option is to use the Find/Replace dialog box. This feature is the same as searching a table as demonstrated in the previous chapter. The dialog box provides some advanced search features (you can search in names, descriptions, or SQL) and lets you replace some characters with others. For example, if you created an object using the word Employee but the correct word is really Collaborator, you can replace Employer with Collaborator.

The second way, which is easier and more low-tech, is to use the Find text box at the bottom of the Universe window. Type the name of your object or class in this text box, and

BusinessObjects selects it in the list, as shown in the following figure.

Creating a List of Values

For each object, you can create a corresponding list of specific values that you associate with the object — various specific names the object can have; the result is called (wait for it) a *list of values* (LOV). So, if you create a query that has (say) a City object, that object would have a list of values — say, Chicago, London, Los Angeles, Sydney, and Sfax — associated with it. If you do nothing, which is the default behavior for dimensions and details, a list of values is created on the fly. In this case, all cities are displayed.

You can use a list of values in several ways. If you're using WebI, you can use the "show list of values" operand that is displayed when you run your query and apply a condition. If you apply any sort of restriction to the values associated with an object, a list of values (LOV) is displayed, showing the available options to the user.

Lists of values require one of two types of data source: either a database file or an external file (such as Microsoft Excel or a text file).

The data in the external file is not dynamic and cannot change, while the opposite is true for database files. If you are using an external file, you can't share it with other users or WebI.

If you are the universe designer in your operation, you have some pretty heavy responsibilities here. It's your job to define the query setting's conditions on a new query called SELECT DISTINCT. Objects use this query to return the list of values. You also have to specify when the list should be refreshed — or even how the list of values should appear on-screen.

To define these properties and options for the LOV file, follow these steps:

1. **Double-click an object in the Universe pane.**

2. **Click the Properties tab in the Edit Properties dialog box (as shown in Figure 8-11).**

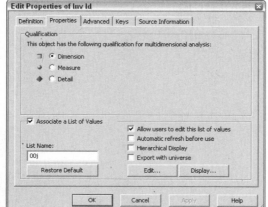

Figure 8-11:
The Edit Properties
·dialog box.

3. **Select the Associate a List of Values checkbox.**

4. **(Optional) If you want to share your list of values with others, check the Export with Universe checkbox (refer to Figure 8-11).**

5. **Click Edit.**

   A Query Panel appears.

6. **(Optional) Modify it but leave your object in first position.**

   For example, you can add the State objects and apply an ascending sort on the State object by clicking the Sort button on the toolbar, as shown in Figure 8-12.

Figure 8-12:
Creating a
custom list
of values.

7. **Click Run.**

8. **Click Display to view the results, which are the same in WebI and
   DeskI.**

   The results appear as shown in Figure 8-13.

Figure 8-13:
Displaying
the custom
list of
values.

Part III

Using Your Desktop for Reporting

The 5th Wave   By Rich Tennant

"Yes, I know how to query information from the program, but what if I just want to leak it instead?"

In this part. . .

*I*t seems that everything these days is Web-based; it's almost a surprise to stumble across any software that still runs using an icon and is found on your C:\ drive. Okay, perhaps that's a slight exaggeration, but it's still true that BusinessObjects lets you create queries and documents from a desktop application called *Desktop Intelligence* (aka DeskI).

The chapters in this part show you everything you need to know to keep BusinessObjects a desktop tool. In addition to the basics (Chapter 9), you find out about queries and how to create them using either the Report Wizard or manually (Chapter 10). Stick around and you even create your first BusinessObjects document in Chapter 11.

Chapter 9

Reporting Live from the Desktop

*T*he term *reporting* is frequently used in business intelligence; in BusinessObjects, *reporting* is the process of viewing, analyzing, and sharing data. The BusinessObjects reporting features are what most users will spend the most time using.

You can use BusinessObjects' reporting capabilities with either of two different applications:

✔ **Desktop Intelligence:** This is a thick-client application that resides on a full-featured desktop computer and works in familiar ways.

✔ **Web Intelligence:** Lovingly referred to as *WebI*, this application resides on the network server. You access such *thin-client* (or *lean-client*) applications as a client, usually via a Web browser.

No, *thick-client* and *thin-client* have nothing to do with an application's weight problem. *Thick-client,* or *fat-client* applications, are installed on a desktop computer in the traditional manner (usually by clicking a `setup.exe` file) and then connected to a network. Conversely, *thin-client,* or *lean-client,* applications are server-based, which means that you access them as a client, usually via a Web browser.

In this chapter, we show you how to get started with Desktop Intelligence. (We cover WebI in Part IV.) Both reporting tools have their advantages and disadvantages. Ultimately, the answer to "which is better?" is answered by a user's specific needs. One major advantage to using WebI in your organization is that a company's IT guy doesn't have to maintain a hundred different desktop application installations. On the other hand, WebI doesn't have all of the features that Desktop Intelligence provides, such as OLAP.

If you're working remotely, WebI may be more convenient; you don't have to be at your work computer to access your reports. If you travel extensively and require immediate access to BusinessObjects reporting, you may want to use WebI. If you work with reports primarily at your office, then Desktop Intelligence is a perfect way to get things done.

Getting Yourself Connected

After someone with administrative network privileges (it could be you) creates a universe and fills it with information from the chosen metadata source, you can get down to working with Desktop Intelligence. (Of course, if you have not yet created a universe, you can also use one of the bundled universes that are available for inclusion during installation.)

Yes, a universe fits on a disc. For more about universes as business-intelligence entities that contain business metadata (but no stray asteroids), see Chapter 5.

To start using Desktop Intelligence, follow these steps:

1. **Choose Start⇨All Programs⇨BusinessObjects XI Release 2⇨ BusinessObjects Enterprise⇨Desktop Intelligence.**

   The BusinessObjects Login dialog box opens, as shown in Figure 9-1.

   If you're not quite sure how to log in to BusinessObjects, contact your BusinessObjects administrator. Don't take the risk of locking yourself out by entering the wrong combination repeatedly (and don't feel it's necessary to use all three attempts!)

2. **Select your system from the System drop-down list.**

   This is the name of the machine hosting your BusinessObjects application.

3. **Enter your user name and password in the User Name and Password text boxes.**

4. **Select your authentication mode from the Authentication drop-down list.**

   Most likely this is Enterprise. You can select Work in Offline Mode if you're not currently connected to the Internet. The Offline Mode is useful if you're not connected to the Internet or your Enterprise network; this means that you don't have repository access.

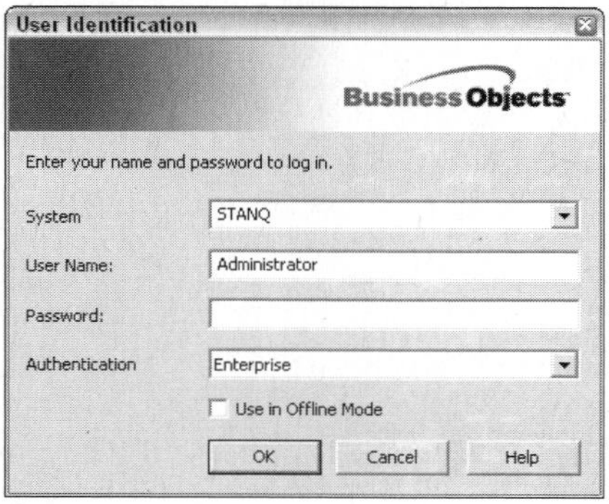

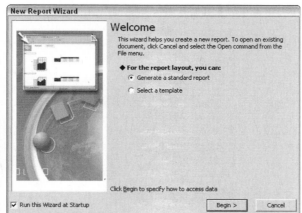

Figure 9-1:
The User
Identification
dialog box.

5. **Click OK.**

When you've successfully logged in to Desktop Intelligence, the New Report Wizard appears, as shown in Figure 9-2.

Figure 9-2:
The New
Report
Wizard.

Your user name must have appropriate privileges set in order to use Desktop Intelligence. For example, if you're not authorized to create a new report, the File⇨New command is dimmed. If you're responsible for your BusinessObjects environment, you can always choose Tools⇨Login As and log in as the Administrator.

Switching to a different user name

Sometimes you may need to log in to Desktop Intelligence as a different user. For example, perhaps your account doesn't have ample rights to perform certain tasks. Or perhaps you're logged in using your personal account but need to perform other tasks as an administrator. Instead of having to waste time by logging out of Desktop Intelligence and then logging in as another user, you can save time by simply switching user accounts.

You can use the Desktop Intelligence Login As feature to change user accounts on the fly.

Desktop Intelligence quickly logs out your current user name and then logs you in again, using the desired account.

To use this feature in Desktop Intelligence, choose Tools➪Login As. Log in with the User Identification dialog box (refer to Figure 9-1), this time supplying the user name and password you want to change to. Desktop Intelligence loads again, using those account settings as if you just launched the application.

Interfacing the Desktop Intelligence Interface

Before you can start working with the reporting features available in Desktop Intelligence, we recommend spending a few moments becoming familiar with the interface (shown in Figure 9-3). While it may seem somewhat unintuitive the first time you use the program, BusinessObjects is very helpful — it almost always has a wizard available to help you get going quickly. If the wizard appears and you want to jump right in to Desktop Intelligence, cancel the wizard and you'll be on your own!

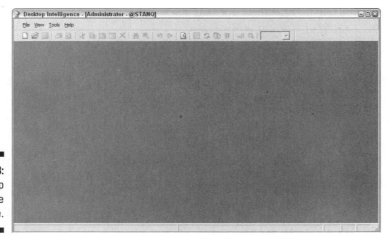

Figure 9-3:
The Desktop Intelligence interface.

When you log in to Desktop Intelligence, the New Report Wizard appears by default. To bypass the wizard, deselect the Run This Wizard at Startup option on the wizard's first screen (refer to Figure 9-2).

Until you start tinkering with reports (discussed later in this chapter), the interface displays only a portion of what you can do with Desktop Intelligence. Don't be misled; that's just the tip of the iceberg! You can perform some fairly hefty tasks without even touching the report:

- ✔ You can import any existing universes that aren't in your machine's universe folder.
- ✔ You can create or modify lists of values or in your universes.
- ✔ You can create or modify user objects in your universes.

The *list of values* is a list of data values for an object; a *user object* is a combination of two or more objects in a universe. (More about those in an upcoming section.)

Importing a universe

DeskI will automatically import the universes you need when you log on; the universes are also refreshed when necessary. However, you can manually import a universe with DeskI.

To import a universe in to Desktop Intelligence, follow these steps.

1. **In Desktop Intelligence, choose Tools⇨Universes.**

   The Universes dialog box appears, as shown in Figure 9-4.

Figure 9-4:
The
Universes
dialog box.

2. **Select the name of the universe you want to import.**

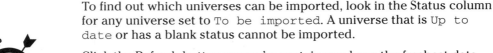

To find out which universes can be imported, look in the Status column for any universe set to `To be imported`. A universe that is `Up to date` or has a blank status cannot be imported.

Click the Refresh button so you're certain you have the freshest data available to you.

3. **Click Import.**

A dialog box appears, stating that the import was successful (as shown in Figure 9-5). The status of the universe changes from `To be imported` to `Up to date`.

Figure 9-5:
A
successful
universe
import!

4. **Click OK and then, in the Universes dialog box, click Close.**

The Universes dialog box closes.

If an error occurs, try importing the universe again. We also recommend looking for any error message that indicates the source of the problem; even if a solution isn't provided, the error message may be sufficiently clear that you'll have a good idea as to how to correct the problem.

Feeling the LOV (list of values)

The *list of values* (LOV) is a list of numbers that describe aspects of a given object in your universe. In Desktop Intelligence, you can use the LOV to select a data source or personal file, edit its role using the Query Panel (as detailed in Chapter 10), select a view for your list of values, or even purge values. The primary use of the LOV is with prompts and the Query Panel Quick filter feature.

The List of Values window shows only classes that have objects with lists of values. You can create and change those objects and values in various ways.

Follow these steps to work with the LOV in Desktop Intelligence:

1. **In Desktop Intelligence, choose Tools⇨Universes.**

The Universes dialog box appears (refer to Figure 9-4).

2. Select the name of the universe whose LOV you want to edit.

You can modify the list of values for any universe you've imported. (If haven't imported a universe yet, see the previous section.)

3. Click the List of Values button.

The List of Values dialog box appears, as shown in Figure 9-6.

Figure 9-6:
The List of
Values
dialog box.

4. Expand the desired class from the collapsible menu, and then select an object.

5. In the Properties section, select whether the List of Values uses corporate data or personal data.

Your choices look like this:

- *Corporate Data:* This option is the default. Leave the Corporate Data radio box selected if you're using metadata from a universe.

- *Personal Data:* If the data source is a personal data file, select this option. If you do so, a dialog box appears, letting you know that you're about to change data types.

If you make any changes to the LOV directly in DeskI, these changes are only available on your DeskI instance. In other words, your changes won't be available to other users via WebI, nor can you share your changes with other users. If your universe designer modifies the LOV that you have changed and then updates the universe, all of your changes are lost.

6. Click Edit.

The Query Panel opens, showing a list of objects available in your universe (it's a collapsible menu, as in the List of Values window).

7. Drag and drop objects into the Query Panel.

This is discussed in greater detail in Chapter 10.

8. Click Save and Close to go back to the List of Values dialog box.

The List of Values window reappears.

9. Click Display.

The List of Values of *X* appears (Here *X* is a placeholder for the name of the selected object.) Figure 9-7 shows the List of Values of Month Name.

Figure 9-7:
The List of
Values of
Month
dialog box.

10. Choose whether to display the values with a tabular or hierarchical view.

The tabular view displays the values similar to how a table is displayed, while the hierarchical view displays the values in hierarchical order.

To see the most recent list of values, click the Refresh button. You can also choose Show Selected Only if you want to show only the objects selected in your query.

11. Click OK to go back to the Lists of Values dialog box.

12. (Optional) Click Purge to delete any obsolete values that are no longer in the universe.

By purging your data, you can be sure that unauthorized people won't be able to see values that they should not see.

13. Click OK to go back to the Universes dialog box.

14. Click Close when you're done modifying the List of Values in all your universes.

Don't forget that if you used a personal data file, WebI has an empty LOV and you're not able to refresh it.

User objects (users in the universe)

You can also create, modify, or delete *user objects* — the organized metadata describing each user in your universe — from Desktop Intelligence. From the User Objects window, you can add, edit, or remove user objects. However, you cannot modify or remove universe objects.

The following steps show how to add a new user object to your universe:

1. **In Desktop Intelligence, choose Tools➪Universes.**

   The Universes window appears (refer to Figure 9-4). This feature is also available from the Query Panel.

2. **Select the name of the universe whose user objects you want to edit.**

   You can use or modify the list of values for any universe you've imported, otherwise it will be imported automatically. (If you haven't yet imported a universe and its accompanying list of values, see the previous section.)

3. **Click the User Objects button.**

   The User Objects dialog box appears, as shown in Figure 9-8.

Figure 9-8:
The User
Objects
dialog box.

4. **Click Add.**

   The User Object dialog box appears, as shown in Figure 9-9. The window features two tabs: Definition and Formula.

    Don't be confused by the similar names. The User Objects and User Object dialog boxes are two different dialog boxes.

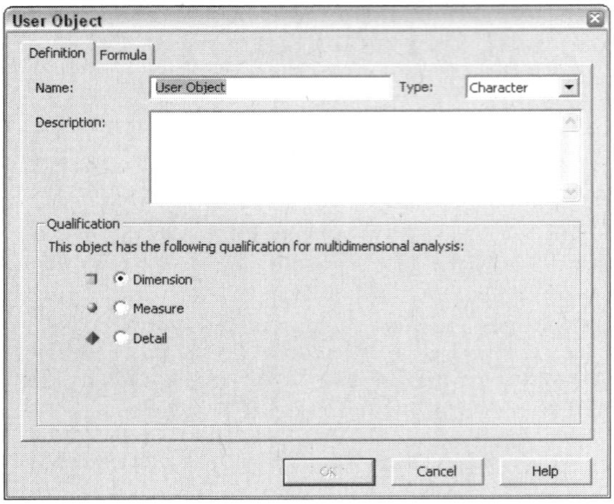

Figure 9-9:
The User
Object
dialog box.

5. On the Definition tab, set the appropriate options.

Your choices are as follows:

- *Name and Description:* Set a name and description for the user object.

- *Type:* Select whether your user object's data type is character, date, or numerical (from the Type drop-down list).

- *Qualification:* You can declare your user object as a *dimension* (numerical data that is a result of previous calculations), *detail* (data such as customer names and addresses), or a *measure* (data on a single object).

  By default, the user object is declared as a Dimension. If you opt to define the user object as a Measure, a Measure drop-down list appears that allows you to select a function to be used with the measure (Sum, Max, Min, Avg, and Count). Likewise, if you declare your user object as a Detail, you can select an associated dimension for which the Detail object provides information.

6. On the Formula tab, create a formula.

The Formula tab lets you create or edit user-object formulas, as shown in Figure 9-10.

- a. *Double-click a value in the Classes and Objects section.*

- b. *Select a function from the Functions section.*

- c. *Select an operator from the Operators section.*

- d. *Test your formula by clicking Test.*

  A dialog box appears, indicating whether the formula is properly assembled.

Figure 9-10:
The
Formula tab.

7. **Click OK.**

The User Objects dialog box reappears, displaying the name of your new user object (as shown in Figure 9-11). The new user object can now be used like another universe object in the Query Panel.

Figure 9-11:
The new
user object.

If you are unable to launch the Query Panel, check in your universe folder and make sure that you have an UDO (user-defined object) file named `MyUniverse.udo` with a 0K file size. Delete this file to launch the Query Panel. UDO objects are stored locally in the `MyUniverse.udo` file. Every time you open the Query Panel, an empty UDO file is created, but is occasionally left behind by BusinessObjects.

To remove a user object from your universe, click the user object's name and then click Delete in the User Objects dialog box. The selected object disappears; the list of user objects is then updated in real time.

To edit a user object, select its name and then click Edit in the User Objects dialog box. The User Object (singular!) dialog box appears. There you can edit the properties you set when you initially added the object.

Before we move on to the next section, there's more that you should know about user-defined objects (UDOs). These are local objects, which means that they cannot be shared with other users and other computers. In some cases in InfoView (for example, when SQL is regenerated), you may have some SQL generation issues, so use this kind of object carefully.

Should you need to share your UDOs, integrate them inside your universe. You can ask your universe designer to do this using Designer. If you'd like to do it yourself, choose Insert⇨UserObjects in Designer, and select the `Myuniverse.udo` file. Your user objects are now part of the universe with all the advantages of sharing and portability!

Setting the (default) style

Before you can start creating and editing reports, you have to set up how they appear in Desktop Intelligence. You can set eye-catching (or purely practical) visual aspects for your reports such as display formats, borders, shading, and other minutiae that give your report an authoritative appearance.

Tweaking your reports can take a decent (or indecent) amount of time. Don't be afraid to keep modifying your style settings until you feel you have it right! Even if you're new to BusinessObjects, if you've worked with Microsoft Excel, adapting to BusinessObjects reports is pretty quick; they have some Excel-like features.

Follow these steps to customize your report styles:

1. **In Desktop Intelligence, choose Tools⇨Standard Report Styles.**

   The Standard Report Styles window appears, as shown in Figure 9-12. The window is neatly organized, which makes customizing your report styles relatively easy:

   • The Report Components section takes most of the left side of the screen. It features five distinct components and their subcomponents, all of which can be set.

   • The right side of the screen contains the various tabs that are available for a particular component or subcomponent. Depending on what you select in Report Components, the tabs change on the fly.

2. Expand a component from the Report Components section and use the various tabs to set preferences.

Each component has a distinct set of preferences, represented by tabs. The components also have various subcomponents, each with its own settings.

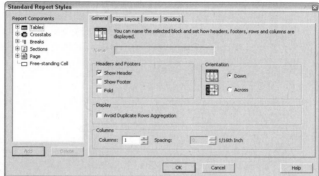

Figure 9-12:
Standard
Report
Styles.

3. Click OK.

You set all the features in the Standard Report Styles window in a similar manner using radio buttons and checkboxes. For example, Figure 9-13 shows the settings for the Alignment tab of any subcomponent.

Don't worry if you feel that you've already specified a similar setting. It's likely you have — but now you can apply that setting somewhere else in your report.

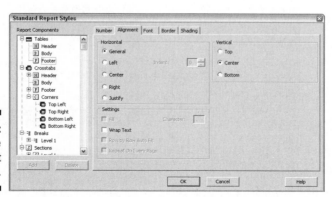

Figure 9-13:
The
Alignment
tab.

So far we've shown just a small sample of the many different features you can set. We recommend you take a closer look at these:

- ✔ **Create additional breaks or sections:** The Standard Report Styles window provides a single sublevel. If you need a second or third sublevel, select the component (or one of its Level 1 subcomponents) and then click Add. A new subcomponent, named Level 2, appears in the hierarchical menu. This subcomponent is the spitting image of the higher-level component — Level 2, by default, has exactly the same properties as Level 1. If you've changed the initial Level 1 settings at all before creating Level 2, those changes appear in both levels.

  You can always click a subcomponent and click Delete if you find a subcomponent is no longer necessary.

- ✔ **Work with values:** If you select Boolean in the Category section, you have two options:

  - *Existing values:* The text boxes in the Properties section automatically fill up with the existing values. Simply change the content of the text boxes as necessary and click Add.

  - *Creating new values:* If you want to create new values, you have two options. Fill in the empty text boxes in Properties. If you click Add or OK, the new values appear in the Format section.

  You can always remove a customized value by clicking the value in the Format section. Just remember that you can't delete a default value, even if you have additional value sets available.

Changing Your Password

For security reasons, it's a good idea to change your password regularly. In Desktop Intelligence, you can change your user password that affects your account across the set of BusinessObjects applications.

Your BusinessObjects administrator most likely applied a setting that requires you to change your password after a certain period of time.

The first time you log on to BusinessObjects, you should change your password for security reasons (if you're not prompted automatically to do so). If you're unable to change your password, it's possible that your BusinessObjects administrator disabled password changing for your user account.

If you change your password, your Enterprise password changes. Changing your password doesn't change your password if you log on to BusinessObjects using any other kind of authentication.

Follow these steps to change your password in Desktop Intelligence:

1. **In Desktop Intelligence, choose Tools⇨Change Password.**

   The Change Password dialog box appears, as shown in Figure 9-14.

2. **Enter your current password, your new password, and then confirm the new password by entering it again.**

   Creating a password for BusinessObjects means following the same security rules as when you create a PIN for your bank card. Don't use a password so long that you're likely to forget it — or, for that matter, one so short that it's easy to guess. Avoid using personal information that people familiar with you might be able to guess, such as birthdays, children's names, favorite sports (or teams), and so on.

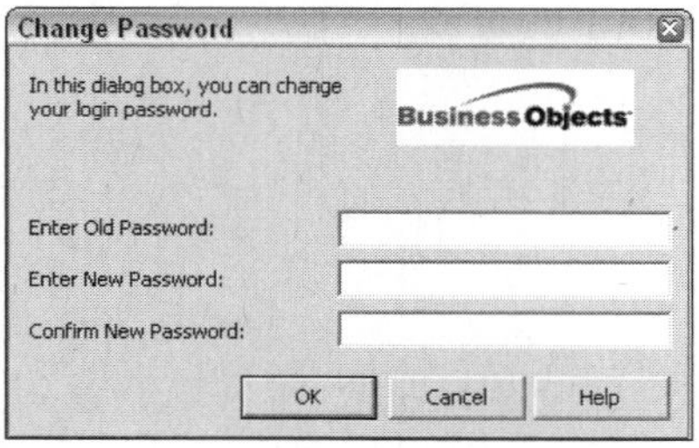

Figure 9-14:
The Change
Password
dialog box.

> **Change Password**
>
> In this dialog box, you can change your login password.
>
> **Business Objects**
>
> Enter Old Password:
>
> Enter New Password:
>
> Confirm New Password:
>
> OK   Cancel   Help

3. **Click OK.**

   The new password goes into effect. You must use the new password the next time you log in to BusinessObjects.

If you cancel the Change Password dialog box, you risk disabling (locking) your account. A warning screen appears, telling you as much; if your account locks so you can't log in, contact your BusinessObjects administrator and ask him or her to unblock your account.

You should keep in mind a few rules when creating your password. By following these rules, you will save yourself a lot of frustration and headaches by avoiding an invalid password warning:

✔ Your password must contain at least 5 characters and no more than 20.

✔ The first character of the password must be alphabetic.

✔ An ideal password contains at least one special character (such as punctuation marks) and two alphabetic characters.

✔ Typically the following characters can be used when creating a password (but check with your administrator):

   • A small range of symbols (@ # $ % ^ & + = -)

   • Letters a through z and A through Z

- Numbers 0 through 9
- Space (except as the initial character).

Of course, your BusinessObjects administrator may establish different rules. The best way to be clear is to check directly with your administrator!

Exploring Your Options

Before you get swept away into using reports, we'd be remiss if we didn't explain a few nuts and bolts of Desktop Intelligence — in particular, the application-related settings that let you determine how it performs.

The Options dialog box has seven tabs, where you can set such features as the user-interface language, file locations for templates and universes, and so on. (See Figure 9-15.)

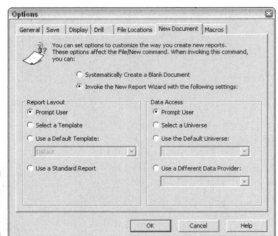

Figure 9-15:
The Options
dialog box.

When you click a tab in the Options dialog box, BusinessObjects provides a one-line description of the tab's purpose. In the following sections, we take a look at each tab.

As you go through the tabs, keep in mind that you don't need to regulate every aspect of Desktop Intelligence. (It's a bit smarter than that.)

General

On the General tab, you can take care of three primary tasks: set the interface language, designate the location of a graphics editor, and set start-up options.

In the Start-Up Options section, we recommend selecting Show Welcome Wizard and Notify Document Reception. It's helpful in several ways:

- ✔ If you're new to Desktop Intelligence, the wizard offers a cheery greeting that helps you get your bearings.

  After you're comfortable with Desktop Intelligence, you can always come back to Options and deselect this option.

- ✔ The Notify Document Reception option is helpful when you send a report to someone; this feature contacts you and lets you know when a report has been received.

- ✔ The Reopen Last Open Documents option opens the last-viewed report by default when you log in to Desktop Intelligence.

The Settings section of the General tab lets you set individual preferences for the application. For example, you can

- ✔ Set how many entries to show in the recent file list.

- ✔ Tell Desktop Intelligence to use an older BusinessObjects format when printing reports.

- ✔ Set a graphics editor for working with graphic files.

More specifically, this tab allows you to

- ✔ **Automatically Import Universe:** Universes are automatically imported in Desktop Intelligence. This is the option that makes it so; we recommend leaving it enabled by default.

- ✔ **Print as BusinessObjects 4.1:** This prints your documents using the standards of the 4.1 release. Unless you need this, we recommend leaving it disabled.

- ✔ **Always Ask Before Opening Documents with Macros:** This is enabled by default for security purposes. We recommend leaving it, just as you probably do in other applications that have a similar feature (for example, Microsoft Word).

- ✔ **Show Recently Used File List:** This is enabled and set to 5 by default. We see no real reason to change it other than personal preference.

The most interesting aspect of this tab, however, is the Language section. BusinessObjects contains an impressive list of installed languages. You can select a language using the Language drop-down list; then click the button to the right of the drop-down list, as shown in Figure 9-16.

Figure 9-16:
The
Language
drop-down
list.

Save

The Save tab, not surprisingly, determines how Desktop Intelligence saves your reports. We recommend these settings:

- ✔ **Automatic Save As:** It would be wise to save the file automatically every five minutes. It's very easy to get absorbed in your work and forget to regularly save your work; this kind of oversight can prove to very costly should anything go wrong, such as a power failure.

- ✔ **Automatic Open After Save As:** Automatically open your document every time you use the save as command.

- ✔ **Refresh Document When Opening:** Refresh a document automatically every time it's opened. By selecting this option, you can be certain that you're always working with the freshest data — a crucial part of reporting!

  Refreshing data can take up to 30 minutes. You may want to schedule your report every night at a "off-peak" time if you have a lot of data.

- ✔ **Protection Password** and **Write Reservation Password:** If you're worried about compromising the security of your reports, you can require a password in order to open the document or to modify the document. This feature only works with Desktop Intelligence; it doesn't work if you are using InfoView to display your document.

Display

The Display tab offers settings you can tweak to fit your style of working; for example, you can select which toolbars to display in Desktop Intelligence, set measurement units for the application, and determine window appearance (deciding whether to include such features as scrollbars). The right side of the Display tab involves report settings. If you've already been using reports, you can include delimiters, grids, or outlines.

The available options include:

- ✔ **Status Bar:** Selected by default, this option displays the status bar in Desktop Intelligence.
- ✔ **Formula Bar:** This option allows you to display the Formula bar in Desktop Intelligence. If you plan on working with your documents in DeskI, we recommend enabling it.
- ✔ **Measurement Units:** This option allows you to display measurements in metric or imperial standard.
- ✔ **Horizontal Scroll Bar:** This option, selected by default, allows you to display horizontal scroll bars in your window.
- ✔ **Vertical Scroll Bar:** Also selected by default, this option allows you to display vertical scroll bars in your window.
- ✔ **Report Tabs:** Also selected by default, this option allows you to display report tabs in your window.
- ✔ **Report Options:** This option lets you set a number of options for viewing your report in DeskI, including alerts, outlines, cell or section delimiters, or grid features.
- ✔ **Height:** This option lets you set the height of the grid if you selected the grid options in Report options.
- ✔ **Width:** This option lets you set the width of the grid if you selected the grid options in Report options.

Drill

The Drill tab provides a number of options for when you work with reports. Working with reports is discussed in Chapter 11; however, we recommend using the default settings.

The Drill tab provides a number of options relating to pop-up menus, drilling, and display options. These include:

✓ **Popup Menus:** This section lets you set the number of entries in the Explore List (Explore List Up to X Entries). You can also select whether to show the number of data rows for variables (Show Number of Data Rows for Variables).

✓ **Drill Toolbar:** Select the Confirmation Message Before Closing option to display a dialog box confirming that you wish to close the application.

✓ **Display Options:** This section lets you change your cursor (Change Cursor to Magnifying Glass), show the next dimension as a tooltip (Tooltip to Show Next Dimension to Explore), or add sums and percentages on measures (Add Sum on Measures, Add Percentage on Measures). Select the Tooltip to Show Next Dimension to Explore option and click the Format Tooltip button to set the appearance of your tooltip.

✓ **Drill Mode:** This section lets you set how you should drill your reports, either by creating a new report (Create New Report), keep an existing report (Keep Existing Report), or by prompting the user (Prompt User).

✓ **Drill Through:** Select the Apply Drill Filters option to drill through a document.

File Locations

The File Locations tab lets you set default file locations for documents, templates, universes, add-ins, XML sources, and filters. To change a file location, simply click the file type and then click Change. The Browse for Folder window appears; simply click the desired folder location and then click OK. The file locations are:

✓ User Documents

✓ User Templates

✓ Universes

✓ Add-Ins

✓ XML Sources

✓ XML filters

Unless you have a compelling reason to change the default locations, we recommend leaving these file locations as they are.

New Document

The New Document tab determines how Desktop Intelligence prepares new documents.

Be careful with the options in this tab; changing these settings can have an impact on the File➪New menu.

You can instruct Desktop Intelligence on how to create a new document:

- ✔ **Open a blank report when you create a new document:** Select the Systematically Create a Blank Document option. Desktop Intelligence takes it from there whenever you create a new document.

- ✔ **Launch the New Report Wizard:** Select the Invoke the New Report Wizard with the Following Settings options. Then specify the settings you want Desktop Intelligence to use.

The best option for you depends on your level of experience with Desktop Intelligence. If you're comfortable working without the wizard, there's no reason not to start with a blank document.

This tab also lets you determine the initial report layout:

- ✔ **Use a specific template:** Choose the Select a Template option.

- ✔ **Run as a standard report:** Select the Use a Standard Report option. We recommend using this option unless you explicitly want a specific template. This displays the report in its default format.

You can also specify the default data-source settings:

- ✔ **Select a Universe:** Documents use a particular universe automatically.

- ✔ **Use a Different Date Provider:** Documents use a different data source than the default provider when you create a new document.

Macros

On the final tab, Macros, you create and apply macros to Desktop Intelligence; you run macros that you can run from the toolbar. A *macro* is similar to a shortcut; it's a recorded command that performs a series of actions. For example, you could create a macro that lets you create a new document in Desktop Intelligence and then save it — all in a single action.

To use macros, follow these steps:

1. **Select one of the five available macro spaces in the Macros tab.**

2. **Enter a tooltip name in the Tooltip text box.**

   This name appears in the toolbar to identify your macro.

3. **Click the button to the left of the Tooltip text box.**

   The Macros dialog box opens as shown in Figure 9-17.

4. Select, apply, create, or delete macros.

Should you opt to create a macro, you must already be familiar with Visual Basic. Macro authoring in Desktop Intelligence is done using a Visual Basic Editor.

Creating a macro is beyond the scope of this book. If you want to try your hand at a macro, check out *Visual Basic 2005 For Dummies,* by Bill Sempf (published by Wiley).

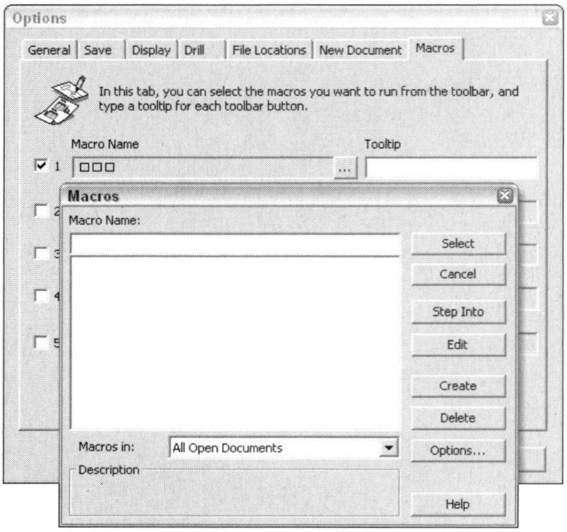

Figure 9-17:
The
Macros tab.

Chapter 10

Building Queries

*I*n the previous chapter, you find out how to define a business object in Universe Designer. In the business intelligence world, a *business object* is an entity that has a meaning for you or your organization. It's much easier for you to work with entities, such as country, product, or sales rather than using the technical SQL definition. In this chapter, you discover how to use the business objects to build your documents.

For example, say you own a clothing store and need to order inventory from the warehouse. You need 20 large red shirts and 15 Hawaiian shirts (size XL), and 30 pairs of black pants (36-inch waist). As the store manager, you don't care about the details, you just want the merchandise quickly so that you can package it nicely and present it to customers.

BusinessObjects works in a similar fashion. You want to package your data nicely in a document, through blocks and charts. Before you can display the data, you must request them from your universe, perhaps even using multiple data providers.

This leads to the word *query*, which has to be one of the most versatile words in the business intelligence language, especially when you're working with BusinessObjects. Just think about it. It can mean many things and take several forms, as a noun or a verb. In earlier chapters, you created a universe; now it's time to use the objects that make up that universe and put on your hard hats. You build a query, which eventually you use to create a document.

If you're having a difficult time trying to figure out what a query is, you can think of it like the brick and mortar that connects the house (your report) to the foundation (the universe). The query really is the building block(s) that comprise your document. In this chapter, you use the query as a data provider to set BusinessObjects Desktop Intelligence up for generating reports.

Queries are really the most interactive part of your BusinessObjects experience. If you don't have a query, you don't have a reporting tool — and where's the fun in that? Even if you're just one of a hundred BusinessObjects users in your office, queries are the one chance you get to be the boss and decide what to use, and how much.

You build queries in this chapter using the Query Panel. Don't worry; that's just a fancy name for the window that you use. The BusinessObjects Query Panel is something like a Burger King. You walk in, have it your way, and then, in theory, are given a made-to-order product that is to your satisfaction.

But enough of these bad analogies; get working with queries!

Using the Query Panel

As with most tasks in BusinessObjects, there is more than one way to use the Query Panel. By now, you probably have a pretty good idea that whatever you can do in Web Intelligence, you can also do in Desktop Intelligence. If so, that's a very astute observation. In the following sections, we first take a look at the DeskI Query Panel, and then the WebI Query Panel.

The DeskI Query Panel

The easiest way to access the Query Panel in Desktop Intelligence is by using the New Report Wizard (see Chapter 9). This ensures that you haven't overlooked any important steps as you're creating a new query. For example, you wouldn't want to, say, forget to select a universe!

After you've run the New Report Wizard, you find yourself face to face with the Query Panel, as shown in Figure 10-1.

Show/Hide Help on Selected Item   Manage Sorts

Default Scope of Analysis   User Objects

Simple Condition   Help

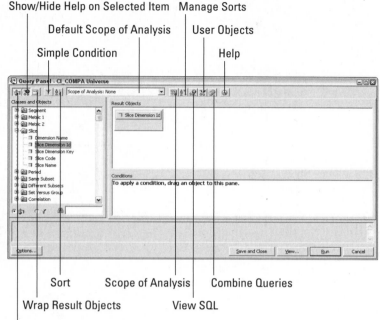

Figure 10-1:
The Query
Panel.

Sort   Scope of Analysis   Combine Queries

Wrap Result Objects   View SQL

Show/Hide All Classes

The Query Panel is neatly broken into the following sections:

- ✔ **Toolbar:** The toolbar is a very helpful area of the Query Panel that lets you take care of an amazing amount of features:

  - *Show/Hide All Classes:* Though we're hard-pressed to find a reason why you'd want to hide these; it's much easier to have them neatly displayed for you,

  - *Show/Hide Help on Selected Item:* You can choose to display a contextual help feature with the Query Panel.

  - *Wrap Result Objects:* You can choose to wrap *result objects*, which are the objects included in a query. You can make these objects appear in rows and columns instead of a single, long row.

  - *Simple Condition:* More pragmatically, if you've already selected at least one object, the simple condition and sort buttons become enabled.

  - *Sort:* Sort the results of your query, in ascending or descending order.

  - *Default Scope of Analysis:* In the middle of the toolbar is a drop-down list that allows you to set your scope of analysis; this is a fancy way of asking how deep into the data do you want to explore.

- *Scope of Analysis:* Related to the Default Scope of Analysis feature, the Scope of Analysis feature lets you manually set the scope or drilling details using the Alerts dialog box.

- *Manage Sorts*: Verify the sorts that are associated with your query or manage multiple sorts.

- *View SQL*: You can verify or analyze the SQL statements in your query using this feature.

- *User Objects*: You can add new objects (user objects) based on the information in your universe using this features.

- *Combine Queries*: This feature lets you add a new tab to the Query Panel so that you can combine queries, usually via the UNION operator.

- *Help*: You can access the online help provided by Business Objects.

✔ Lest you think we went through this way too fast, not to worry, we discuss the toolbar in ample detail in the following sections.

Instead of using multiple queries, we recommend combining multiple queries. Only one query is sent to the database. Multiple queries are sent when you have Join or Synchronization in your SQL statement (multiple measures, different context involved).

✔ **Classes and Objects:** This box displays a hierarchical list of classes and objects (basically a representation of your universe's data) that you can use to add to the query as either an object or a condition. Every element is preceded by an icon indicating whether it's a dimension, measure, predefined condition, or detail.

✔ **Result Objects:** This large area is where you drag-and-drop your classes and objects. Along with the Conditions area, this is where you make up or determine your query's content.

✔ **Conditions:** This area is used in conjunction with the Results Objects area, where you drag-and-drop conditions to apply in your query.

In the Conditions area, you create your query filtering conditions by dragging and dropping predefined conditions, or by creating your own conditions by dragging and dropping dimensions and then defining your own parameters

✔ **Options:** This feature lets you set options for the current query.

✔ **Save and Close:** Perhaps you want to create a query, but aren't quite ready to run it yet and generate your report. Click this button to save your progress and then exit the Query Panel.

If your query takes time to execute, you can save your query and set up your report: define your block formulas, tables, sections, and so on.

✔ **View:** Perhaps you are ready to generate your report, but you're con-cerned about how it's going to look once you've created it. Rather than go through the hassle of creating a query and then having to get rid of it, click this button, which works like the Print Preview function in a word processor.

View allows you to execute the query but you don't have access to the report part. It's useful when you want to check your query result and see which rows are returning by the query and if they fit your expectations.

✔ **Run:** When you're ready to go and nothing can dissuade you, click this button to create your query.

✔ **Cancel:** If it all seems too much, you can click Cancel to abandon your work and quit the Query Panel. Don't forget that once your query is cancelled, you're not getting it back. If you click this button within the New Report Wizard, you go back to the Select Universe page of the wizard.

If you're not sure of what each class or objects represents in the Query Panel, click the Help button on the Query Panel toolbar. A frame appears across the bottom of the Query Panel, displaying a descriptive text for whatever element you click in the Classes and Objects area, as shown in Figure 10-2.

Figure 10-2:
The Classes and Objects help.

The Web1 Query Panels

The Query Panel in Web Intelligence is simply a nightmare. Don't get us wrong; there are plenty of things to like about it, once you figure out what you want to use.

For starters, you have three different ways of using the Query Panel:

✔ **The Query — HTML version** is a purely HTML version of the Query Panel. While it's quick to load and respond, it also has less versatility than the next option, which is the Java Report Panel.

✔ **The Java Report panel** is Java based, which means that it can be slow and that some browsers might not enjoy the experience. On the upside, it is quite robust and offers more features.

✔ **The HTML — Report Panel version** is a no-nonsense Query Panel that lets you walk step by step (or, in this case, tab by tab) through query creation.

Deciding which version of the Query Panel to use depends largely upon your administrator's preferences. In this chapter, we use the Query — HTML version. If you are comfortable with BusinessObjects, you may want to use the more powerful applet instead as it provides a number of features the Query — HTML version doesn't, such as combined queries, subqueries, and ranking. This can prove useful when developing a report using test data and then putting it into production.

The Query — HTML Query Panel is very similar to the DeskI Query Panel, as shown in Figure 10-3.

It contains the following:

- ✔ **Toolbar:** This toolbar lets you

  - *Add a Query:* You can scrap what you're doing and start a new query. This allows you to create more than a single query, much like a muti-data provider in DeskI.

  - *View SQL:* View the SQL for the query.

  - *Query Properties:* View the query properties.

  - *Run Query:* Run the query.

  - *Cancel:* Cancel the query.

- ✔ **Universes:** This portion of the Query Panel displays the available classes and objects that you can use to create your query. You can either choose to display by objects or by hierarchies from the drop-down list.

- ✔ **Result Objects:** As in DeskI, this is where you drag-and-drop your objects to be used in creating the query.

- ✔ **Query Filters:** As in DeskI, this is where you drag-and-drop your objects to be used as filters in creating the query.

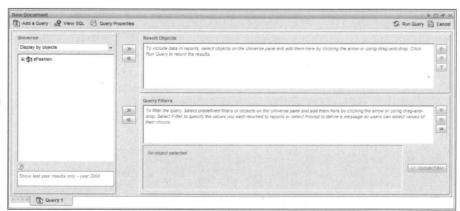

Figure 10-3:
The Query —
HTML Query
Panel in
Webl.

Creating a New Query

Now that you've made your acquaintance with the Query Panel, you can jump right in and actually create a query. This is the first step to creating your own Desktop Intelligence and Web Intelligence documents.

Querying in DeskI

If you're used to working with Desktop Intelligence, follow these steps to create a query:

1. Open Desktop Intelligence, and choose File⇨New.

The New Report Wizard appears.

2. Click Begin and then Next.

The Select a Universe page appears.

3. Select an available universe and click Finish.

The Query Panel appears.

4. Expand the Objects and Classes menus and drag and drop objects from the hierarchy menus to the Result Objects area.

You have to select at least one object; however, keep in mind that your document only provides as much data as you request. For example, if you select the Period object, the document displays the data set for that specific selection, as shown in Figure 10-4.

5. Select any objects to act as filters and drag it to the Conditions area.

Conditions are rules that you can apply to the Query Panel when it generates your reports. For example, of all the returned data, you are only interested in seeing products that are blue. You can select Color and drag it to the Conditions area.

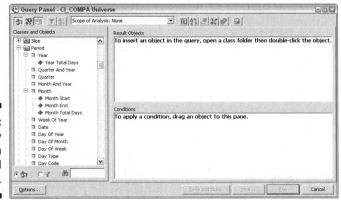

Figure 10-4:
The Query Panel with objects and classes.

Using SQL through the Query Panel

In addition to creating queries, you can use the Query Panel as a tool if you're designing a universe or developing a document — but you have to know a little bit more about SQL to get the most out of that capability. When you define your query by putting objects in the Results pane (or by defining conditions using the Conditions pane), the tool builds an SQL query for you automatically. To see the SQL generated, click the View SQL button on the Query Panel toolbar.

The window that shows you the SQL looks much the same whether you're viewing it in DeskI or in WebI:

✔ **On the left side, a tree view represents all database queries generated by the application.** The query engine may decide (according to your universe design) to build more than one SQL query.

In general, if you put more than one measure into your Results pane, the query engine creates one query per measure.

✔ **Within Web Intelligence, you have a list of the different queries you've designed:**

On the right side, you can see the SQL generated for each statement. That way you know which SQL query is sent to the database, and whether it's correct.

You can also copy the query and execute it to check the data returned. This option is very useful when you're using a tiered SQL query tool.

Advanced users can also modify their SQL queries online in one of two ways:

✔ **In DeskI:** Check the Do Not Generate SQL Before Running option.

✔ **In WebI:** Use the Custom SQL option.

Either way, you end up working with the data returned by your query.

---

6. **Follow the instructions that appear as a highlight in the Conditions object.**

   Here we added Color, double-clicked an operator from the list of operators, and then selected an operand type. For example, you can decide to click Show list of values and select Blue.

7. **Click Run.**

We don't blame you for thinking that you're done with the query at this point. After all, it seemed pretty straightforward, didn't it? To be honest, that's all there is to creating a query, but we'd be remiss if we told you there was nothing else to know about the Query Panel.

There's an important difference between filtering in the Query Panel and applying a report filter — and it has an effect on how long your document takes to load:

✔ **When you apply a filter in the Query Panel,** you retrieve a very limited amount of data — in our case, only Blue products — such that a 10,000-row query takes maybe a second to run. In the resulting document, you can access *only* the data concerning Blue products.

✔ **If you're using a report filter,** your query returns data for all products; a 200,000-row query may take 10 seconds to execute. In the resulting document, you have access to all the data for all the products — in this case, all 200,000 rows — which makes the document 20 times bigger. Such a monster document takes a lot longer to open because the engine has a lot more rows to process.

Querying in Web Intelligence

To be honest, there aren't a lot of differences between performing a simple query in DeskI and in WebI. In fact, the only differences are menu names! Here's how to prepare your query in WebI:

1. **Log on to InfoView.**

2. **Choose New⇨Web Intelligence Document.**

3. **Double-click the universe that you wish to use in the New Web Intelligence Document window.**

4. **In the Query Panel, select the desired objects and filters by dragging and dropping them into either the Objects or Filters area.**

5. **Click Run Query.**

Looking under the Query Panel's hood

Creating a new query was easy enough, but you've really just scratched the surface of what BusinessObjects XI Release 2 can do! In this section, we show you how to use the basic features that are available and may be of great use to you as you create your own queries.

After you create your query, you find yourself looking at a nice new document, like the one in the HTML — Query Panel, as shown in Figure 10-5.

What might you want to do with this report? Here are a few ideas:

✔ **Edit your report:** Perhaps the report doesn't have the level of detail you need. Click the Document button and select Edit Query to go back to the query panel and make changes to the selected objects and classes.

✔ **Filter your data:** Perhaps you've ended up with too many store states and just want to see stores in California. Right-click the State column and select Quick Filter and then select California. (For more about Quick Filter, see the next section.)

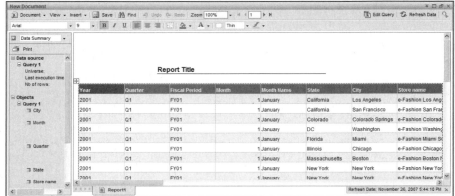

Figure 10-5:
The new report in the HTML — Query Panel.

Limiting the results you get

Suppose you end up with results showing stores in too many states, and you only want to see the stores in California. You can do this operation at the report level or at the query level.

✔ **If you're limiting results at the report level,** right-click the State column and select Quick Filter. Doing so creates a block, section, or report filter — with no impact on your query. The resulting document still has data for all states stored inside it. If your document has many reports, your filter won't impact others reports, and they display data for all states.

✔ **If you're limiting results at the report level by using the Quick Filter mode in the report,** select your objects in the Result Objects panel, and then click the yellow icon. You are prompted to select a value from the Universe Objects list of values. From there you can limit your results.

✔ **If you're limiting results for your entire document,** display it at the query level. You start by creating a new condition [State equals California], and then run the query. Now all data displayed from this data provider is California.

The Quick Filter has a few limitations that are important to keep in mind:

✔ The Quick Filter filters only the report; it has no effect on the query, and it doesn't appear in the Query Panel.

✔ If you have a document with multiple reports, your Report Quick Filter filters only the current report, not the entire document.

✔ Quick Filter is only available if you've deployed ASP.NET with interactive HTML viewing.

Drilling through your document

There are many features available with BusinessObjects and its Query Panel, but the most important feature is undoubtedly the Drill feature.

After you start analyzing your new query results, it's likely you'll want to take an even closer look at what you find. Using the Drill feature, you can descend level by level to the root of the information you seek.

For example, Figure 10-6 displays stores listed (among other criteria) by state. There are stores in Colorado, but just by looking at the report, you can't tell where in Colorado the stores are. By clicking the Drill icon (it looks like a magnifying glass) in the Query Panel, you can go to the Colorado link and see the relevant city, as shown in Figure 10-7.

Figure 10-6: The list of available stores, pre-drill.

					Report Title	
Fiscal Period	Year	Quarter	Holiday (y/n)	Month	State
FY01	2001	Q1	N	1	California
FY01	2001	Q1	N		Colorado
FY01	2001	Q1	N		DC
FY01	2001	Q1	N		Florida
FY01	2001	Q1	N		Illinois
FY01	2001	Q1	N		Massachusetts
FY01	2001	Q1	N		New York
FY01	2001	Q1	N		Texas
FY02	2002	Q1	N		California
FY02	2002	Q1	N		Colorado

Figure 10-7: The State column, drilled one level.

					Report Title	
Fiscal Period	Year	Quarter	Holiday (y/n)	Month	City
FY01	2001	Q1	N	1	Colorado Springs
FY02	2002	Q1	N		Colorado Springs
FY03	2003	Q1	N		Colorado Springs
FY03	2003	Q1	Y		Colorado Springs
				1	
Fiscal Period	Year	Quarter	Holiday (y/n)	Month	City
FY01	2001	Q1	N	2	Colorado Springs
FY02	2002	Q1	N		Colorado Springs
FY03	2003	Q1	N		Colorado Springs

At this point, you have two options:

- ✔ Drill up to your initial state by clicking the upward arrow that appears in the header of the drilled column.

- ✔ Drill down another level by clicking the link of the corresponding city.

In this case, the drill displays the name of the store in that city. If you're not sure whether to drill to the next level, simply hover your mouse over the link in Drill mode and a message appears indicating the next drill level.

When a link no longer appears in the data, no more levels of data are available for drilling.

Here's a rundown on how Drill Through works:

- ✔ In DeskI — and by default in WebI — when you drill out of the existing scope (for instance, by clicking Colorado State and going from the State level to the City level), the tools add City in the Result Objects list. After you run your query, you still have access to the other states; you can navigate from one to another through the top-level list box.

- ✔ WebI has another option, however: Query Filter. To find it, go to the document properties (in an HTML viewer); Query Filter is hidden on the Document menu in the toolbar, in the Java applet.

- ✔ To display the report properties in the General section, you select Document properties; the document properties panel appears at the right side of the applet.

Using the Drill Through option, drilling from the level of (say) Colorado state creates a Query condition [State = Colorado]. Thus, after drilling down below Colorado in your report, you have access to only "Colorado" data — but there's an advantage here: If you retrieve less data, then you only have to look at (say) Cities of the Colorado state, and not *all* cities. Clearly, how you use this option depends on the amount of data you're managing.

Drill Up/Down has some significant differences from Drill Through:

- ✔ **Drill Through is more explicit in Desktop Intelligence than in Web Intelligence.** In particular, the Drill Up/Down option displays New Query, as in Drill Up (New Query).

- ✔ **After your query executes, your document stores the resulting data.** Then, when you drill up or down, you navigate inside this data without generating any further queries against the database.

- ✔ **Drill Through allows you to extend your scope and add some more data in your query.** For instance, in your query you have tour sales revenue by Country, State.

> Here's an example: To navigate from Country to State (or vice versa), you use the Drill Up/Down feature, but if you're working from the State level and you want to analyze the County level, you have to extend your query by using the Drill Through feature.

Handling Multiple Data Providers

WebI and DeskI use essentially the same concepts to deal with data — in much the same way the manager of a furniture store deals with furniture: The manager asks different service providers for items to sell (query), the providers send her what she's ordered (execution), she stores the furniture in her shop (storage), and finally she uses what she has in stock to arrange her shop nicely and bring in all those happy customers (filtering).

BusinessObjects handles data in the same straightforward way: When you create a document, the first step is to choose your providers (in this case, deciding which universes to use). Then you use the Query Panel to create your query, execute it (in effect, asking your data provider for the data you need), store the resulting data in your document; even if what you get isn't always visible, it's always tucked away in the *microcube* (where data from the data provider is stored for use in reports), and then use the reporting feature to display a portion of what you have in tables, sections, and charts. When you're formatting the data in your document, you aren't taking in any more data from your provider; you simply work with the data stored in your microcube. In DeskI, you can see what you have by using the View Data dialog box (choose Data➪View Data).

When you create a query with Desktop Intelligence, you need to select a data provider. That data provider can come in many forms — for example, it could be one of your universes, or an OLAP server, a VB procedure, various XML files, or even a personal data file.

Sometimes your queries may require several different sources to get the job done. To use the store manager analogy, imagine a shop that stocks several different kinds of merchandise — say, garments, furniture, and computers. The stock has to be supplied from several different sources. Well, Web Intelligence and Desktop Intelligence documents offer the same capability in terms of data: You can access various sources — in the BusinessObjects vocabulary, different data providers — to get results for your query.

From the BusinessObjects point of view, all data providers have the same purpose: feeding data to your microcube.

Both DeskI and WebI can access multiple data providers, but each presents you with a different panel as a starting point, and each has its own way to handle the multiple providers.

Using multiple data providers in DeskI

DeskI offers several different ways to add new data providers. In general, you create the first one by using the DataProvider Wizard. Then, if you need to add more data providers, you simply use one of these methods:

✔ **Adding a provider while inserting a new block:** Choose Insert⇨Table/Crosstable or Chart (depending on the block type you want to insert). The New Table Wizard opens, offering four ways to select your data (see Figure 10-8).

The first of these options, Use Existing Data from the Document, doesn't generate a new query; it uses your existing query. The other three options are ways to create a new data provider.

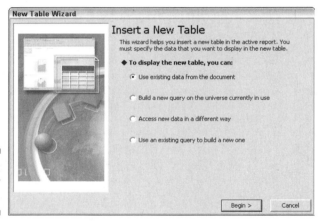

Figure 10-8:
Select your
data.

✔ **Creating from scratch:** You can insert a new data provider without inserting a new report component. Simply choose Data⇨New DataProvider; a wizard offers you the same three options.

✔ **Using the Data Provider dialog box:** In your document, you can access the content of your microcube by using the Data Provider dialog box:

1. *Choose Data⇨View Data.*

   From here you can see the data returned by your query.

2. *Give your query a more meaningful name.*

   For example, you could rename the query from `Query1 from myUniverse` to `Sales of blue shirts`.

3. *Choose from among the ways you can manage the information about your data, from whichever provider, in this window.*

   You can review historical statistics of how often you've refreshed your data, export the result of your query to another database (or even to an Excel sheet), and synchronize data from several providers.

Adding data providers in WebI

You can also manage different data providers in Web Intelligence — but WebI only lets you access universes. If you need to access personal data, don't use Web Intelligence for this purpose.

To add a new query to your document in WebI, follow these steps:

1. **Select Edit Query in the document.**

   You are now in the Query Panel.

2. **Click the Add a Query button on the toolbar.**

   Web Intelligence creates a new query.

3. **Select a universe based on your new query, and then build your query as usual.**

   This feature is not available from the HTML report format.

If you really need access to personal data through Web Intelligence, one way to get it is to create a universe based on (say) your Excel file and then export it to the repository. You can use the resulting universe as you would any other BusinessObjects universe.

If a single data provider isn't enough to get you the information your organization requires, you can add a second data provider to your query — or more — in Web Intelligence.

Linking your data sources

However, before you can use data from multiple various sources together, you must link them so that they can be synchronized. What this does is create a bond between common fields between the two data sources. For example, one data source may have an `Employee ID` field while the other has an `ID` field that has similar purposes. If you use a join to synchronize these fields, the data is linked.

You can synchronize your data providers using either Desktop Intelligence or Web Intelligence — but each program uses different wording to describe the process. Web Intelligence talks about *Merged Dimensions* and *Queries*; Desktop Intelligence refers to *Linked Dimensions* and *Data Providers*.

Here are a few rules to keep in mind when linking:

✔ You must link your data otherwise BusinessObjects returns skewed data that doesn't accurately reflect your data.

✔ You can only link dimension objects.

✔ You can link an unlimited number of dimension objects.

✔ Objects don't have to have the same name.

In DeskI

If you're working in DeskI, you use a tool called the Data Manager to link the dimensions. The workflow to link together dimensions is similar to Web Intelligence:

1. **Create a query in DeskI.**

2. **Highlight the desired object, and click the Link button.**

3. **Select which dimension from the other data provider you want to link to.**

4. **Select the other object to link in the new window.**

5. **Close the Data Manager, and generate your query!**

In WebI

By default, you have to synchronize similar objects. If you've used the same object in two queries, you see a third object created when you choose the Available Objects view in the left panel. This third object combines the two objects that come from the two different original queries — that's the default behavior, anyway. But if you have two different objects with the same *meaning* (say, `Employee Id` and `id`) and you want to synchronize them with Web Intelligence, you have to go to the Java Applet. Here's how that process looks:

1. **Edit your document in the applet and then click the Merge Dimension button on the toolbar.**

   If you are working in InfoView, make sure that you're using the Query — HTML panel or the Java Applet in InfoView using the Web Intelligence tab of the Preferences page.

   The Merged Dimensions dialog box appears (as shown in Figure 10-9):

- *Available Dimensions:* This part shows all the dimensions from your different queries that are not part of a merged dimension.

- *Merged Dimensions:* This part shows the merged dimensions.

2. **Merge your desired dimensions by choosing them in the upper part of the dialog box and then clicking the Merge button.**

3. **Type a name for your newly merged dimension.**

   You can use this merged dimension with data from both queries.

BusinessObjects requires the use of merged dimensions when you're using multiple queries or multiple data providers. BusinessObjects won't let you use unmerged dimensions that come from different data providers; you must either merge or link them.

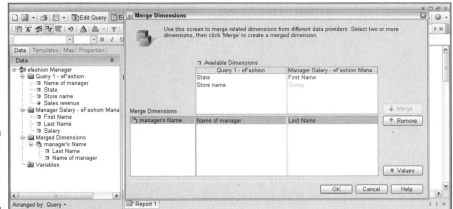

Figure 10-9:
The Merged
Dimensions
dialog box.

Changing a Query to a BusinessObjects Universe

If you're using BusinessObjects at the corporate level, you may have to develop a document based on a development environment, migrate the document to a test environment, and only migrate it to a production environment when you have the bugs worked out. In such a situation, you might have two databases with the same structure but with radically different sizes — say, a small set of data in the test database and millions of rows in the production database. What this situation calls for is changing a query into a BusinessObjects universe.

Here's an overview of how that process unfolds in WebI:

1. **Develop your document based on the small database.**

   The idea here is to create a small-scale model of the universe you want, limiting response time so you can tweak it (using some BusinessObjects magic) the way you want. That way you won't have to re-create your document using production data.

2. **Create a copy of your document.**

   This is a standard precaution in informatics: *Always work with a copy instead of the original.* You never know what might happen to your document before you can deploy it.

3. **Edit your query on the Property tab by clicking the small button close to the name of your desired universe.**

   A dialog box appears, in which you can choose the new universe for the query.

4. **Choose the universe based on your production data,**

5. **Close the dialog box and map the objects in your test universe to those in the production universe.**

6. **Run the query.**

   You're done — you have a document based on your production data.

To do the same thing with Desktop Intelligence, you have to edit the data provider, which involves fewer basic steps:

1. **Select your data provider.**

2. **On the Definition tab, click the button close to the name of your desired universe.**

Chapter 11

Documents in BusinessObjects

· ·

· ·

Many users have confused two elements of BusinessObjects for years: the difference between Business Objects (the company) and BusinessObjects (the product) and — oh, yeah — the difference between reports and documents. You can find out about the former in Chapter 1; we talk about the latter in this chapter.

Also in this chapter, we show you how to work with documents with Desktop Intelligence (*Desktop Intelligence,* or DeskI, is a desktop application installed on your computer that lets you create queries and generate documents). We show you the basics of working with Desktop Intelligence to create a new document or open an existing document — and just to cover all the bases, we explain what a document is in BusinessObjects.

This chapter works specifically with Desktop Intelligence. If you plan on using WebI, see Chapter 13. Both DeskI and WebI have distinct advantages that make both a viable option as a query and reporting tool. However, if you're looking to simply access documents created by your colleagues or create a report without using advanced features that are available in DeskI, then you might prefer using WebI.

Reporting is the key element of BusinessObjects for most users. If you use BusinessObjects, most of your involvement includes generating, refreshing, and broadcasting reports that are based on data someone else in your organization has provided.

Knowing the Difference between Documents and Reports

The whole question of documents versus reports is curiously stubborn. Despite Business Objects' best explanations and user documentation, people still seem confused about this terminology and often use the two words interchangeably.

On the surface, the words *seem* to refer to the same thing — but getting a handle on the differences will help you avoid any potential confusion when you're working with other users.

The notion of a report is something that is more closely affiliated with Crystal Reports instead of BusinessObjects. A *report* can be any of several things:

- **In InfoView:** If you create a graphic representation of your data using InfoView, it's saved as a document. Your document can contain any number of reports.
- **In Desktop Intelligence:** If you create a document in Desktop Intelligence, a report is a tab inside the document. The difference is that you can use data coming from multiple data sources in your report.
- **In BusinessObjects generally:** A graphic representation of your data-source data.

A *document* is less ambiguous, even if DeskI creates documents the same way as WebI. In Desktop Intelligence, you use your data sources' data to create a document. This document can contain multiple reports.

In short (and as a rule), a document is the larger entity that can contain a number of individual reports.

Creating a New Document

The quickest way to create a document in Desktop Intelligence is by using the New Report Wizard. Undoubtedly, the easiest way to create a document or report in Desktop Intelligence is through the New Report Wizard. If you or your administrator keep the default Desktop Intelligence settings, getting to the New Report Wizard is as easy as launching Desktop Intelligence.

We recommend that you use the New Report Wizard until you feel you've mastered document creation with Desktop Intelligence. The wizard walks you through the creation process step by step; there's no chance of inadvertently forgetting a step (as you might if you're manually creating a document).

To create a new document in Desktop Intelligence using the New Report Wizard, follow these steps:

1. **Open Desktop Intelligence by choosing Start⇨All Programs⇨ BusinessObjects XI Release 2⇨BusinessObjects Enterprise⇨ Desktop Intelligence.**

2. **Log on to Desktop Intelligence using your user name and password.**

   The application launches; the New Report Wizard appears, as shown in Figure 11-1.

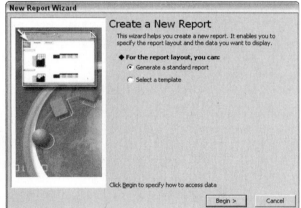

Figure 11-1: The New Report Wizard.

3. **Select a report layout and then click Next.**

   Check with your BusinessObjects administrator and see whether your company has a template that you should use when creating a document; if so, choose the Select a Template option. If not, you can choose to create a standard report.

4. **If you opt to select a template, select a template from the available list in the Available Templates section, and then click Next.**

   A preview of the template appears when you click a template in Available Templates.

To select a template that's stored somewhere else on your computer, click the Browse button.

If you're satisfied with a particular template, you can define it as the default template by selecting the Default Template checkbox.

5. **Choose the data source that you will use to create your report.**

   A report needs a data source from which to pull data that is included in your report.

   If you select Universe, select one of the available universes in your BusinessObjects environment from the drop-down list.

   If you don't want to use a universe, Desktop Intelligence lets you choose from one of five different data sources — including an XML data provider, stored procedures, or even an Excel file. Whichever data source you use is entirely up to you. You should use the appropriate data source that exists for your organization.

6. **If you selected a universe, click Next. If you selected another data source, click Next or Finish, depending on your choice of source.**

   If you selected another data source, select the file or source and make the necessary configurations. For example, if you chose a personal data file, you click the Browse button to find the file, and then set a delimiter and select any desired settings as shown in Figure 11-2.

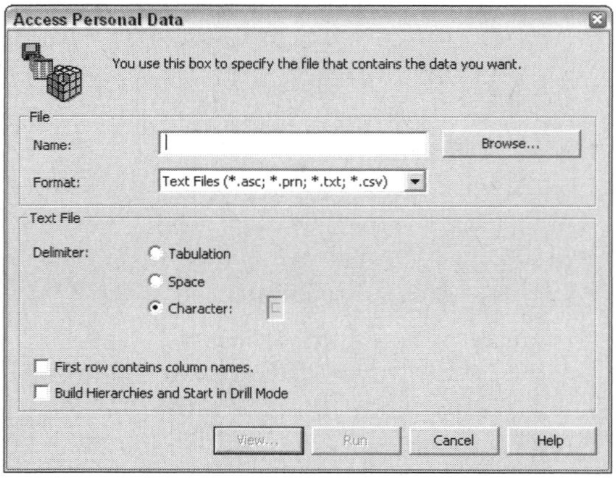

Figure 11-2:
Choosing a
personal
data source.

7. **If you clicked Next in the previous step and you're working with another data source, click Run. If you're working with a universe, click Finish.**

   If you're working with another data source, for example, a text or Excel file, the report displays using the file's contents.

   If you're using a universe, the Query Panel appears, as shown in Figure 11-3.

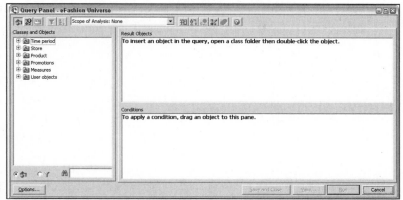

Figure 11-3:
The Query
Panel.

8. **If you're using a universe, select the desired classes and objects from the expandable and collapsible menus.**

The classes and objects represent the contents of your universe, which are neatly organized in hierarchical menus:

   a. *Select an object, drag it to the Objects window, and drop it there, as shown in Figure 11-4.*

   b. *Click the Filter icon (which represents conditions) and the list of pre-defined conditions in your universe is displayed.*

   c. *Drag any necessary predefined conditions to the Conditions window and drop them there. You can also double-click the pre-defined condition for the same affect.*

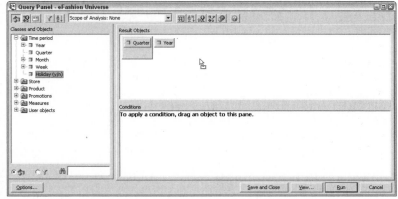

Figure 11-4:
Preparing
for your
report.

9. **Decide what you want to do with your report:**

- Click View to preview the report in its current state prior to being run.
- Click Save and Close to save your report-in-progress in DeskI.
- Click Run to run your report.

Your report appears, depending on your selected objects or conditions, as shown in Figure 11-5.

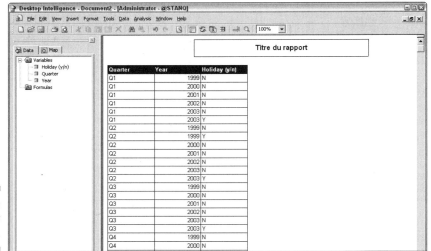

Figure 11-5:
Your new
report.

Saving Your Document

After you complete your report, you may want to save it as a document for later. If you're creating a personal report, you can simply save it to your hard drive. However, most likely you want to save it to a *repository*, which is part of the BusinessObjects administration database system that includes space for documents that can be shared among users.

If you plan to make your document available to other members of your team, save your document to the repository so it's easily accessible.

First, choose File⇨Save and save the document to your userDocs folder. From there, you can upload it to your repository:

1. **When your document is saved, choose File⇨Export to repository.**

   The Export window appears, as shown in Figure 11-6.

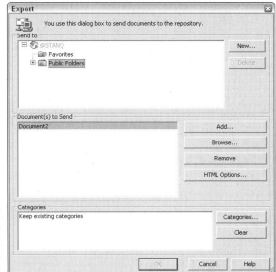

Figure 11-6:
The Export
window.

2. **Select where to export the document.**

   You can either select an existing folder in the repository, or you can create a new folder by clicking New and entering a folder name.

3. **In the Document(s) to Send window, select the document to add and click Add.**

   You can always remove the document by clicking its name and then clicking Remove. If the document you're looking for isn't displayed, look for it by clicking Browse.

4. **Select the desired category for your document.**

   Click the Categories button to select an appropriate category for your document. Click the Manage button in the Select Categories dialog box to create or edit categories in your repository, as shown in Figure 11-7. There is a difference between folders and categories: A document belongs to a single folder but can belong to multiple categories.

5. **Click OK twice.**

   When you've successfully exported your document, a dialog box appears and indicates that success.

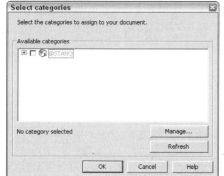

Figure 11-7:
Working
with
categories.

Opening a Document

If you've already created a document, you can always open it with
BusinessObjects Desktop Intelligence.

If you saved your new document to your local hard drive, choose File⇨Open
in Designer. However, if you or another user saved a document to your
repository, you can import the document.

To import a document that you've saved to a repository, follow these steps:

1. **In Designer, choose File⇨Import from Repository.**

   The Import window appears, as shown in Figure 11-8.

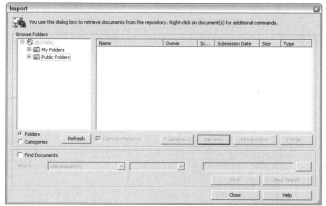

Figure 11-8:
The Import
window.

Open your eyes

If you have a well-fed repository, you may have some difficulties finding your document. Don't worry, you don't have to add spring cleaning to your already long To Do list at work — just use the Find feature to track down what you're looking for.

1. **Click the Find Documents box at the bottom of the Import window.**

   The Find options appear, as shown in the following figure.

2. **Select the directory to search by clicking its name in the Browse Folders area.**

You can't perform a search from the root (top-level) directory; you must select at least a subfolder.

3. **Select or enter criteria for your search in from the Where drop-down boxes.**

4. **Click Search.**

   Your document appears in the document list if it's found.

---

2. **In the Browse Folders section, click the folder containing the desired document. If you are using Categories, select the category; if browsing through folders, select a folder.**

   The documents that are in the folder appear in the primary window.

3. **Select the name of the desired document.**

4. **Retrieve the document by clicking it, which returns the most recent version of the document.**

   In addition to retrieving your document, you can do other things:

   - Click the Properties button to find out more about the document (such as file size, source, and a timestamp).

   - Click the Retrieve Inst button to return an earlier version of the document.

   - Click the Delete the Document button to delete it.

5. **Select a location to save the document and then click Save.**

   The document is now imported from the repository and is available on your hard drive.

If you need to send a document to a colleague, choose File➪Send to Mail.

Making Your Document Work for You

Great — you've created your first document. Of course, you've barely scratched the surface of what you can do with BusinessObjects Desktop Intelligence. You can do some pretty simple stuff, for example, give your report a name, but you can actually perform some neat tricks with your data so the data works for you. For example, you can change how the data appears graphically, as well as how it appears within the actual table.

Naming your document

Why leave your document hanging with a generic title? Not only does it look bad, but your audience probably will have trouble understanding what the document is all about.

To rename your new document, follow these steps:

1. **Double-click the title in the box at the top of the new document.**

   The current title is selected and a cursor appears; this is your sign that you can simply rename the document.

2. **Type the new name in the box.**

   Be sure you're actually just renaming the document and not the report *in* your document! Choose your fields carefully when editing!

3. **Click outside the title box.**

   Even though you're done working with the title box, you're not necessarily finished with it. For example, now is the perfect opportunity to make changes to the report title font or size.

4. **(Optional) To modify the title box attributes, right-click inside the title box.**

   From here, the world is your playground as you can do several things, including:

   - Formatting the title

   - Apply a standard style to your title

   - Work with variables in your report

   We discuss each of these in the next sections.

Naming your report

If you simply want to name the report (which is nothing more than renaming the tab), double-click the tab or choose Tools➪Rename. You might also want to make your report more readable with some simple formatting.

Dressing up your report title

When you right-click your report's title and choose Cell Format, you can work with basic text attributes in the Cell Format dialog box.

On the Appearance tab, shown in Figure 11-9, you can apply basic text-editor features such as font, font style (italic, bold, and so on), font size, color, or even apply effects. As with most text editors, a preview window is available so you can view considered changes in real time before committing.

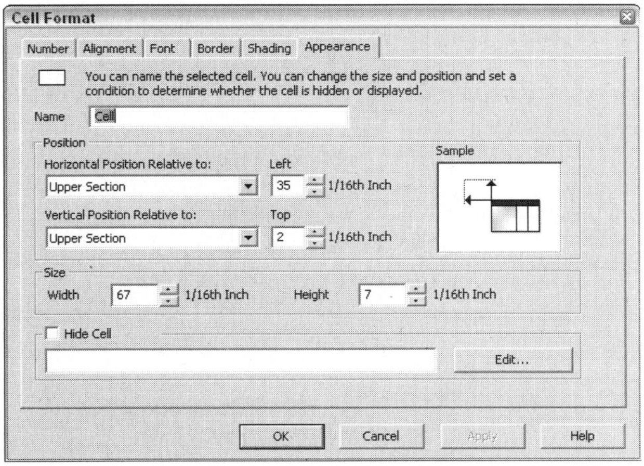

Figure 11-9:
The Cell
Format
dialog box.

You can do more than play around with the title's font. You can also choose the correct alignment, border, and shading you'd like on your report title:

- ✔ **Alignment:** The Alignment tab lets you do things, such as centering or left-justifying your report title, or even determining how it should appear in the title box — perhaps you want your vertical alignment centered, or at the top? Other interesting features include word wrap, which wraps your title onto a second line if necessary, and a feature that allows you to display the report title on every page of your report.

- ✔ **Border:** The Border tab, as you might imagine, lets you set properties for the border of the title box. Perhaps you'd like the border to be slightly more pronounced or in magenta; in that case, you can do that here in several mouse clicks.

If you find a border unnecessary for your report, you can remove it here by clicking on the offending border, much like you do in Microsoft Office applications.

Shading: The Shading tab lets you apply any shading or fills to your title box. If you want to add a gradient, so your title box has a slight blue tint to it, you can use the Shading and Background Color areas of this tab to do just that.

Don't get too carried away with shading; applying a colored background can often get in the way of your text. As nice as a colorful report may be, make sure it doesn't hinder the message of your report, which is best conveyed by its content.

When you're done customizing your report title, click OK to return to your report.

Applying standard styles

In Chapter 9, we discuss how to create standard report formatting styles in the BusinessObjects Desktop Intelligence Options page. This is where you can finally put that hard work to good use.

Imagine you spruced up your report title and then heard from the boss that you need to keep it simple and use the defined corporate style. If you worked with the Options page to create a standard style that would be applied throughout the document, you can quickly revert to that standard.

Right-click the title box, and select the Apply Standard Style option to revert to the standard. Your title once again has the predefined style.

Working with variables

You can also work with the title box through the use of variables; while the actual report title is a *constant* — its name or value doesn't change unless you change it — you can still edit it through the Variables page.

To do so, right-click the title box and choose Variables. Under the Constants menu, you can see the name of your report. If you click Edit, you can modify the *formula* (your report title) and then click OK and then Replace.

Setting the table

The report table is the meat and potatoes of the report. This is the physical representation of the portion of data selected from your data source. This table displays the information that you requested in the Query Panel; in other word, it's a cross section of your data source.

Data is presented in a simple table, as shown in Figure 11-10. There are many ways to work with the data presented in your document; however, if you're using BusinessObjects at work, it's more likely that you'd work with documents using Web Intelligence instead of Desktop Intelligence. Nevertheless, it's still a good idea to know how to work with your report's tables.

So, what exactly can you do? There are the basics, such a formatting your table, or performing a calculation. There are also the more advanced tasks: flipping, charting, and drilling down the data.

		My Report

Quarter	Year	Holiday (y/n)
Q1	1999	N
Q1	2000	N
Q1	2001	N
Q1	2002	N
Q1	2003	N
Q1	2003	Y
Q2	1999	N
Q2	1999	Y
Q2	2000	N
Q2	2001	N
Q2	2002	N
Q2	2003	N
Q2	2003	Y
Q3	1999	N
Q3	2000	N
Q3	2001	N
Q3	2002	N
Q3	2003	N
Q3	2003	Y
Q4	1999	N
Q4	2000	N
Q4	2001	N
Q4	2002	N

Figure 11-10:
The report's
table data.

Flipping your data

You can change how your columns appear, specifically their direction. For example, take a look at how the table appears in Figure 11-10. If you click the top of the header of a column, a black arrow appears, as in Figure 11-11. The column appears with a black background, which indicates that the entire column is selected. Right-click the column and select Rotate Table. Your table changes and appears as shown in Figure 11-12. You can flip the table by selecting a cell inside the table.

Figure 11-11:
The black
arrow
means
you've
selected the
column.

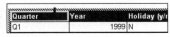

Quarter	Year	Holiday (y/n
Q1	1999	N

Figure 11-12:
The new
look report.

My Report					
Quarter Q1	Q1	Q1	Q1	Q1	Q1
Year 1999	2000	2001	2002	2003	
Holiday (y/n) N	N	N	N	N	Y

Charting your data

Perhaps displaying a table isn't that hot of an idea; maybe you need something that gives a better indication of your data. If you have a measure in the Y-axis and a variable in your X-axis (which you can set in the Query Panel), you can magically change your table to a chart.

Simply click anywhere in your table and then right-click a cell. Select Turn to Chart and the table appears as a chart, provided your table has a variable on the X-axis and a measure on the Y-axis, which you can set back in Desktop Intelligence. If you don't have the right information in your axes, a warning box appears, as shown in Figure 11-13.

Figure 11-13:
A stern
warning for
you if you
don't meet
require-
ments.

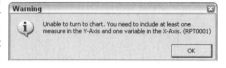

Warning ⊠

ⓘ Unable to turn to chart. You need to include at least one
measure in the Y-Axis and one variable in the X-Axis. (RPT0001)

OK

Drilling your data

Perhaps you want to take a closer look at your data; in that case, you can use the Drill feature, which lets you dig deep and examine individual bits of data.

The following steps show you how to get an up-close-and-personal look at your database data:

1. **Click the cell containing the data that you wish to drill and then click the Drill icon or choose Analysis➪Drill.**

   A new report is created, which is in drill mode.

2. **Right-click a cell in your table and select Scope of Analysis or choose Analysis➪Scope of Analysis.**

   The Scope of Analysis lets you set the range of your drill down; in other words, you can set the boundaries for your drill by selecting which dimensions to include, as shown in Figure 11-14.

Figure 11-14:
The Scope
of Analysis.

3. **Right-click anywhere within the table and select Drill Through.**

4. **Select an object, such as year, and then click OK.**

   This indicates on which object to drill and return precise, individual data. The drilled data is displayed, as shown in Figure 11-15.

Figure 11-15:
The drilled
data
appears
on-screen.

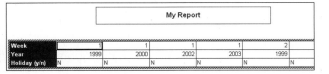

You can always move up or down a level by right-clicking inside the table and selecting Drill Up or Drill Down.

If you mouse over your table, a magnifying glass cursor appears if you're able to drill down. Double-click the cell to drill down (or use the contextual menu). If a text label appears and tells you to right-click, it's telling you that you can't drill down any farther.

Part IV
Making Web Intelligence Work for You

The 5th Wave   By Rich Tennant

DATA MINING

Hold on Brad – I forgot the canary.

DOWN

In this part. . .

Sometimes a full-client application isn't always the most convenient way of going about things; fortunately, BusinessObjects lets you handle most everything Desktop Intelligence does using Web Intelligence (WebI). WebI lets you perform query and reporting tasks using a browser-based interface. This is perfect if you're a road warrior who travels with a laptop that might not be powerful enough to fully run BusinessObjects locally. Simply connect to your Virtual Private Network and fire up your Web browser. Before you know it you'll be admiring Kansas City's Q3 results.

Chapter 12 shows you how to work with InfoView and make it your own by customizing it. You also discover how to perform queries and create reports (Chapter 13). If you need to share your reports with colleagues to prep for an upcoming meeting, you can even find out how to export or send reports to others in your BusinessObjects environment and beyond (Chapter 14).

Chapter 12

Getting Your Hands Dirty with InfoView

*I*n this chapter, you get started with what is basically the rock star of BusinessObjects: InfoView! InfoView is the Web-based application that allows you to do what BusinessObjects Desktop Intelligence does and then some! For example, you can perform queries, create and update documents, and save them to a repository, just as you can with Desktop Intelligence. But you can also do more — such as schedule reports to be refreshed or choose formats for displaying your documents.

If you're using BusinessObjects at your place of business, it's very likely that you're using InfoView to handle your reporting needs. Even though Desktop Intelligence is a very capable product, InfoView has some distinct advantages. For example, using InfoView means that

✔ Everyone on your network can access InfoView, no matter where they are (assuming they can access the network).

✔ Your system administrator doesn't have to install BusinessObjects software on every network computer.

✔ You can work with the familiar Internet Explorer browser, instead of having to familiarize yourself with the look and feel of a new piece of software.

BusinessObjects officially supports only specific versions of Internet Explorer (versions 5 through 7). However, it is likely that you can use other commonly used browsers, such as Firefox, with few difficulties in InfoView. There may be rendering issues using other browsers, but you should be able to get what you need done. However, Firefox doesn't work with Performance Management due to compatibility issues with SVG.

Before you can start creating documents, you need to feel comfortable finding your way around InfoView, accessing it, and customizing its look and feel.

After you discover the basics of using InfoView and *WebI* (short for Web Intelligence) as it is affectionately referred to by BusinessObjects users, you'll find that querying and reporting can be fun! Before we get ahead of ourselves, this chapter simply focuses on getting your feet wet with InfoView. If you're looking to make a quantum leap and jump right in with query and reporting, flip ahead to Chapter 13.

InfoView and WebI aren't interchangeable terms to throw around lightly! *InfoView* is a business intelligence portal that allows you to manage various kinds of documents (DeskI documents, WebI documents, Crystal reports, and so on) and perform tasks, such as scheduling and publishing. *WebI* is a report engine and is the equivalent of a Web-based DeskI.

Logging On to InfoView

As you can imagine, logging on to InfoView is the first step you'll take to getting started. Before you can log on to InfoView, make sure that

✔ **You're connected to your network, either directly or via VPN.**

A *virtual private network* (VPN) is a networking system that uses encryption to create a secure path through the Internet so you can log on to your network remotely. It's used primarily for corporate networks rather than home networks.

✔ **You have the URL, or Web address, of your InfoView installation.** If you don't know the URL, contact your system administrator.

When you have these two issues squared away, you're ready to get started!

Follow these steps to log on to InfoView:

1. **Open your Web browser.**

   We recommend using Internet Explorer or Firefox. If you're using a different Web browser, visit the Business Objects Web site and make sure that your browser is compatible with this release.

2. **Enter the URL, or Web address, for InfoView.**

   If you don't know the URL, contact your system administrator. Usually, it will look similar to this:

   ```
   http://servername:8080/businessobjects/enterprise115
   ```

   The InfoView logon page appears, as shown in Figure 12-1.

3. **Enter your user name and password in the text boxes.**

   Do not modify the System or Authentication fields unless instructed to do so by your system administrator. If you modify these settings without system administrator approval, you most likely won't be able to access InfoView. If you are used to desktop products, use the same user name and password.

4. **Click Log On.**

   When your logon is validated, the InfoView Home page appears, as shown in Figure 12-2.

   In the next section, we show you how to change which page is displayed at logon.

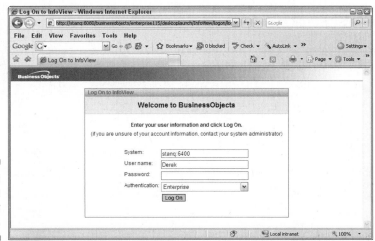

Figure 12-1:
The InfoView logon page.

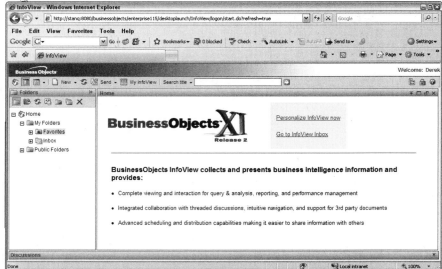

Figure 12-2:
The
InfoView
Home page.

Customizing InfoView

The first time you log on to InfoView, you see its bare-bones default configuration. This may be perfectly fine for many users, but you can liven things up! For example, you can change the opening page to display a preferred report instead of the default Home page.

You do all InfoView customizing through the Preferences page. You can access Preferences in two ways:

- ✔ Click the Personalize InfoView Now link on the Home page (refer to Figure 12-2).
- ✔ Click the Preferences icon (located on the right side of the InfoView toolbar), as shown in Figure 12-3.

The Preferences page is composed of seven tabs; each tab represents a different aspect of InfoView.

Figure 12-3:
The
Preferences
icon.

Preferences

Generally speaking

The General tab (see Figure 12-4) lets you handle InfoView basics.

In the My Initial View section, you can tell InfoView which page to open when you launch the application:

- ✔ **Home:** By default, InfoView opens the Home page.
- ✔ **My InfoView:** This view (discussed later in this chapter) reflects your preferences. If you decide to display InfoView with multiple columns displaying specific documents, this button displays the defined layout.
- ✔ **Favorites**: This opens the Favorites folder, which is a list of any documents that have been saved as favorites, much like a bookmark in your Web browser.
- ✔ **Inbox:** This opens your Inbox, which contains any documents received or stored in this location.
- ✔ **Folder:** Choose a folder from the folder hierarchy displayed in the Folders panel, on the left side of the screen. These are the folders in which you store your documents.
- ✔ **Category:** Choose either the Personal or Corporate category; when saving a document, you can apply a category to the document.

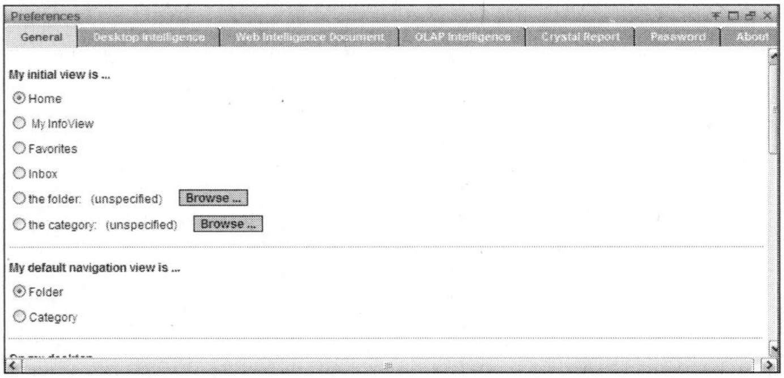

Figure 12-4:
The
General tab.

The Default Navigation View Is section allows you to set how you want to navigate InfoView; you can navigate by folder (a hierarchical format) or by category. There is no particular advantage to either approach; use whichever feels right to you.

The On My Desktop option lets you determine how many objects appear on a single page. By default, the maximum is set to 10. There isn't a real reason to change this setting unless you feel that you can comfortably fit additional objects on your screen without rendering the page too busy to read.

The For Each Document, Show Me option lets you determine what information to display for a document listing. By default, all available options are selected. Unless you feel that your screen is too busy with all this information, we recommend leaving the selected options as is.

You can determine how you wish to view documents in InfoView using the View My Documents option. For example, you can tell InfoView to display the document in the same browser window as InfoView. You can also choose to display all documents one at a time in a separate browser window or to display each document individually in multiple browser windows. By default, this is set to display documents in the InfoView portal.

The General tab also lets you instruct InfoView on what to do when you close the browser window using the When I Close My Browser Window option. You can tell InfoView to automatically log you off of InfoView, to never log you off of InfoView, or to ask if you want to log off. For security reasons, we suggest that you tell InfoView to either log you off or to ask you about logging off when shutting your browser window. This, coincidentally, is also the default setting.

Failure to log off could result in other users accessing your InfoView session. It is imperative that you opt to log off of InfoView (and not to ask your permission) when closing your browser window if you are using a computer where others may have access or if you are using a public computer.

The My Interface Locale option lets you set the browser locale — you specify the country you're in. The selected locale determines which formatting rules (such as number and date/time settings) to apply to InfoView. The locale also determines the language of the application; you can display menus in English, French, Spanish, and so on.

The My Current Time-Zone Is drop-down list lets you select any time zone in the world or opt to use the time zone settings of your BusinessObjects server. You should set this option before you schedule anything because the default time zone depends on the server that is running the BusinessObjects environment and not the time zone of your computer!

Be sure to click Apply before moving on to the next tab!

Desktop Intelligence

The Desktop Intelligence (DeskI) tab lets you choose the display format for documents (by default, HTML is the selected display format). You may opt to use PDF (assuming you have Adobe Acrobat Reader installed) or to open as a Desktop Intelligence document in Desktop Intelligence if you're using Windows.

You must have DeskI stored locally on your machine to use the Desktop Intelligence format.

We recommend using the PDF format if you only intend to view a report, print your document, or to save it locally to your computer. If you plan to work with report *prompts* (queries that require you to enter a value) or to drill through data, then you must work in HTML.

Web Intelligence Document

The Web Intelligence (WebI) Document tab is similar in nature to the Desktop Intelligence tab. This tab lets you determine how to display documents created using InfoView for viewing in InfoView. Unlike the previous tab, it lets you go far beyond display formats, as shown in Figure 12-5.

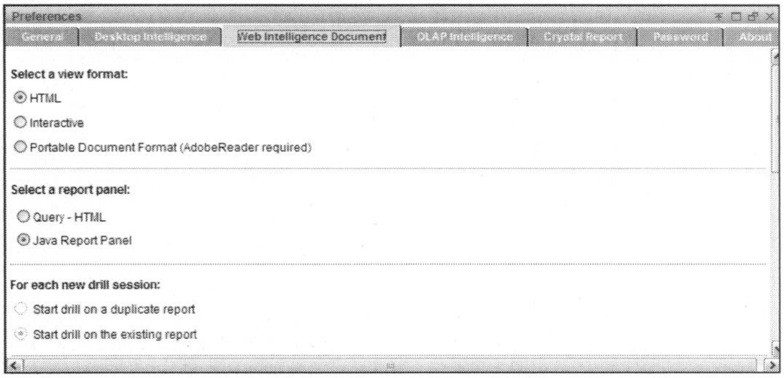

Figure 12-5: The Web Intelligence Document tab.

On this tab, you can select the desired display format, such as HTML or PDF, from the Select a View Format section. You can use a third type of document format, Interactive (which is similar to HTML), to work with prompts, perform sorts, and modify data formatting.

The Select a Report Panel section lets you select what kind of report panel to use when building reports. InfoView lets you choose between the Query — HTML panel and the Java Report Panel, which is the default option (shown in Figure 12-6). The Java Report Panel lets you work with a more graphics-oriented panel; you can also drag and drop objects into your query. The HTML panel has the advantage of being HTML-based (which means no potential third-party application errors can affect performance) and has a wizard-like interface, which is ideal for inexperienced users. (Our normal preference is to use the Java Report Panel, which has more reporting, formatting, and querying options available than the HTML panel.)

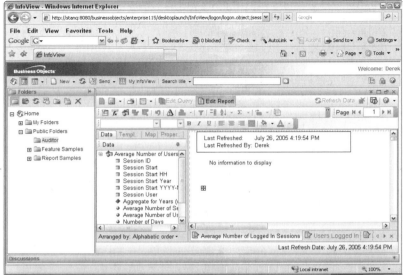

Figure 12-6:
The Java
Report
Panel.

In the For Each New Drill Session section, you can choose how you want to drill reports — directly in an open report or (if you feel more comfortable) in a copy of the report in another window instead of drilling into your original report.

If you're worried about making changes to your document and not finding your way back to the original, change the default option and work with a report duplicate.

The For Each New Drill Session options appear just below the Select a Report Panel option. These options let you decide whether to be prompted if additional data is required. For example, when you're drilling down a level, InfoView may require you to run a new query. (Should that occur, and you have selected this option, InfoView lets you know.)

There are three General drill options:

- ✔ **Prompt if Drill Requires Additional Data:** Displays a prompt if your document requires extra info before carrying on.

- ✔ **Synchronize Drill on Report Blocks:** If you drill down on a table, the table and chart for your data displays drilled values if this option is selected. If selected, your table continues to display drilled data values, but your chart won't because it hasn't been synchronized.

- ✔ **Hide Drill Toolbar:** Lets you hide the drill toolbar.

The Select MS Excel Format option lets you set priorities for Microsoft Excel. There are two choices in this section, though their titles are somewhat ambiguous! Basically, you can display data as either an Excel spreadsheet or as a text file. Again, this is a question of personal preference, as well as perhaps network performance. (We prefer working with reports as Excel spreadsheets, though this is not the default option.)

The Select a Format Locale drop-down list lets you pick which country's display formats to use. The default option, Use Interface Locale, is sufficient for most users. This selection uses the country/language combination of your application and applies the display rules (for date, time, currency, numbers, and so on) for that locale. To apply a different standard, select another locale from the drop-down list.

The When Viewing a Document option lets you select which locale to use when formatting document data. The default option (Use the Document Locale to Format the Data) lets you use the formatting locale to dictate the formatting rules to apply. The other option (Use the Document Locale to Format the Data) lets you apply the formatting rules that were applied to the document when it was created.

The Select Default Universe section lets you select a default BusinessObjects universe to use when creating reports. By default, no universe is defined as the default. Click the Browse button and select an available universe, as shown in Figure 12-7.

Figure 12-7:
The list of available universes.

OLAP Intelligence

One of the great things about business intelligence is all the great terminology you'll encounter — OLAP, ROLAP, LDAP, and so on. In this particular case, this tab helps you select a display format when working with OLAP.

OLAP, otherwise known as *Online Analytical Processing,* quickly performs dynamic multidimensional analysis of information in a relational database.

This tab has but a single option — View My Reports Using — and you can choose one of two: the ActiveX or DHTML (default) viewer. Either option is fine; it comes down to a question of priorities. This DHTML viewer, shown in Figure 12-8, uses a Web browser window and provides considerably more options than ActiveX, while offering fewer security vulnerabilities than ActiveX. On the other hand, ActiveX offers better performance than its Web-based counterpart.

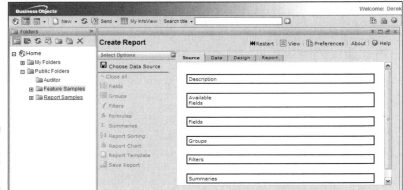

Figure 12-8:
The DHTML
viewer.

Crystal Report

You use the Crystal Report tab (see Figure 12-9) when you're viewing Crystal Reports documents in InfoView. We cover the features of this tab, but stop short of covering how to use Crystal Reports. For that information, we suggest *Crystal Reports 2008 For Dummies* by Allen Taylor (Wiley Publishing).

Figure 12-9:
The Crystal
Report tab.

The View My Reports Using The section lets you choose your viewer of choice:

- ✔ **ActiveX:** If you plan on using the ActiveX viewer, you must make sure that your Web browser supports ActiveX controls. Your Web browser's options or preference pages allow you to set security settings, including whether or not to allow the use of ActiveX in your Web pages.

- ✔ **DHTML:** The DHTML viewer lets you work with a browser-based window for viewing and working with reports. This is the default choice.

- ✔ **Advanced DHTML:** The Advanced DHTML viewer has the same features as the DHTML viewer, but also has an integrated search feature. Frankly, if you're leaning toward the DHTML viewer, we recommend using the Advanced DHTML viewer instead.

- ✔ **Java:** Java is a viable option if your Web browser supports Java Virtual Machine (JVM).

The "best" viewer is the one you're most comfortable working with.

The DHTML Viewer Printing Uses The section lets you determine how to print documents or reports if you're using the DHTML Viewer. The default option (ActiveX Printing Control) lets you print from a control (button). The other option (Acrobat Reader Printing Control) lets you print from the Adobe Acrobat Reader (once the report is exported to PDF format). We prefer using Adobe Acrobat because we're comfortable with it.

You only need to set the DHTML Viewer Printing Uses The and Rendering Resolution (DHTML Viewers) sections if you plan to use one of the DHTML viewers. Otherwise you can leave the default settings in place.

The Preferred Measuring Units for Report Page Layout section lets you decide if you want to use a metric or Imperial unit of measurement. Whether to use inches or millimeters is purely a question of comfort.

The Rendering Resolution (DHTML Viewers) section is solely for users working with the DHTML viewer (see — there's a reason that it's the default viewer!): You can send page-rendering DPI, which means you must set the print level for the DHTML viewer. If you're comfortable reading a smaller font, you can use 96 DPI; if you prefer a larger font, we recommend using 120 DPI.

Password

The Password tab is a rather straightforward tab that leaves little to the imagination. This is where you can change the password that you use to log on to InfoView.

Should you forget your password, you can contact your BusinessObjects administrator who can help you reset your password. If you're the BusinessObjects administrator and you've forgotten your password, you're in trouble.

To change your password, follow these steps:

1. **Click the Passwords tab in InfoView Preferences.**

2. **Enter your old password.**

3. **Enter your new password.**

4. **Enter your new password again for confirmation.**

5. **Click Submit.**

While changing your password is easy, picking a good password can be a trying exercise. For security reasons, do not pick a password that others are likely to guess based on your personality or hobbies. At the same time, be practical — you're likely to forget a password like %4@fsK8. Because writing down a password makes as much sense as being a Disney fan and selecting MickeyMouse as a password, it's better to find a compromise between the two!

What's it all about?

The final tab, About, provides copyright information and other legalese. It doesn't offer much information that can help you with InfoView.

I Did It MyInfoView's Way

If the Preferences page is where you customize your InfoView, then MyInfoView is where you put it all together and show off. Okay, if you're more modest than that, MyInfoView lets you "build your own InfoView" and specify not only the content but where it should appear.

The MyInfoView page lets you display frequently used elements, such as InfoView folders and reports, or even Web sites in frames. You can pick the layout of your frames that accommodates all the content you want to display.

The MyInfoView page is one of the potential Home pages you can define. You can customize your content and tell InfoView to load this page when you open it so your customized content appears straightaway. We recommend using MyInfoView to save you time and effort; instead of hunting around for InfoView content, you can put it at your fingertips.

When you browse the MyInfoView page for the first time, it's pretty barren, as shown in Figure 12-10.

Click the Resize buttons at the top-right of the MyInfoView frame to maximize viewing space.

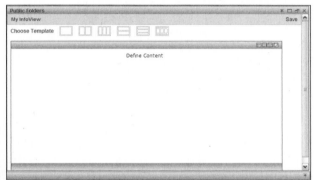

Figure 12-10:
MyInfoView.

Contemplating your template

Before you start worrying about content, think first about your MyInfoView layout. It's like building a house; first you establish your foundation. In this case, the MyInfoView template is your foundation.

MyInfoView gives you six different template options. Follow these steps to set up your template:

1. **Log on to InfoView and click MyInfoView.**

   The MyInfoView page appears; at the top of the page (above the Define Content window) is a series of six templates that resemble column layouts.

2. **Click the desired template from the list of available templates.**

   You can hover your mouse pointer over the template to find out its name.

   A dialog box opens, warning you that you're about to overwrite any existing changes.

3. **Click OK in the dialog box.**

4. **Click Save back in MyInfoView.**

   Your template is saved to MyInfoView. If you log out of InfoView and come back to MyInfoView, MyInfoView appears on-screen using the template you saved.

If you decide that you're tired of the selected template, you can apply a new template by repeating these steps.

If you've already defined content and try to change templates, you lose any existing frame content.

Defining content or being happy with MyInfoView

After you select the right template for MyInfoView, you can define the content for each of the frames. Before doing so, however, familiarize yourself with the five buttons found in your frame, as shown in Figure 12-11.

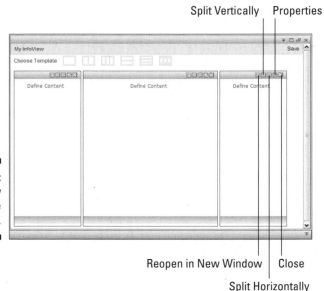

Figure 12-11: MyInfoView frame buttons.

✔ **Reopen in New Window:** Opens the frame in a new browser window. This is a useful button because once populated, you may find that you don't have enough room in the frame to actually view all of the content.

✔ **Split Vertically:** Splits the existing frame vertically into two columns of equal size.

✔ **Split Horizontally:** Splits the existing frame vertically into three columns of equal size.

✔ **Properties:** Displays the Dashboard Properties window. We show you how to change the properties in the upcoming steps.

✔ **Close:** Closes the relevant frame. The remaining frames are resized to use the space vacated by the deleted frame. Note that this button only appears once you've selected one of the other buttons first.

Follow these steps to define content for your MyInfoView frame:

1. **Once you have put your template in place, click Define Content.**

   The Dashboard Properties window appears.

   You can also access the Dashboard Properties window by clicking the Properties button.

2. **Select either a Web Address or an Object to display in the frame. If you opt to use a Web address, enter a valid URL. If you prefer an Object, select a folder or a report to display.**

3. **(Optional) In the Header section, enter a header name.**

   If you entered an URL in Step 2, you can give it a name for easy reference by entering it in the Caption field. If you choose an object in Step 2, the name of the selected folder or file automatically appears in the Caption field. For both Web addresses and objects, you can add an URL that makes the header clickable. Also, be sure that the Header check box is selected!

4. **(Optional) In the Footer section, enter a footer name.**

   The Caption field is empty by default. You can enter a footer text in the text area as well as an URL. (This section works exactly the same as the Header section.)

5. **Select which borders to apply in the Border section.**

   By default, all borders — top, bottom, left, and right — are selected, as shown in Figure 12-12.

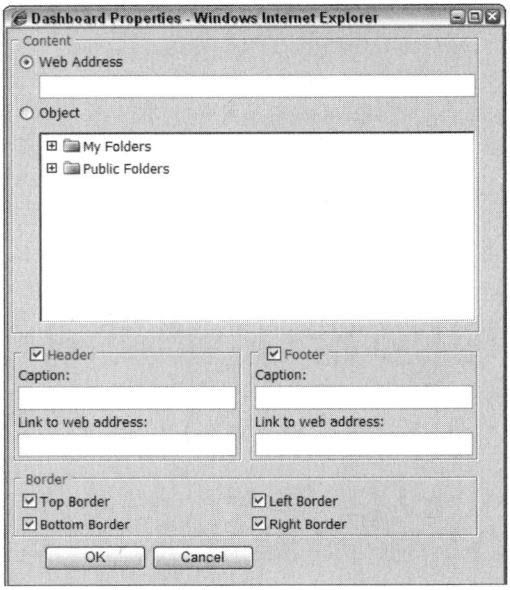

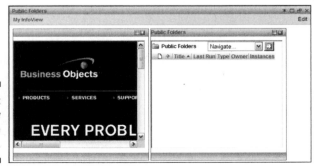

Figure 12-12:
The Dashboard Properties window.

6. **Click OK.**

The updated My InfoView page appears, as shown in Figure 12-13.

7. **Save your changes by clicking Save.**

If you want to display MyInfoView as your Home page, you can go to the Preferences pages and change the Home page (see the section "Customizing InfoView" earlier in this chapter). When you launch MyInfoView and decide that it's time to make changes to your page, you can click the Edit link (as shown in Figure 12-13) and repeat the steps.

Figure 12-13:
MyInfoView with the Edit link.

Chapter 13

Setting Up Your Documents

. . . .

In This Chapter

▶ Creating a new document

▶ Creating other types of files

▶ Using prompts

▶ Saving and printing documents

. . . .

*I*f we've said it once, we've said it a million times: If you're using BusinessObjects, you may be almost destined to use WebI — for lots of tasks, including report creation.

It's not hard to see why: Creating documents and reports in WebI is easy.

One reason is that WebI (and InfoView) nestles nicely into the framework of your favorite Web browser. And here's another: It has a very user-friendly design that doesn't overcrowd screen real estate.

This chapter extols the virtues of WebI. Exclusively. If you plan on using Desktop Intelligence instead, see Chapter 9.

In this chapter, we show you how to create a new document. It's all about making choices. To create a document (for example), you must select one of your available universes — an important decision, because the universe you pick contains the data you use as you create your reports. We also offer pointers on using *prompts* (fields that let you add a unique values for particular objects) to build your document, so you can zero in on the precise data you need. You can even use multivalue prompts, too, so you can add several countries, for example!

Then we show you how to save your document and even print it for good measure! There are many ways, as well as many places, for you to save your documents.

Creating a Document

Using InfoView, you can create many different types of documents —
including Desktop Intelligence documents, publications, WebI documents,
hyperlinks, analytic reports, and so on; you can even add a Microsoft
Office document through InfoView. What you are allowed to create depends
solely on the access given to your user account from the BusinessObjects
administrator. For example, you may be able to add a Microsoft Office
document through WebI but are unable to create a WebI document.

In this section, we show you how to create a Web Intelligence document.

For more information on creating a Crystal Report in InfoView, refer to *Crystal
Reports 2008 For Dummies* by Allen G. Taylor (published by Wiley).

The following steps walk you through the creation of a document in InfoView:

1. **Choose New⇨Web Intelligence Document from the InfoView toolbar.**

   The list of available universes appears, as shown in Figure 13-1.

2. **Select the name of the desired universe.**

   Web Intelligence launches and the report panel appears; what it looks
   like depends on the type of panel you selected in InfoView Preferences.
   (For these steps, we selected Java Report Panel.)

   You can change your report panel by clicking the Preferences icon on
   the InfoView toolbar and selecting the Web Intelligence Documents tab.

3. **On the data tab, expand the menus; then drag and drop the desired
   objects into the Results Objects pane (shown in Figure 13-2).**

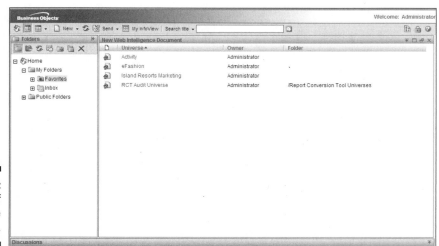

Figure 13-1:
The list of
available
universes.

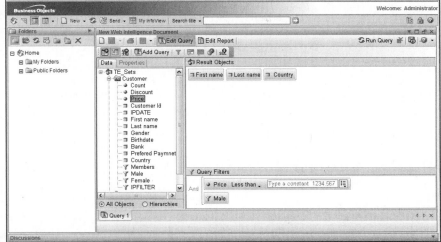

Figure 13-2:
The Results
Objects
pane.

4. **(Optional) If you're finished, click Run Query to display your report on-screen, or you can add filters in Step 5.**

5. **Add filters (represented by a gold filter icon) by dragging and dropping them into the Query Filters pane.**

   Alternatively, you can add an object and make it a customized filter.

6. **Click Run Query.**

   WebI generates a report based on the selected objects and filters you applied in the Query Panel. Either the report appears or a prompt appears, as shown in Figure 13-3. (A later section, "Using Prompts," explains how to fill in prompts.)

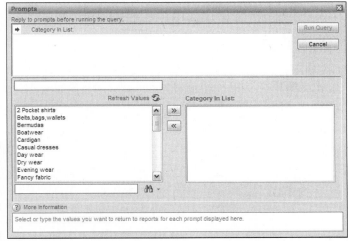

Figure 13-3:
A request to
fill in a
prompt
appears.

Creating Other Types of Files

In the previous section, we showed you how to create a Web Intelligence document. In this section, we show you how to create other things in InfoView.

Log in to InfoView and click the New button on the toolbar to reveal the extensive list of document types:

- **Desktop Intelligence:** Just in case you missed Desktop Intelligence, selecting this option launches it so you can create a report using your desktop-based application.

- **Publication:** This option creates a new instance (including a title, keyword, and category) that then appears in the selected folder.

- **Web Intelligence Document:** You can use this option to create a new report in InfoView through the Query Panel. We discuss the Query Panel in Chapter 10.

- **Hyperlink:** This option stores a link to a frequently visited site in your BusinessObjects environment. Simply provide title, description, keyword(s), location, and (oh yes) a valid URL.

- **Analytic:** Creates a dashboard that graphically represents system metrics, using the Performance Manager Analytics Tools (an application that is part of BusinessObjects Enterprise since BusinessObjects XI R2).

- **OLAP Intelligence Report:** Creates a new OLAP (Online Analytical Processing) Intelligence Report.

- **OLAP Intelligence Connection:** Sets up a new OLAP connection; an OLAP connection is required if you want to create a new OLAP Intelligence Report.

- **Single Dashboard:** Creates a single dashboard, or framework, much like that you can set up in the My InfoView page.

- **Crystal Report:** Creates a Crystal Report.

- **Report Data Source:** Sets up the data-source connection for your Crystal Report.

- **Document from local computer:** This neat little option lets you add third-party documents to your BusinessObjects environment. For example, you can add a Microsoft Office document (Word, Excel, PowerPoint), or even Adobe Acrobat (PDF) and text files, as shown in Figure 13-4.

- **Folder:** If you have the right permissions, you can use this option to create a new folder in your BusinessObjects environment.

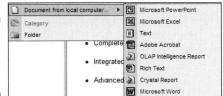

Figure 13-4:
Add a file
from your
computer.

Using Prompts

Prompts are interactive conditions that are useful when you want to change your conditions at refresh time. Otherwise, you can use static conditions if such interactivity is not necessary. For example, if you're the manager of the Chicago outlet, you can set `Chicago` as a static condition and `products` as a prompt. By doing that, you can choose different products for your outlet every time you refresh your document.

Prompts give you an interactive role in document creation; they give you on-screen places to enter specific values that affect the data you want returned. In effect, prompts are conditions you can impose that define the environment, other conditions, or whatever else is required to produce the desired data.

The three report panels (Query HTML, Java, and HTML) all work much the same. If you're new to filters and prompts, we recommend using the Query HTML report panel, which has a particularly easy interface. In this section, we use the Query HTML report panel, which you can select by choosing Preferences⇨Web Intelligence Document.

The following steps show how to set up a prompt:

1. **Log in to InfoView, and choose New⇨Web Intelligence Document.**

   WebIntelligence launches and the Query HTML panel appears (if it doesn't, change it in InfoView's Preferences).

2. **Select a universe.**

   In this example, select the eFashion universe.

3. **Expand the Time period menu; drag the objects you want into the Result Objects window.**

   We selected three objects: Year Quarter, and Week now appear in the Result Object window.

4. **Expand the Store menu and drag the objects you want into the Result Objects window.**

   We selected two objects: City and State. These two objects now appear in the window, next to the Time Period objects, as shown in Figure 13-5.

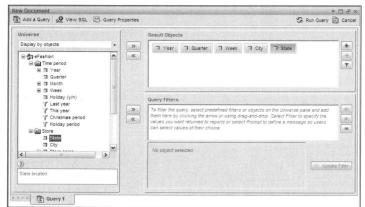

Figure 13-5:
The Query
Panel with
objects.

You can remove an object at any time prior to running the query by dragging it out of the Result Objects or Query Filters windows. You can also select the object and press the Delete key.

 5. **Under the Time period menu, drag the filters you want into the Query Filters window.**

Your selection appears in the window (we selected the Year filter).

If you use a predefined filter, you don't have to set any additional parameters. Predefined filters are already specific about the detailed information they filter from the data and provide in your report.

 6. **Expand the Product menu, and drag and drop the objects you want to the Query Filters window.**

Your selection appears in the Query Filters window (we selected the Category object, shown in Figure 13-6).

Notice that in this step, you bring an object — not a filter — into the Query Filters window. Because the object isn't already a filter, you have to adjust it a bit to get it in shape for use. Figure 13-6 shows how the Query Panel changes appearance to accommodate an object used as a filter.

 7. **Decide whether you want to create a filter or a prompt, using the Filter or Prompt radio buttons.**

A filter grabs specific values as data passes through it. A prompt does the same thing, except you can enter a value to specify what's grabbed.

If you decided to use Java Report Panel instead of the Query — HTML Panel, the Prompt radio button doesn't appear. You must add the object as a filter and select Prompt from the drop down list on the right side of the object.

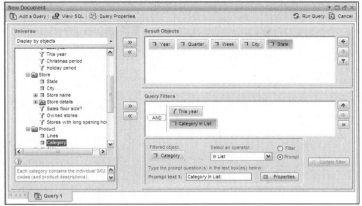

Figure 13-6:
The object
as a filter.

8. **Select an operator from the Select an Operator drop-down list.**

   The operator list contains a list of 16 operators, such as the equals (=) or greater-than (>) signs. These operators help you create the conditions for the values that your report's users will enter.

9. **In the Prompt Text 1 text box, enter a question for your prompt.**

   A default text is provided, but you can replace it with more descriptive text in the form of a question. We suggest putting a different prompt name.

10. **Click the Properties button.**

    The Properties window appears (as shown in Figure 13-7), where you can specify additional settings.

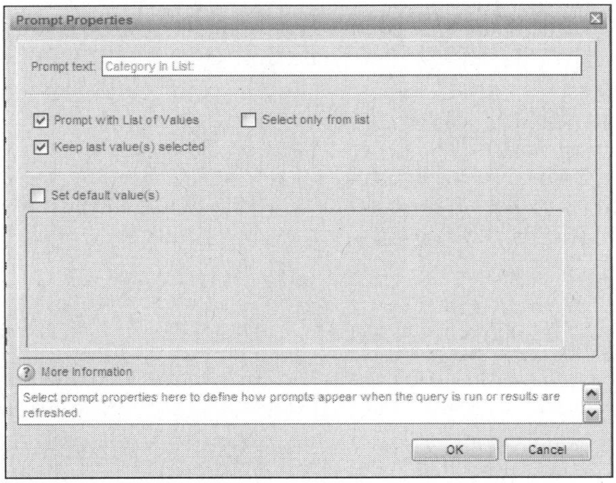

Figure 13-7:
The
Properties
window.

11. **Leave the default settings in place for now; if you wish to provide a default value for your prompt, enable the Set Default Value(s) option. Click OK to go back to the Query Panel.**

    The default settings provide users with a list of values from which to choose a prompt value; the value last used remains if the report's users decide to keep it unchanged.

    If you enable the Select Default Value(s) option, you can type a default value (or click Values to select a value from a list).

12. **Click Update Filter.**

    The prompt is now established for your report. When you generate your document, or refresh your data, the document asks you to submit a value for the filter.

Save a Document, Save a Life

After you've created a document, you'll probably want to save it for future use. BusinessObjects provides you with a number of options for saving your reports. Fortunately, the software doesn't assume that everyone who needs access to your report has access to BusinessObjects to be able to read it.

First you have to decide where this document is going to be needed. You have two general options:

- ✔ If your document is a *personal document* created for your own use, save it somewhere in My Folders.

- ✔ If your document is a *corporate document* that you want to make available to several groups or users, store it somewhere in Public Folders.

 You may also want to save your document to your computer, in one of various formats that don't require BusinessObjects, such in Adobe PDF format, text (CSV), or Microsoft Excel. This is particularly helpful if you've created a document that may contain one to many reports.

Another concern is how to categorize your document. BusinessObjects lets you create various *categories*, brief descriptions or keywords that you can apply to your document for easy access.

Saving your document

The following steps show how to save your document as a personal or corporate document:

1. **Click the Save icon on the document's toolbar.**

The Save Document window appears.

2. **Enter a document name for the title, a description, and any appropriate keywords.**

3. **Select whether to refresh the data when the document is opened.**

   We recommend selecting this option.

   We don't recommend checking the Permanent Regional Formatting check box in case users are in multiple countries.

4. **Select a folder location for your document.**

   Use My Folders for a personal document; use Public Folders if you're creating corporate documents.

5. **Select a category for your document.**

   Depending on the nature of the document, you can expand either the Personal or Corporate categories and then select an existing category, as shown in Figure 13-8.

6. **Click OK.**

Your document appears in the location to which you saved it, as shown in Figure 13-9.

Figure 13-8:
The categories.

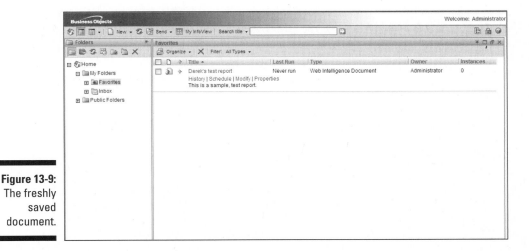

Figure 13-9:
The freshly saved document.

If you save a document to your desktop, you haven't yet saved it to your repository (see the upcoming section, "Making Saved As documents available"). Be sure to do a standard save if you want to store the document in either My Folders or Public Folders.

Adding new categories

It's likely that your initial categories were set up by your BusinessObjects administrator or perhaps another colleague. As your *repository* (the place where your documents are stored) grows over time, you'll probably have to add more categories to your repertoire.

To add new categories, follow these steps:

1. **In InfoView, go to the Folders panel and click the Categories icon.**

   The Categories panel appears, as shown in Figure 13-10.

2. **Select an existing category type (Personal or Corporate), and in the toolbar, choose New⇨Categories.**

   You can't create a new category if you haven't already selected a category.

   The Create a New Category window appears, as shown in Figure 13-11.

3. **Add a category name, a description, and any relevant keywords.**

   Be sure to provide as much information and detail as possible so other users know when to use this category.

Figure 13-10:
The
Categories
panel.

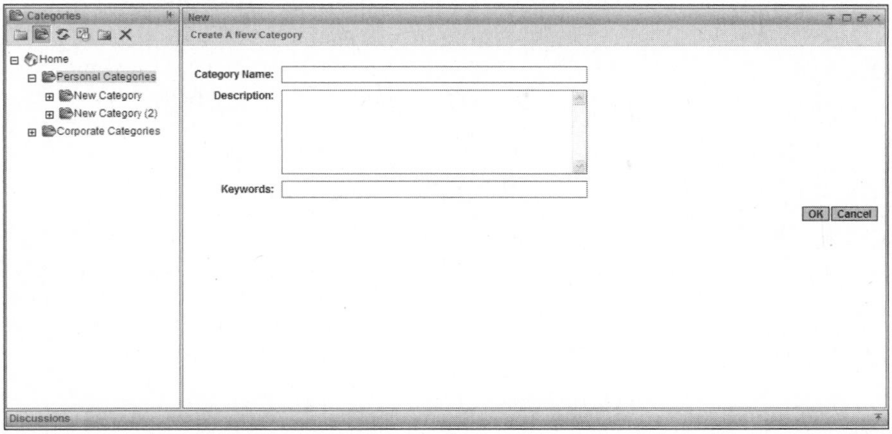

Figure 13-11:
The Create
a New
Category
window.

4. **Click OK.**

The new category appears in the Categories panel, as shown in Figure 13-12.

Figure 13-12:
The new
category
appears.

Saving documents in other formats

You don't necessarily have to save your document as a Web Intelligence document. You can also save the document in a third-party format so other people can access it.

InfoView lets you save the document in any of four formats: Microsoft Excel, PDF, CSV, and CSV (with options).

If you opt to save your document as a Microsoft Excel, PDF file, or a CSV (text) file, InfoView converts your document on the spot and displays a Save As dialog box. All that's left for you to do is to save the document as you would any other file in Windows.

If you opt to save the document using the CSV (with options) format, there is one slight change. The Save as CSV–Options dialog box appears (as shown in Figure 13-13); there you can configure your formatting settings. You can set text qualifiers, column delimiters, character sets, or add a new character set. If you're satisfied with the settings, you can designate them as your new default values. After you've made your changes and clicked OK, the standard Save As dialog box appears.

Data displayed in a Microsoft Excel spreadsheet isn't the same content as displayed in an Adobe PDF file or a CSV file. In Microsoft Excel and Adobe PDF format, you have the full WebI document with charts, multiple documents, formula results from document filters, and so on. In CSV format, the database query results appear and data comes directly from the database without any document formatting, filtering, or any reporting features.

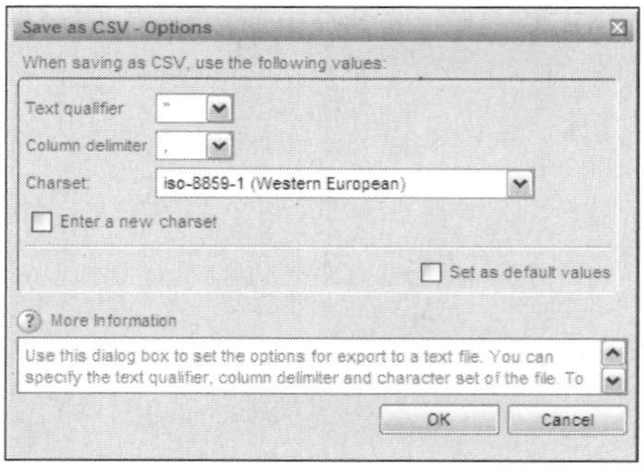

Figure 13-13:
The CSV
(with
options)
dialog box.

If you opt to use any of these formats, other users can't modify the document content. Any changes made are reflected only in the file modified; if the document has also been saved to the repository, any changes aren't saved there.

Which format option you choose depends on your personal preferences and document compatibility. If you plan to use the Microsoft Excel or PDF formats (for example), anyone viewing the document has to use Microsoft Office or Acrobat Reader to view the files.

Making Saved As documents available

Say you've created a document for someone in Microsoft Excel format; your colleague liked it so much that she wants you to put it in the repository, specifically in the Corporate folders.

If you've saved the file to your desktop, you can save it to the repository by choosing New⇨Document from Local Computer⇨Microsoft Excel from the InfoView toolbar.

A Find File dialog box appears; select your file and then supply the other pieces of information requested, such as a title, description, keywords, and location. After you select your file, the rest of the process is the same as saving a document for the first time. When you've done that, the Microsoft Excel file appears in the desired location, as shown in Figure 13-14.

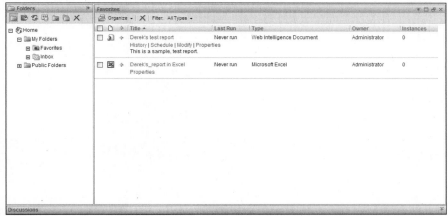

Figure 13-14:
The Excel file in its new home.

Printing Your Document

Printing your document in InfoView can be a lesson learned the hard way if you're not careful. An open document in InfoView isn't necessarily the easiest way to print your document; we'll show you how to make this process go a little more smoothly.

If you're looking to print a document that was created in one of the other formats, you can simply open the file and print it in the usual way. If you want to print a document in InfoView, things are done a little differently.

Plain and simple, if you want your document to print properly, it must first be in PDF mode. If your document is in HTML, you must change the view. If you try to print your document in HTML format, it doesn't print properly.

The following steps show you how to print your document as a PDF document:

1. **If your document in InfoView appears in HTML format, choose View⇨PDF mode in the document toolbar.**

   The document appears in PDF format.

2. **Click the Adobe print icon located in the Adobe toolbar within the document, as shown in Figure 13-15.**

   A Print dialog box appears.

   You can also save your document to your hard drive using the Save button in the Adobe toolbar.

3. **Choose the printer you want to print to, specify how many copies you want, and click Print.**

   Your document prints as a PDF document.

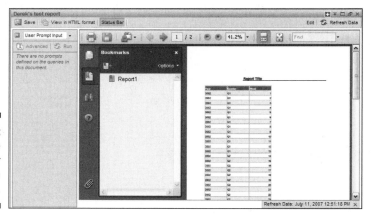

Figure 13-15:
The Adobe toolbar when in PDF mode.

You really don't want to print your document any other way. If you attempt to print as HTML, the rendering almost certainly won't be to your liking and it can be near impossible to decipher. Printing your document as a PDF guarantees readability.

Chapter 14

Working with Your Completed Documents

*U*p to this point, most of this book has been about reports and documents. We've covered how to create them, how to maximize your data to find what you're looking for, we've even looked at mundane tasks like saving and printing your documents.

What we've not covered concerning documents — until now — is how to communicate with your documents.

Not every InfoView user is responsible for creating reports and documents — but every InfoView user is a pretty sure bet to *access* reports and documents and eventually *share* them with colleagues.

One of the most important aspects of business intelligence is the capability to share or broadcast data. InfoView gets you to the heart of this capability through a very user-friendly, Web-based environment. This chapter discusses what to do with your documents after you've created them — you didn't think you were *finished*, did you?

Accessing Saved Documents

Reporting in BusinessObjects is a two-way street. As much as you might enjoy using the Query Panel and create informative reports and documents in minutes, sometimes you're going to have to share the fun with your colleagues — and then make use of their documents.

Fortunately, you're never more than a few mouse clicks away from accessing documents in InfoView. Your documents are almost always in one of two places: My Folders and Public Folders, which are shown in Figure 14-1.

Logically speaking, you can access documents created and saved by others using the Public Folders. The My Folders folder contains documents that you have explicitly saved to this folder, be they your own documents or others' documents, in either the Inbox or Favorites.

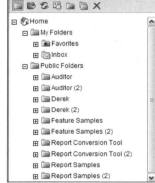

Figure 14-1: The InfoView My Folders and Public Folders hierarchy.

Finding a saved document

If you've been using BusinessObjects long enough, you may have so many documents at your disposal that finding what you're looking for is a real challenge. Like most applications, InfoView has a search feature to quickly find the document(s) that you're looking for.

The Search Title box is built right in to the InfoView toolbar, as shown in Figure 14-2. Type either the entire report title or part of the document title you're looking for in the text box and then click the search icon.

Even though you can enter partial titles in the Search Title box, you cannot use wildcards. For example, if you want to find a document with the word "Analytic" in the title, you can use "Analytic", "aly", and so on; however, if you type "Ana*" or "Analy*.*", your search yields no results.

Figure 14-2: The Search title feature.

If you enter a document title or letter combination that matches a document that is in either My Folders or Public Folders, it appears as shown in Figure 14-3. From here, you can perform a number of important tasks using the document, such as open, send, or print the report.

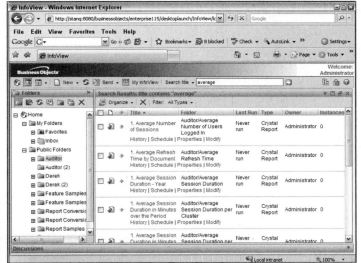

Figure 14-3:
The Search
title results.

Going straight to the man

Perhaps you've grown overly accustomed to all the documents that are available in your BusinessObjects environment. In that case, you can go straight to the saved document that you seek. The ease with which you find the desired document depends largely on how well your colleagues or administrator have maintained a tidy set of folders.

If care has been taken to maintain appropriately labeled folders or perform regular maintenance or spring cleaning, you should be able to find a specific document relatively quickly.

As we discussed in Chapter 13, you can create or designate which folders to use when saving documents. To access these documents, expand the Public Folders hierarchy in the Folder pane. When you find the appropriate subfolder, expand it so that the list of documents for that subfolder appears in the main InfoView window.

The contents of Public Folders vary by BusinessObjects environment because its content layout is entirely up to you or your organization.

Getting the Lowdown on Your Document

Whether you know it or not, the page that appears when you open a sub-folder in either My Folders or Public Folders, or when you perform a title search, is extremely important. Sure, this page may look a little bare, but it actually lets you find some very important information about your document and lets you perform some equally important tasks.

The folder display, as shown in Figure 14-4, shows basic information, such as the type of document in the folder (is it a Webi document? A Crystal Report?), the document title, owner, number of instances, as well as the last time the report was run.

What's more important is the set of links located below the document title. If these links aren't displayed, click the downward arrow located between the document type icon and the document title. The arrow now appears upward and four links appear for the document: History, Schedule, Modify, and Properties.

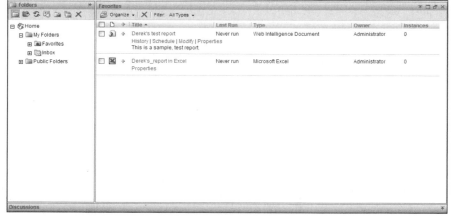

Figure 14-4:
Ample information is available for each document.

Knowing your history

If you click the History link, a History page appears featuring a number of buttons and options. The History page displays any historical instances and provides information about such events — for example, the time the instance occurred, the instance title, who ran the instance, its status, and any reschedule information.

If you're just starting out with InfoView, it's highly likely that you won't have any historical instances. If this is the case, InfoView definitely calls this to your attention, as shown in Figure 14-5.

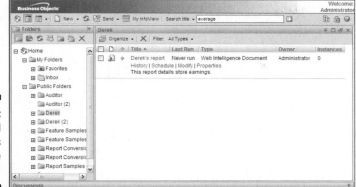

Figure 14-5:
Not all
documents
have
instances!

I'll put it on my calendar

The previous section mentions features that only occur when you schedule an instance. The options available to you on the Schedule page vary, depending on the type of document you're working with in InfoView. If it's a Web Intelligence document, the Schedule page looks like the one shown in Figure 14-6.

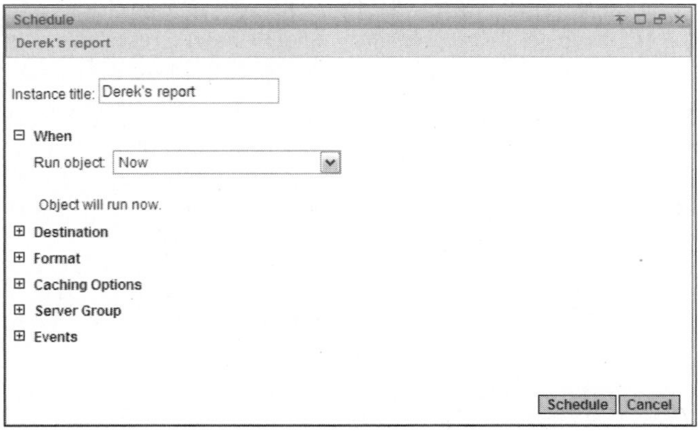

Figure 14-6:
The
Schedule
page for
a Web
Intelligence
document.

The following steps show you how to set up and schedule an instance in InfoView:

1. Click Schedule from the list of documents.

The Schedule page opens.

2. Enter a title in the Instance Title text box.

Be sure to give the instance a name that clearly represents it so you don't have to guess later on.

3. Expand the When menu and select when to run the document.

This drop-down list features a pretty extensive range of time options. Pick the one that suits your needs; this is when the document will be regenerated or run.

4. Expand the Destination menu and select the destination location.

Three options are available in the drop-down menu; for each option, additional settings appear.

We recommend using the default settings — that is, the Job Server settings — if you're using either the Inbox or Email Recipients fields (shown in Figure 14-7). That way you don't have to type details that you might not know. See the section, "Sending Documents to Colleagues" for more information.

5. Expand Format and select a format to generate.

If you're creating a Web Intelligence document, you can save the instance as a Web Intelligence document, a Microsoft Excel worksheet, or a PDF.

6. Expand Caching Options and select the appropriate option.

This option lets you decide which document formats to *cache*, or store (Microsoft Excel, Standard HTML, and Adobe Acrobat). You can also cache formatting locales that will be used during scheduling; locate the desired language and use the arrows to select the locale.

You can use the Locale feature to select a language spoken in a specific country. For example, if you're looking for a French locale, keep in mind that the language has separate entries for France, Canada, Switzerland, and so on.

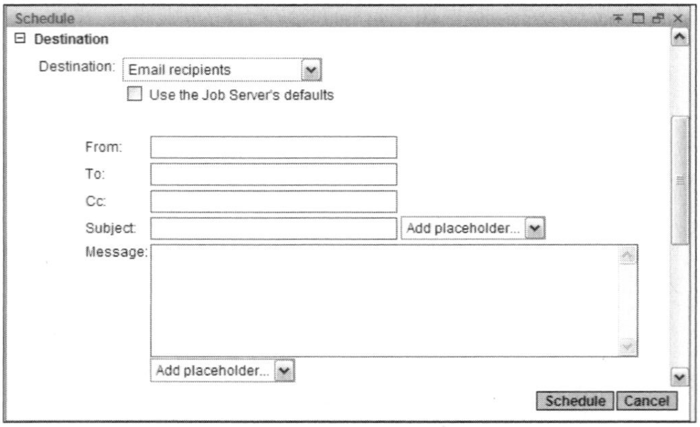

Figure 14-7:
The E-mail Recipients field.

7. **Expand Server Group and select which server to use for generating the instance.**

   We recommend using the default setting, which uses the first available server.

8. **Expand Events and select any available events.**

   You can use the arrows to switch events between windows.

9. **Expand Prompts and click Modify Values.**

   The Query Panel appears (as shown in Figure 14-8); there you can modify the values of your prompts. Make your changes and then click Apply. The selected values are used when the document is refreshed (a mandatory step) before being sent to its destination.

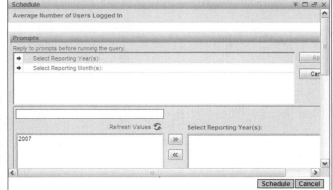

Figure 14-8:
Modifying prompts during scheduling.

10. **Click Schedule.**

    The scheduled instance appears in the History window, as shown in Figure 14-9.

At the top of the window, two checkboxes are designed to do two specific functions:

- ✔ **Show Only Instances Owned By Me:** Check this box to display only the instances owned by you.

- ✔ **Filter Instances By Time:** Check this box to filter instances that occurred during a specific time frame. If checked, you can set the specific time period using the drop-down menus and set the specific date(s) using the pop-up calendar located next to the text boxes. When you're finished, click Apply Filter to set it in motion.

Figure 14-9:
The
scheduled
instance.

Below the checkboxes, and above the column headers for the list of inci-
dents, is a toolbar with these handy capabilities:

✔ **Pause** and **Resume:** If you have an instance that is scheduled, you can
pause or resume it.

A scheduled instance must have a Pending or Recurring status or these
two buttons don't work.

✔ **Delete:** You can delete an instance regardless of status by clicking the
checkbox next to it and then clicking Delete.

✔ **Show All Instances:** Decide whether to show all instances (regardless of
status) or to only display completed instances.

✔ **Refresh:** Refresh your list of historical instances.

Viewing the properties

If you ever need to find information related to your document, document, or
application, the Properties window provides that information. In your Inbox
(or any other folder, for that matter), you can do so by clicking Properties.
The Properties window (shown in Figure 14-10) displays basic-but-important
information about your file.

You can view, but not modify, the following information:

✔ **Title:** The title you've chosen for the instance.

✔ **Description:** Any descriptive text that may have been added when
saving the document.

✔ **Keywords:** Any keywords that may have been added when saving the
document; these are helpful for searching for the document.

✔ **Created:** The date the instance was first created.

✔ **Last Modified:** The date the instance was last updated and saved.

✔ **Last Run On:** The date the instance was last generated.

✔ **Locale:** The formatting language and country applied to the instance.

✔ **Categories:** Whether the document is saved under the Personal or Corporate categories.

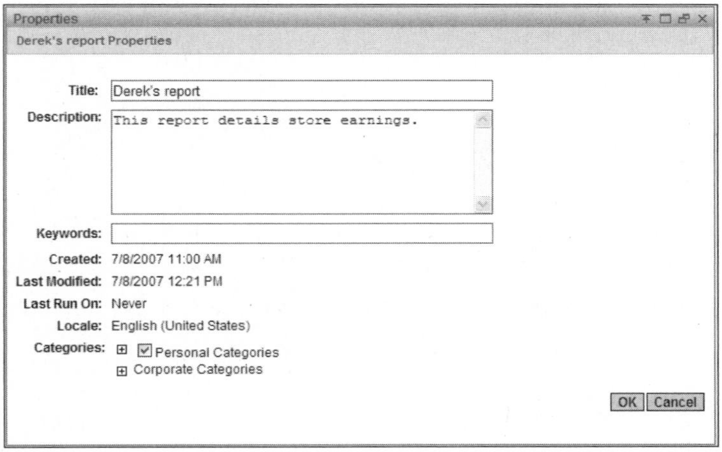

Figure 14-10:
The
Properties
window.

Properties	⌐ □ ⧉ ×
Derek's report Properties	

Title: Derek's report

Description: This report details store earnings.

Keywords:

Created: 7/8/2007 11:00 AM
Last Modified: 7/8/2007 12:21 PM
Last Run On: Never
Locale: English (United States)
Categories: ☐ ☑ Personal Categories
☐ Corporate Categories

OK   Cancel

Making changes

The final option available to you for your document is the Modify feature. This feature lets you modify your document. To get started, click Modify for your document in your folder.

The default Report Panel appears and lets you modify the document in much the same way you would have created it. (For more about how to use the Report Panels, go to Chapter 13.)

Viewing Documents

There's actually more to viewing documents than you may think. While it's true that being able to consult documents is a primary use of InfoView, you can do that in multiple ways — viewing, exporting, or sending your documents along to colleagues.

You can define how you view documents with InfoView Preferences, as discussed in Chapter 12.

Follow these steps to pick your document and view it (in several ways):

1. **Go to your Inbox or whatever folder your document is located.**

   The list of available documents appears.

2. **Click the document title.**

   The document appears according to your default settings, as shown in Figure 14-11.

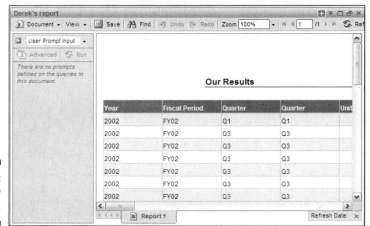

Figure 14-11:
An InfoView document.

cal menu under the document title in the navigation map.

At this point, you can do a number of things with the document, depending on your needs. As shown in Figure 14-11, a toolbar just above the document provides options you can use to make full use of your document.

Your documents, please

You can use the first option — Close — on the Document menu to close the document. You can also (more importantly) edit your document. Choose Document➪Edit and the Java applet viewer opens the already open document, where you can add objects to it via drag-and-drop, as shown in Figure 14-12.

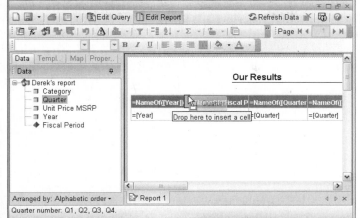

Figure 14-12:
Adding
an object
to your
document.

You have two ways to edit your document: Either click Edit Report or click
Edit Query from the Report window (so you can modify your document
query in the Query Panel). You can modify a single document query; the
query can belong to all documents in a Web Intelligence document.

Back in the HTML viewer, the Documents menu also has three distinct
options for saving your document:

- ✔ **Save:** This option saves the document, using its initial save settings, to
  the location where it was initially saved.

- ✔ **Save As:** This option changes where to save the document. You can also
  modify the title, applicable keywords, and the description.

- ✔ **Save to My Computer As:** This option saves the document to your document in various formats (explained in greater detail in Chapter 13).

A document with a view

The View menu provides three different *modes* (ways of viewing your
document), as well as two additional display options.

The three modes are

- ✔ **Page:** The Page mode is ideal if you want to adjust your document's
  appearance and formatting. For example, if you decide you want to
  include charts or specify table colors, this is the ideal view to use.

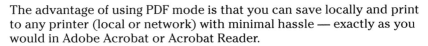

✔ **Draft:** This mode doesn't look very different from the Page mode — but this is the view you work in if you're getting your hands dirty with your data. For example, if you want to add formulas or sort the data in a table, this is the mode for the job.

✔ **PDF:** Using the PDF mode displays your document in the main window as a PDF document. When you finish modifying your PDF or decide to view it in HTML, click View in HTML format.

The advantage of using PDF mode is that you can save locally and print to any printer (local or network) with minimal hassle — exactly as you would in Adobe Acrobat or Acrobat Reader.

You can use the remaining two options in the View menu to toggle between displaying the Left Panel (at the left of your document, where you can modify prompts or other aspects of your document) and the Status Bar (located beneath your document). Both are selected by default. We recommend leaving them selected unless you have compelling reasons to disable them.

The other, lesser menus

The toolbar has a number of other buttons you can choose. Most of these work just like Microsoft Office features.

Here's a rundown of what they do:

✔ **Save:** This Save button works just like the Save option on the Document menu.

✔ **Find:** The Find button works like any other Find feature; it works in your current document. You can match cases, or search for whole words based on your text.

✔ **Undo/redo:** You can undo or redo your latest task(s) for up to two actions.

✔ **Zoom:** Increase or decrease the magnification of the document.

✔ **Next/Previous Page:** The next buttons let you move forward or back a page (assuming your document has multiple pages). If you have more than one page, you can also enter the page number of the document.

✔ **Refresh Data:** Refresh your document with your default settings. This button automatically refreshes the data in your data source; you don't even have to refresh your prompts. If you are using multiple data providers, you can either refresh all data providers or just one.

✔ **Drill:** You can drill down or zoom in to take a closer look at the details of your data, as shown in Figure 14-13.

Figure 14-13:
A drilled-
down
document.

Sending Documents to Colleagues

As we've mentioned on several occasions throughout this book, InfoView lets you send your documents over e-mail. This feature is particularly helpful if you have to send a document to someone outside the office (for example, a client) who may not have access to your BusinessObjects environment or office network.

You can send a document or documents to others in four ways:

- ✔ InfoView Inbox
- ✔ E-mail
- ✔ FTP
- ✔ Specifying a file location

Your BusinessObjects Administrator must configure these options, with the exception of the InfoView Inbox. If these features aren't enabled and configured, you can't use them. The same configuration is needed when you schedule a document instance.

Before sending a document, you must first go to the folder where the document is located. The following sections show you how to send a document for each option, starting from the Inbox.

Sending to the Inbox

Sending your document to the InfoView Inbox is just another way of saying that you're transferring the document to another folder.

The following steps show you how to do this.

 1. **Select the desired document by finding it in your Inbox and clicking the checkbox.**

    You can select as many documents as you like.

 2. **From the InfoView toolbar, choose Send⇨To BusinessObjects Inbox.**

    The Send window appears.

 3. **Select Inbox from the Destination drop-down list.**

 4. **Select the Use the Job Server's Defaults checkbox.**

    If you can't use the Job Server's default settings (or if you want to customize those settings), deselect this option.

    The window expands, as shown in Figure 14-14.

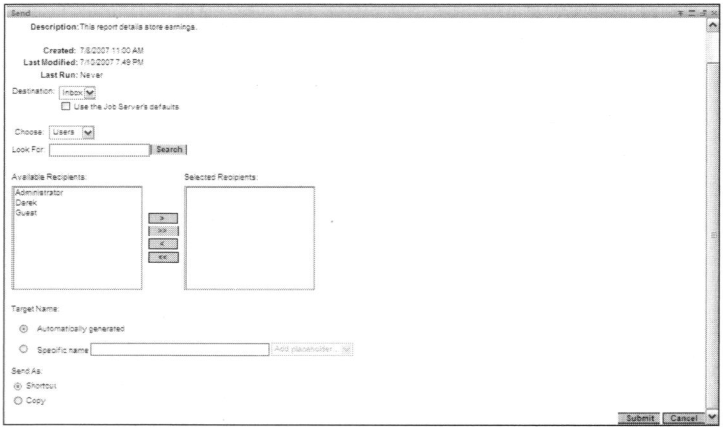

Figure 14-14:
The
expanded
Send
window.

 5. **Select Users or Groups from the Choose drop-down list.**

    The Available Recipients box fills with your selections.

 6. **Select the users or groups to whom you want to send the document, using the Available Recipients box.**

    Your document(s) appears in the Inbox of the selected users or groups.

 7. **Select a target name.**

    You have three naming options:

    - Let BusinessObjects name the document automatically (that name appears in the Inbox).
    - Select a placeholder (such as a title, e-mail address, ID, and so on).
    - Type a specific name.

 8. **Select whether to actually copy the document to the Inbox or provide a shortcut instead.**

If you decide to create only a shortcut, the document remains in its original location and acts as a link that the recipient can access to view the document. In that case, the document isn't literally sent.

9. **When your changes are complete, click Submit.**

The document appears in the recipient's Inbox, as shown in Figure 14-15.

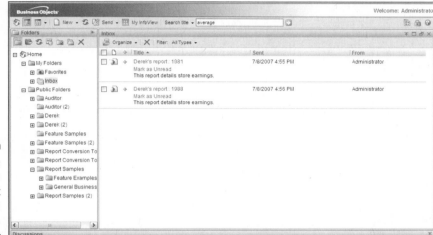

Sending an e-mail

You can also e-mail a document (or any other type of document stored in your folders or Inbox) to another user.

We recommend using the Job Server's configuration when you use this feature; otherwise you may find it difficult to enter your server details manually. Use the Job Server configuration unless you have a good reason (a *really good* reason) not to use it. If you're using BusinessObjects in the context of a large corporation, it's likely that you won't have the Job Server details handy or won't have access to these configurations.

When you send an e-mail using the default configurations, you can send your document to any e-mail recipient that is saved on the job server. The security upside is that you can't send anything you shouldn't to outside users. The downside is that you can only send to the number of people who can actually receive the document.

If your system administrator is feeling nice, this is one of those good reasons not to use the default Job Server configuration. If you manually enter the domain and server information, you can also enter your e-mail recipient's address manually: Simply select your document, fill in the necessary information, not to mention your recipient, any message for the recipient, and so on, and send!

Sending over FTP

Using the FTP option, you can transfer a document (or any other type of document stored in your folders or Inbox) to another user by storing it on an FTP server. We recommend using the Job Server's configuration to use this feature; otherwise you may have a hard time entering your server details.

When you send a document using the default configurations, you can send your document to an FTP server that is already set up through the Job Server.

If you opt not to use the Job Server default configurations, you can type the name of an FTP server.

Sending to a file location

The File Location option is handy for transferring a document (or any other type of document stored in your folders or Inbox) to another user by storing it to somewhere on your hard drive. Here, too, we recommend using the Job Server's configuration to save yourself some fuss.

When you send a file using the default configurations, you can send your document to a file location that is already set up as an unmarked portion of your hard drive through the Job Server.

If you opt not to use the Job Server default configurations, you can specify where you want to store your file(s) by typing the path to that location.

Exporting Documents

If you use BusinessObjects at work, you may hear colleagues ask about exporting documents — but they may actually be referring to sending (rather than exporting) them.

You can actually go about exporting a document in three ways:

✔ **Send a document:** You can transfer it to the Inbox, e-mail it to someone, transfer it to FTP, or send it to a specific file location. (See the earlier section, "Sending Documents to Colleagues.")

BIAR files

Even though BIAR files are potentially a big topic all by themselves, it's handy to know about their purpose in case you encounter these often-used files at the office. You can create BIAR (Business Intelligence Application Resource) files in BusinessObjects for easy importing and exporting. A BIAR file collects folders, universes, documents, categories, and so on and saves them in a single file that can be installed in another BusinessObjects environment with minimal work on your end.

Note, however, BIAR files are pretty advanced stuff; we recommend getting thoroughly familiar with using BusinessObjects before you try using them. In fact, Business Objects recommends contacting its support staff to help determine (a) where to find your BIAR file(s) and (b) whether you should use this feature.

✔ **Save your document:** You can save your document to your computer or a network drive using the Save to Computer As option. You can save it in one of several formats, including Microsoft Excel, PDF, or CSV (if you want a plain-text file). See the earlier section, "Viewing Documents," for details.

✔ **Import your document:** Using the Import Wizard, you can export universes and documents from one BusinessObjects repository to another. This option, which we discuss in this section, is only for advanced BusinessObjects users and administrators.

Follow these steps to use the Import Wizard to transfer documents:

1. **Choose Start⇨All Programs⇨BusinessObjects XI Release 2⇨ BusinessObjects Enterprise⇨Import Wizard.**

   The Import Wizard appears.

2. **Click Next.**

   The Source Environment screen appears, as shown in Figure 14-16.

3. **Enter the login and password for the source CMS (BusinessObjects environment) and click Next.**

   The Destination Environment screen appears.

4. **Enter the login and password for the destination CMS (BusinessObjects environment) and click Next.**

   The Select Objects to Import screen appears. You can choose a BIAR file as a source or destination environment. However, for a XI Release 2 or older environment (BO 6.5, Crystal Reports 10) it can only be for a source.

5. **Deselect all options and then select Import Users and Users Groups; click Next.**

The Import Scenario screen appears.

6. **Select the second option (updating the destination system using the source system as a reference), and then click Next four times.**

Here you're skipping screens that aren't germane to this task; click until you reach the Ready to Import screen (shown in Figure 14-17).

7. **Click Finish.**

The wizard imports your documents.

Figure 14-16: The Source environment.

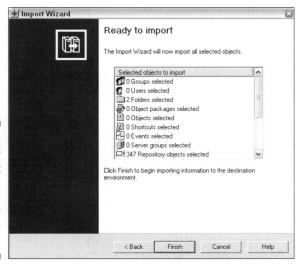

Figure 14-17: The Ready to Import screen shows exactly what is imported.

Part V
Keeping Track of How Your Organization Is Doing

The 5th Wave   By Rich Tennant

DATASUK
Service & Support

"Please answer the following survey questions about our company's performance with either, 'Excellent', 'Good', 'Fair', or 'I'm Really Incapable of Appreciating Someone Else's Hard Work.'"

In this part. . .

This part helps you take your use of the BusinessObjects XI Release 2 Enterprise suite to the next level.

In these following chapters, you move on from the simple reports you build with WebI and DeskI to find out how you can use the suite's Performance Management tools to create dashboards, metrics and analytics to keep track of how your organization is doing.

Chapter 15 is all about dashboards: what they're for, how to create one, and how to make them more visible by putting one right on your home page.

In Chapter 16, you discover how to make effective use of analytics in conjunction with Business Objects technology.

Chapter 17 introduces you to the final weapon in your performance management arsenal: metrics. We walk you through creating your own metrics and goals, and help you see where they fit into the big picture and appreciate the value they add to a business intelligence suite.

Chapter 15

A Different Kind of Dashboard

*I*f you need to analyze specific data on a particular subject, the usual approach is to search for a document whose name you already know in your list of available documents in InfoView, open the document, and browse through it for the data you're looking for. Alternatively, you could build this data into the report itself, or you could create a new report from the universe you're using. In any case, you already know what information you're looking for.

It's also quite possible, however, that what you need is an at-a-glance macro view of what's going on in your business. That's where a dashboard comes in handy.

A *dashboard* is a portal made up of pages and tabs that organizes data according to the information it contains. This portal can be secured in such a way as to customize what users can see depending on their role in the company. A CEO, for instance, might have access to the whole dashboard, while a sales manager would see sales data (perhaps filtered geographically) but would not have access to worldwide HR information.

Each page in a dashboard contains analytical tools and interactive charts, which display and highlight key performance indicators — such as trends over time, comparison with goals, strategy maps, alerts, and such. They also contain links to reports so you can drill down on information, always going from a macro view of your data into more and more detail.

Accessing Dashboard Manager

Dashboards are designed to provide you with a consistent view of your business data and alert you about critical information, allowing you to monitor your company's activity more effectively. The BusinessObjects tool that lets you do this is Dashboard Manager.

The supported environment for Dashboard Manager is less complete than for the BusinessObjects XI Enterprise Release 2 platform as a whole. In particular, the .NET version of BusinessObjects XI Enterprise is not supported. Specific features (such as dynamic viewers) may require you to install browser plug-ins. Check the Business Objects Web site for details.

To get started, you first need to open the Dashboard Manager tool:

1. **Log in to InfoView.**

2. **Click the Performance Management icon, as shown in Figure 15-1.**

    The Performance Management area opens.

Figure 15-1:
Click the
Performance
Management
icon to
access
Dashboard
Manager.

Performance Manager

If you can't see the Performance Management icon, make sure that the product has been correctly installed by clicking License Keys in the CMC (Central Management Console, see Chapter 3) and checking to make sure you have a key for BusinessObjects Dashboard Manager.

Creating a Dashboard

Basically, there are two kinds of dashboards. Corporate dashboards exist to share information company-wide; personal dashboards are designed for your own individual work needs.

This section shows how to create a corporate dashboard, and then how to create a personal dashboard.

Constructing a new corporate dashboard

When you open Dashboard Manager for the first time, you're presented with the default demo dashboard that contains different tabs for each activity (Sales, Marketing, Products, and others) of a fictional company called Total Electronics, as shown in Figure 15-2. We're guessing, however, that you might be more interested in creating a dashboard that displays data for *your* company.

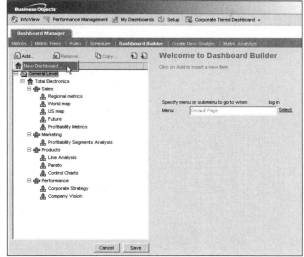

Figure 15-2: The default dashboard.

To create a new, empty dashboard, follow these steps:

1. **Click Dashboard Builder in the Dashboard Manager top toolbar.**

   The Dashboard Builder page opens.

2. **Click Add, and then select New Dashboard.**

3. **Enter the name of your dashboard in the Name box on the right side of the page.**

4. **Click Save, browse to the location in the repository where you want to save your new dashboard, and then click OK.**

   The new dashboard name has been added to the Dashboard structure.

Constructing a personal dashboard

In Part V, we showed you how in InfoView you can save a document in the My Folder and Corporate Folder areas. Well, dashboards follow a similar logic.

A Corporate Dashboard is an enterprise application, made by business intelligence specialists, secured and published through the company according to users' activities. In this case most users have read-only access to this dashboard.

If you want to give users more autonomy, you can allow individuals to make their own dashboard from reports and data they can access according to their profiles, using the My Dashboard area, which provides a simplified way to build dashboards. Personal dashboards can't be shared with other users.

To create a personal dashboard, follow these steps:

1. **From the Performance Management toolbar, click the My Dashboards icon.**

   The My Dashboards Information page appears.

2. **Click the Add link to create tabs in the My Dashboard area.**

   Your dashboard is now saved in your Favorites folder in InfoView (instead of a public folder).

After you've created menus, you have the same workflows and features as a corporate dashboard for customizing content and layout.

Filling Up Your Dashboard

So you have a new dashboard — but it's looking pretty bare. Your next step is to decide the structure of your dashboard and start filling it with content.

Adding a menu

In Dashboard Builder, the first stage of adding content to your dashboard is to add tabs (called *menus* in the Dashboard Manager) so you can organize your dashboard in line with the main activities of your organization that you want to monitor. Next, you structure each menu (remember, that's what Dashboard Manager calls *tabs*) by adding windows and links that lead to other windows and pages. Here's how that process looks:

1. **Select your new corporate dashboard in the Structure panel.**

2. **Click Add.**

3. **Choose New Menu from the list of available options, and give it a name.**

   A new menu is added to your dashboard. Figure 15-3 shows a dashboard with four menus: Sales, Marketing, Products, and Performance.

Figure 15-3:
A dashboard with four menus: Sales, Marketing, Products, and Performance.

Adding a submenu

A menu can contain several first level pages, called *submenus*. To add a sub-menu, follow these steps:

1. **Select a menu from your corporate dashboard in the Structure panel.**

2. **Click Add.**

3. **Select New Submenu from the list of available options, and give it a name.**

   A new submenu is added to your dashboard menu. (Refer to Figure 15-3 where the Sales menu has a submenu with five items.)

Inserting an analytic

In order to add content to this new page, click Customize. Your page opens in edit mode across two tabs: Content, the default tab that allows you to add content to the page; and Layout, which allows you to modify what the page looks like.

You might as well start with some useful business tools called *analytics,* which help you analyze and interpret data by showing a macro-view of data at a glance. From the Content tab (see Figure 15-4), you can drag and drop any elements from the Analytics list on the left. These elements are organized in different directories:

- **Analytic Catalog:** A list of analytics delivered with the product, based on the default demo data.

- **Analytics Services:** The interfaces used to create dashboard content — pages, metrics (measurements), analytics, and so on — as described in more detail in Chapters 16 and 17.

- **Corporate Analytics:** All corporate documents in InfoView.

- **Existing Analytics:** A list of analytics already in use in an existing dashboard, which helps enable their reuse.

- **List of Analytics:** All documents and components in InfoView, including personal documents.

- **New Analytic:** A catalog of analytics templates.

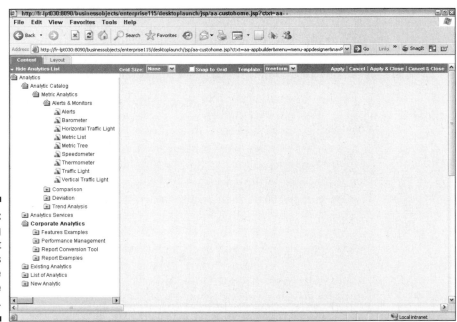

Figure 15-4:
Customizing the content that appears in your page in the Content tab.

To add a component to your page, follow these steps:

1. **Open the folder that contains the analytic you want.**

   For example, if you want to add the Speedometer analytic based on the demo data, you open the Analytic Catalog folder, the Metric Analytics folder, and then finally the Alerts & Monitoring folder.

2. **Place your cursor over the analytic, click, drag the analytic to your page, and then release the cursor to drop it into place.**

   Your page now contains the analytic you choose. Figure 15-5 shows a Speedometer with the default data Net Sales All Old, in a resizable window.

We show you how to create new analytics in Chapter 16.

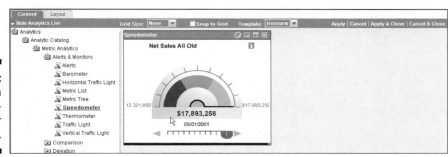

Figure 15-5:
Adding a Speedometer to your dashboard.

Adding free text and Web pages

Instead of using predefined analytics, you can also choose to insert free text — or even a Web page — into a window on your dashboard:

1. **Open the New Analytic folder in the Analytics list.**

2. **Click Text Analytic, and then drag it into an existing window on your page.**

   A new window called Text Analytic is added into your page

3. **To edit the text, click Edit.**

   The same tabs appear as when customizing your window (Content and Layout).

4. Type the text you want to display directly in the text area.

You can customize the style in which it is displayed by entering your text using HTML tags to format the style, as shown in Figure 15-6. If you want to add a logo or other image, copy it into the `images` subdirectory on your server; by default, if you're using the Tomcat server, this is

```
$Tomcat Directory\webapps\businessobjects\enterprise115\
            desktoplaunch\images
```

Alternatively, you can ask your administrator to do it for you. Then, using a text analytic, insert it as an HTML image tag. For example

```
<img src=" ../images/myDummyLogo.png">
```

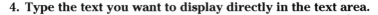

Figure 15-6:
Formatting the style of free text on your dashboard using HTML tags.

5. To add a Web page, add the Web Page Analytic into a window, edit the analytic, and then enter the URL in the content panel.

This feature can be useful if you need easy access to applications on your company intranet, or to a site on the Internet that can help you analyze your data more effectively.

Adding BusinessObjects reports or other documents

If you want to add BusinessObjects reports (either WebI or DeskI reports), or indeed any other documents, just drag them from the Corporate Analytics or List of Analytics in the Analytics List and drop them into your page as you would for any other analytic.

You can only add BusinessObjects reports and other documents to your dashboard if you've published them to InfoView first!

Defining Your Layout

After adding content to your dashboard page, you can now think about defining a layout for the whole page or for each window independently. A window is only the default container of each analytic component. You can personalize each window, modify their styles, turn them into hyperlinks or buttons, or display their content directly into the main page. This section describes how to define a dashboard layout.

Applying a predefined style to your dashboard

By default, the application provides six styles. You can choose any of them for your full dashboard or for a specific window:

- ✔ **At the page level,** you can manage (for example) the dashboard pages background color. The style defined at this level becomes the default values for all new analytics added to it. For existing analytics, you have to modify the style manually.

- ✔ **At the window level,** you can manage (for example) each window's title bar style and background. You can select the same style for your page style and then dress up windows in completely different styles if you choose. You can also transform a window into a link to a new page or display it like a simple part of your main page.

To apply a style to your component, follow these steps:

1. **At the page level, select the Customize link; at the window level, click the Edit button.**

   In each case, the page or the window opens with the Content tab showing.

2. **Click the Layout tab.**

3. **Add a title and a description.**

   The title is displayed at the top of the window.

4. **Specify the kind of display of the window content:**

   - *Hide window borders:* Using the Display As radio buttons, you can hide window borders. In this case the analytic is displayed as a simple part of the page, without interactivity.

   - *Transform the window into a link to a new page*: In this case, the main page displays a hyperlink with the title text opening a new page containing the window content. Associating an image to this hyperlink adds a button to the hyperlink.

5. **Select your style from the Style Sheet drop-down list.**

   An overview of the style appears on the right.

Adding a custom style

If you don't like the predefined styles that come with the dashboards, you can define your own style.

You need some Cascading Style Sheet (CSS) knowledge. You may want to have your administrator on speed-dial because you'll need to modify files on the server.

Here's how to create your own style:

1. **Define a name for the new style.**

   You need a business name (for example, BO for Dummies) and a folder name (for example, dummies).

2. **Modify the following properties file with your business and folder names:**

   ```
   $Business Objects Dir$\Performance Management 11.5\server\conf\style.xml
   ```

3. **Go to your Web application directory at**

   ```
   $Tomcat Dir$\webapps\businessobjects\enterprise115\desktoplaunch\styles
   ```

4. **Add a new folder with the folder name from Step 1.**

5. **Copy all files from an existing sample.**

   From the Windows folder, for example.

6. **Modify** style.js **with your new folder name.**

7. **Define your own style by modifying the style.css file and add different image files.**

   Figure 15-7 shows a customized dashboard.

Organizing Your Dashboard

After you fill your dashboard with the content you want to monitor, you may also want to organize this content, in such a way that makes it easier for you to see whatever information is most important to you first.

Figure 15-7:
Dashboard
with a
"Dummies"
style.

You can organize how your content is displayed in several ways:

✔ **Move windows:** Click somewhere in the window you want to move, drag it to where you want to move it to, and then release the mouse button.

✔ **Resize windows:** Click the arrow button in the bottom-right corner of the window, stretch or shrink the window to its new size, and then release the mouse button.

✔ **Use a preconfigured template:** Choose one from the Template drop-down list in the toolbar. Figure 15-8 shows the 2-2 template, which gives you four equal-size windows in which to drag and drop content from the Analytics list.

✔ **Remove a window:** Click the X at the top-right of the window.

When shuffling and resizing your windows, check the Snap to Grid checkbox to ensure your dashboard retains at least a semblance of order!

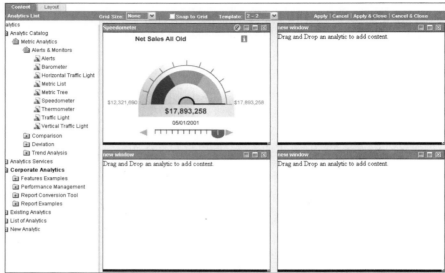

Figure 15-8:
The 2-2
template
in action.

Viewing Dashboards

After you build your dashboard and stuff it full of useful content, you may want to see what the finished result looks like.

Opening your dashboard

To view your dashboard, go to the Performance Management home page. There you can find your corporate dashboard and the menus it contains listed by application in the Access Corporate tiered dashboard section. To open a page of your dashboard, simply click the relevant link.

To view your personal dashboard, go to the Performance Management home page and click the My dashboards section. To open a page of your personal dashboard, simply click the relevant menu.

Making sense of a window

Your dashboard is an interactive application made up of different pages, windows, and links.

To improve visibility and ease of use, you can maximize or minimize each window independently.

Each analytic contains interactive features specific to its type. In the Speedometer, for instance, you can

- ✔ Place your mouse pointer over the Information icon to display the most recent refresh date and time.

- ✔ Move the slicer along the Time axis to observe how your Net Sales value varies for each month over the period you're interested in.

- ✔ Use the color-coding of the gauge and the needle to track trends over time.

The default format for analytics is Adobe SVG, but you can choose to display some analytics in Flash format by browsing to the Preference page, clicking the Performance Management tab, and then checking Use Macromedia Flash When Available.

Making a Dashboard Your Home Page

So you've created beautiful dashboards that provide you with quick and easy access to key information about your organization's activities. Fine. But there's no point creating them if you never take the time to look at them.

If you want your dashboard to help you deal with potential issues before they occur, it must be one of the first applications you consult every day. And the best way not to miss what it has to offer is to make your dashboard the home page of your portal.

To make a dashboard your home page, follow these steps:

1. **Log on to InfoView.**

2. **Click Preferences on the Header panel toolbar.**

3. **On the General tab, select a dashboard from the My Initial View Is section:**

    - *Corporate:* Click Select to browse in the Dashboard builder directory structure.

    - *Personal:* Choose a personal dashboard from the drop-down list, as shown in Figure 15-9.

Figure 15-9:
Choosing a dashboard as your home page.

⊙ Select a PM Corporate Dashboard:	My Dashboard [Select ...]
○ Select a PM Personal Dashboard:	Stuart Mudie dashboard ▾

Chapter 16

Making Better Decisions through Analytics

In This Chapter

▶ Appreciating and making effective use of analytics

▶ Basing a new analytic on a measure from a BusinessObjects universe

▶ Using analytics with BusinessObjects technology

*J*ust as the previous chapter compares reports and dashboards — with dashboards providing an at-a-glance macro view of what's going on in your business, and reports providing specific, more detailed data — so this chapter makes a similar comparison: In this case, charts inside reports provide the specifics, and analytics inside dashboards help shape the macro view of your data.

While a chart in a report displays detailed data in a particular area, the aim of an analytic is to highlight an indicator or trend in order to allow you to monitor it more effectively.

Understanding the Value of Analytics

In BusinessObjects, an *analytic* is a logical tool for visualizing data in a specific way. Creating an analytic involves selecting the template and data to use, and then personalizing how it's rendered, tailoring it to the data you want to analyze (trends, history, or whatever).

A major difference between analytics and charts is that analytics are interactive — inside an analytic, you can monitor the time dimension. Analytics can show, for instance, whether your sales are going up or down, identify those countries where business is increasing significantly, or reveal which product is contributing the most to your bottom line.

Analytics are classified in several groups:

- ✔ **Trend analysis analytics** monitor trends over time, such as interactive metric trends, or Raw versus Smoothed and Dual metric comparisons, which are based on WebI documents.

- ✔ **Alerts and monitors** warn you about an issue or give a global view of the health of an indicator and include gauges, alerts, metric lists, and metric trees.

- ✔ **Comparison analytics** like Pareto charts, or Kiviat and radar diagrams based on WebI documents.

- ✔ **Performance management analytics** measure achievement against goals, such as goal analytics or strategy maps.

Depending on their function, you can build some analytics using data from a BusinessObjects universe, a metric, or a goal; others may come specifically from a metric; and still others may come from a goal. (We go into more detail about metrics and goals in Chapter 17.)

To help understand the value of analytics, this section takes a look at three of those most commonly used: barometers, traffic lights, and Pareto charts.

Barometer

In the physical world, a barometer is a tool designed to measure atmospheric pressure and (based on the result it obtains) predict trends in the weather. In a similar way, the barometer analytic shows trends in a measure by displaying its variation over time.

The barometer is one of the six *gauge analytics*, which are found in the Alerts and Monitors folder.

The barometer analytic that appears in the default demo is made up of three colored areas, each equal in size:

- ✔ **Red:** Contains the lowest values in the key performance indicator.

- ✔ **Green:** Contains the highest values.

- ✔ **Orange:** Contains the values that fall in the medium range.

For a *satisfaction index* (such as the example shown in Figure 16-1), the closer a value is to 100%, the better — so the colored areas of the barometer have been defined to match this requirement. The highest and lowest values for the time range defined on the slider (67% and 78% in our example) are indicated on the boundaries of the chart.

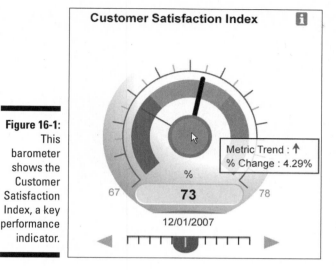

Figure 16-1:
This barometer shows the Customer Satisfaction Index, a key performance indicator.

The slider underneath the barometer lets you position the arrow for a given period of time. The bold needle represents the value for the selected period; the thin needle shows the previous period. The tooltip tells you the percent change in comparison to the previous period and gives an indicator of the trend.

Figure 16-1 shows that the index value is 73% on December 1, 2007. Although this value only falls in the medium area (compared to the time-range data), the previous month's value was in the red area, so the percentage change between November and December is 4.29% and the trend indicator is up.

Traffic light

As every good driver knows, a traffic light tells you whether to go ahead, exercise caution, or stop immediately — with the aim of preventing "problems" farther down the line.

Similarly, the traffic-light analytic (shown in Figure 16-2) — which is another type of gauge analytic, and found in the Alerts and Monitors folder — provides an indicator of the health of a particular measure for the current period, based on predefined criteria that determine what is "good" and "bad."

Figure 16-2:
This traffic light shows a red-light warning signal to indicate that the stock average is not as high as it should be.

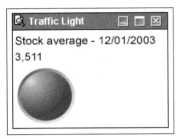

Traffic Light

Stock average - 12/01/2003

3,511

Pareto chart

A *Pareto chart* displays the best contributors of a category for any given measure. It is one of the comparison analytics and is found in the Comparison folder.

In a Pareto chart, solid bars represent the value of each item in the category, sorted in descending order. The cumulative curve (the thin, red line) shows the overall total for the category as each contribution is added. The number of bars is limited — with five bars being typical — and the final bar represents the value of all the other items in the category.

Pareto charts provide a visual representation of the *80–20 percent rule* — a classic business rule stating that 80 percent of any effect is caused by 20 percent of the contributing factors.

The Pareto chart shown in Figure 16-3 indicates that the net sales of the PC Components product line accounts for almost half of all sales: around $12 million out of a total of $23 million. Click the cumulative curve for bar B and a tooltip appears, revealing that the net sales generated by the PC Components and Electronics product lines have a combined value of $16.9 million.

Notice that not every possible product line is specifically represented in this chart. When you create an analytic, you explicitly define the number of bars it is to contain. In this example, the number of product lines and the number of bars is the same: five. If there had been more than five product lines, the fifth bar would have shown the sum total of net sales for all the other product lines.

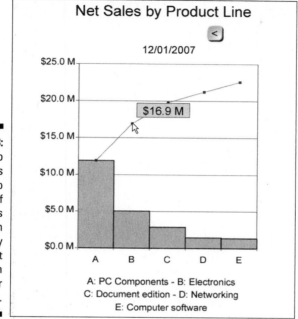

Figure 16-3:
This Pareto
chart shows
a macro
view of
net sales
broken
down by
product
line on
December
1, 2007.

Creating Analytics Based on Universe Measures

You start creating an analytic from (no surprise here) the Create New Analytic page. You can access that page in two ways:

- In InfoView, choose New⇨Analytic (as shown in Figure 16-4).
- In the Performance Management application, click the Create New Analytic link in the Dashboard Manager tab.

By default, the most commonly used analytics are displayed when the application opens.

When you've chosen the analytic you want, you go into Edit mode, which is where you define the data you want to measure and set the parameters for how the results are to be rendered.

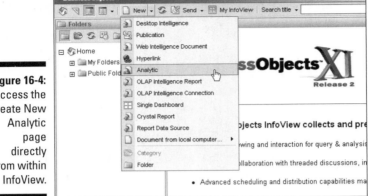

Figure 16-4:
Access the Create New Analytic page directly from within InfoView.

Each analytic's dialog box contains at least two parts: the settings for data definition and the settings for visualization.

Depending on the specifics of the analytic you choose, the way in which you select data or the visualization settings may differ.

Figure 16-5 shows a Speedometer (see Chapter 15), along with the Pareto Chart and Barometer. It also features an Interactive Metric Trends analytic, which — as its name suggests — is generally a metric-based analytic (see Chapter 17); a Map to show how values change over a geographic area; and a Thermometer, which is another kind of gauge analytic that we show you how to build in the next section.

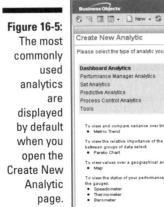
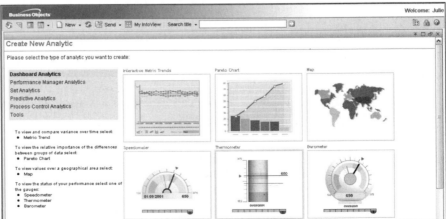

Figure 16-5:
The most commonly used analytics are displayed by default when you open the Create New Analytic page.

Building your own Thermometer

To show how analytics work, we show you how to create a new Thermometer analytic that shows monthly profit by product line. The Thermometer analytic works similarly to other analytics.

To do so, follow these steps:

1. **Click the Thermometer template on the Create New Analytic page.**

2. **Select the data you want to display in your analytic.**

   You have a choice: You can display metrics, goals, or data from the universe. For this example, we selected Universe Query from the Select Data to Display drop-down list, as shown in Figure 16-6.

Figure 16-6:
Select the
data you
want to
display
in your
analytic
from a drop-
down list.

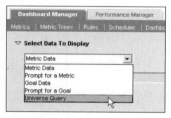

3. **Click Define Query to open the Query Panel to define the data from a universe.**

   Although a Thermometer analytic displays only one value of a measure at a time, the interactivity of the analytic allows you to delve into one or two dimensions to track variations in the measure. To do so, you have to associate dimensions with the measure when you define the query.

4. **To view profits on a time and product line axis, select the following objects from the Sales universe: Year-month, Line, and Profit.**

   You can add objects by selecting them in the Universe Objects list, and then moving them to the Result Objects and Query Filters lists by clicking the >> button, as shown in Figure 16-7.

5. **Click OK to close the Query Panel.**

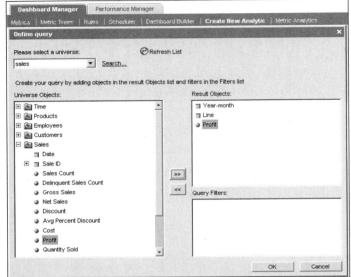

Figure 16-7:
Setting
Profit as one
of the Result
Objects to
display.

6. **Select the objects defined in your query to be displayed in the analytic:**

   • *Measure To Display:* Select Profit.

   • *Dimension for X-Axis and Slider:* Select Year-Month.

   • *Dimension for Slice's List:* Select Line.

7. **Select a template from the Render Style section.**

   For the thermometer analytic, choose the Thermometer template.

8. **Set the color-coding rules according to data trend in the Graph Properties section.**

   By default, three zones are defined: green, orange, and red. They're split in equal sizes that are automatically calculated from the values of the measure.

9. **(Optional) Customize the default configuration and adapt it to suit your data:**

   Set global boundaries

   • To define fixed min and max values of the global data range, select the boundaries manually.

   • To set minimum and maximum values equal to the minimum and maximum values of the measure, check the Calculated Automatically Based on Measure Value radio button.

Set boundaries for each zone

- To fill fixed boundaries for each zone, select Zones Entered by Value from the Zone drop-down menu, select a colored zone, and fill the boundaries values manually.

- To use the same workflow to fix a percent for each zone, select Zones Entered Manually, by % from the Zone List drop-down menu.

Set color zones

- To increase or reduce the number of zones, click the + or – buttons. To modify the default color of each zone, select a colored zone and use the palette to change it.

- To give a correct range to profit measure, change the color of the three predefined zones. For instance, you could make the first zone, which corresponds to the lowest levels of profit, red, and make the third zone, which corresponds to the highest levels of profit, green. See Figure 16-8.

Figure 16-8: Modify the default color of each zone in your graph. Using the palette, set the second color zone as yellow

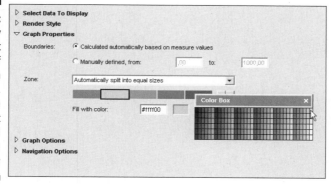

10. Add a title to your analytic in the Graph Option section.

The metric name is used by default; in the case of a universe-based analytic, you have to add a metric name.

11. Set the display options:

- Un-check the Dimension Slider box to remove the slider from the analytic.

- Un-check the Dimension Value box to remove the ability of choosing a product line through a list.

- Check the Metric Value box to display the thermometer level indicator in bold font.

- Check the Metric Previous Value box to display the thermometer level indicator in regular font.

Adding a symbol can be a useful way of displaying the currency of the displayed measure or marking a measure as a percentage, if the measure doesn't have a symbol already attached in the universe. To add a symbol, simply type it in the Symbol field.

The `profit` measure of the Sales universe already has the $ currency attached, so it's displayed with the value in the analytic automatically.

12. Improve interactivity of the analytic by defining hyperlinks:

- *To set a hyperlink to a report or any document from the analytic title,* from the Navigation Option section, click Browse to select a document from the InfoView list.

- *To set multiple links from the analytic with the Multiple Links dialog box,* click the Multiple Links button to open the Edit Navigation Link Menu dialog box (see Figure 16-9). Click the Add button, and for each hyperlink, click the Browse to select a document from the Infoview list.

- Click the Move Up and Move Down buttons to order your hyperlinks.

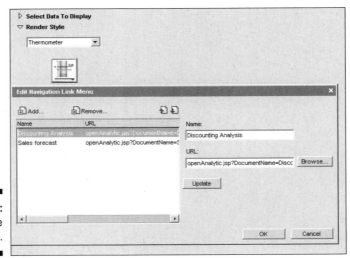

Figure 16-9: Set multiple links.

13. **Click OK.**

The Monthly Profit by Product Line thermometer is displayed, as shown in Figure 16-10.

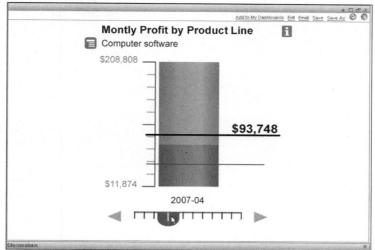

Figure 16-10:
Move the slider to show data for a particular date.

Viewing your data

When you move the slider position to April 2007, the analytic shows that for the computer-software product line, the profit for this period (with a value of $93,748) was in the orange zone — but with significant growth from the previous month (shown in the middle of the red zone).

To visualize the profit for another product line, click the List icon or the text itself to display the list of product lines and select a different value, as shown in Figure 16-11.

To refresh the date you're seeing, hover your mouse pointer over the Information icon: A tooltip displays the date of the last refresh of the analytic, as shown in Figure 16-12.

To refresh the analytic, click the Refresh button in the top-right menu.

To browse to linked documents, click the title of the analytic to display the list of linked documents, as shown in Figure 16-13.

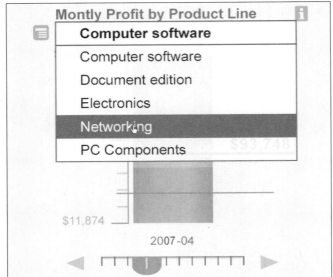

Figure 16-11: Select the value for which you want to display data from a drop-down list.

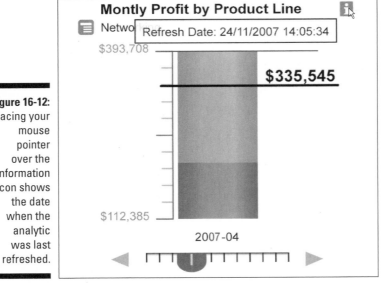

Figure 16-12: Placing your mouse pointer over the Information icon shows the date when the analytic was last refreshed.

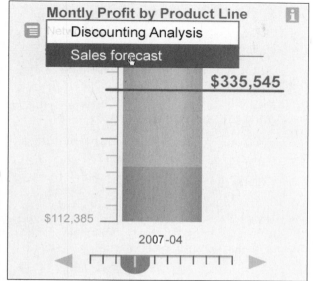

Figure 16-13:
The list of
linked
documents
in this
analytic.

Saving the analytic

To save your analytic as an InfoView document, click the Save or Save As link
in the top-right menu to open the Save dialog box. Add a title, description,
keywords, refresh, and display mode, as shown in Figure 16-14.

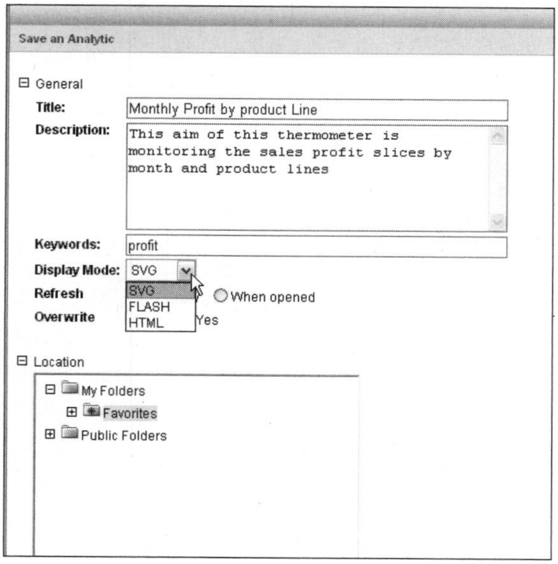

Figure 16-14:
Specify the
format in
which to
save your
analytic.

You can choose from these display modes:

- ✔ **SVG (Scalable Vector Graphics):** Interactive default format of many analytics (such as gauges).

- ✔ **Applet:** To get the analytic into editing format, some analytics propose SVG as snapshot and Applet for interactive display.

- ✔ **CSV (Comma-Separated Values):** Save your analytic in this format if you expect to export the data of the analytic.

- ✔ **Flash (Macromedia)** used for more interactivity and zero footprint. This display format is not available for all analytics.

- ✔ **HTML:** For 508-compliancy (the standard for disabled people — for more information, see www.access-board.gov/508.htm).

After you've chosen a display mode, you can access your analytic from the InfoView folder (as you would any other type of document). InfoView identifies your analytics by displaying the icon shown in Figure 16-15.

Figure 16-15:
The analytic
icon.

Analytics

A word about formats

By default, the format in which gauges appear on-screen is Adobe SVG. If the Abode SVG 3.x. component is not installed on your computer, the product proposes that you install it from the Web (recommended for MS Internet Explorer users).

If you want to display your gauges in Flash format, the Macromedia plug-in (Adobe Flash Player 9) has to be installed first. Otherwise your analytics won't be displayed properly.

To set Flash format as your default display format, go to the Preferences page; from Performance Management tab, check the option labeled *Use Macromedia Flash when available*.

Users of the Firefox browser normally prefer to use the Flash rendering for designing analytics.

Inserting an analytic into a dashboard

From the analytic page, click the Add to My Dashboard link to add the analytic to the personal dashboard. From there, you can either add the analytic into an existing page of your personal dashboard or into a new page. The analytic is placed into the dashboard at a default location. You can customize the page to modify its settings. Figure 16-16 shows what this looks like.

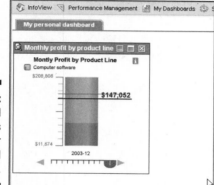

Figure 16-16:
You can add analytics to your personal dashboard.

To add the analytic into a corporate dashboard, follow these steps:

1. **Save your chosen analytic in the public folder tree.**

2. **Customize a page of your dashboard.**

3. **Drag and drop the analytic from the Corporate List to your dashboard page.**

   Figure 16-17 shows an analytic added to a corporate dashboard.

You can also create a new analytic directly from the Dashboard Design page. Here's the drill:

1. **Drag and drop the analytic template of your choice from the New Analytic folder.**

   The analytic opens in Edit mode.

2. **Add the content of the analytic.**

   In this case, type its data and rendering characteristics.

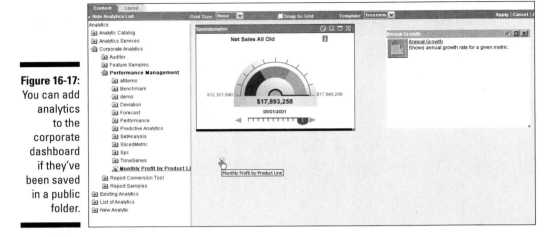

Figure 16-17:
You can add analytics to the corporate dashboard if they've been saved in a public folder.

Creating a Map Analytic Based on a Universe

A map analytic displays how the results of a measure break down geographically. It lets you drill into each area to get more detailed data. The map analytic shown in this section contains common geographical levels: World/continent/ countries and specific levels for each country. For instance, it contains state and county levels for the United States, and a region level for France.

In this section, you create a map analytic based on the `geodata` universe that comes with BusinessObjects.

To create a map analytic from your own data, you must create a universe that has the same characteristics as the `geodata` example. To verify it has been configured properly, check out Chapter 17.

The characteristics of the `geodata` universe are pretty basic.

✔ It contains one `geo` class with geographical dimensions and one `sales` measure, as shown in Figure 16-18.

✔ The `geohierarchy` table defines relationships between each level.

✔ The three lookup tables give both the name and the long name for each code defined in the relationship table.

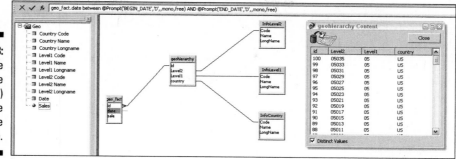

Figure 16-18:
A universe
with one
class (Geo)
and one
measure
(Sales).

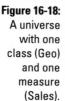

✔ Data relationships and hierarchies are used for navigation from level to level within the analytic.

Maps use the values for `Country`, `level1`, and `level2` — so use the same values in your own universe as those defined in the maps' properties.

✔ From the `geo_fact` fact table, the following auto-join has been defined on the `date` object:

```
geo_fact.date between @Prompt('BEGIN_DATE','D',,mono,free) AND
                @Prompt('END_DATE','D',,mono,free)
```

✔ `BEGIN_DATE` and `END_DATE` are keywords used by the BusinessObjects engine. Don't change the case; don't translate them because the end user doesn't use them.

This auto-join defines the time period to display in the analytic. If it is not defined in the universe, the Time Window section isn't available in the map analytic properties.

Additionally, the universe contains three hierarchies that define the parent-child relationships between objects (see Figure 16-19):

✔ `Geo Code` with objects: `Country Code, Level1 Code, Level2 Code`

✔ `Geo Name` with objects: `Country Name, Level1 Name, Level2 Name.`

✔ `Geo Long Name` with objects: `Country Longname, Level1 Longname, Level2 Longname.`

✔ `Level1` is the child of the `Country` level, such as `state` for `United States` and `region` for `France`.

✔ `Level2` is the child of `Level1`: so `county` for `the United States` and `departement` for `France`.

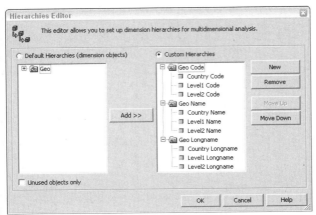

To create your map analytic, follow these steps:

1. **In InfoView, choose New⇨Analytic and then open the Map template on the Create New Analytic page.**

   The analytic's template opens in Edit mode.

   A map analytic requires very specific settings for data definitions but accepts settings for rendering properties that are common to most other analytics.

2. **Select the map to be displayed as first level, the highest level from the Select Data to Display section.**

3. **Check the Use a Universe radio button.**

   You can use data from a universe or a metric. For the purpose of these steps, we've based this map analytic on a universe.

4. **Select Map from the Map drop-down list, and Longname from the Match Object By drop-down list.**

5. **Click the Select Objects button.**

   The Select Objects dialog box opens, as shown in Figure 16-20.

6. **From the Subject Area drop-down menu, choose a universe class.**

   For a map analytic, select Geo as the subject area.

7. **From the Measure drop-down menu, select the measure to display.**

   For a map analytic, select Sales as the measure.

8. **From the Classification list, choose the higher dimension to display.**

   For more accuracy, choose Country Longname.

9. **Select the aggregation to apply on measure from the Aggregation Method drop-down menu.**

   For a map analytic based on a universe, choose Sum.

10. **Select the hierarchy corresponding to your chosen classification type from the Dimension Hierarchy drop-down menu.**

    For a map analytic, choose Geo Longname as the hierarchy for your dimensions.

11. **Depending on the type of classification object you want — code, name, or long name — choose the appropriate match from the Match Map Object By drop-down menu.**

    The idea is to identify the retrieved data for the map engines in order to ensure good matching.

    If you use other data from this universe (instead of the data shown here), you may end up with data missing from your map because the geodata default database is not complete.

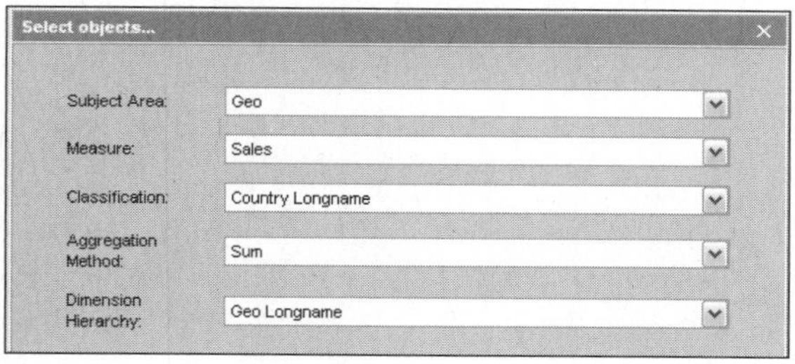

Figure 16-20:
The Select
Objects
dialog box.

Select objects...		
Subject Area:	Geo	
Measure:	Sales	
Classification:	Country Longname	
Aggregation Method:	Sum	
Dimension Hierarchy:	Geo Longname	

12. **Adjust the visualization settings according to the Sales measure.**

    • Define the number of ranges to use in order to define the number of color zones. For each zone, define a color and boundaries:

      Boundaries can be calculated automatically with equal values. For example if you define four zones, the boundaries cover the values from 0 to 25 %, 25 to 50%, 50 to 75% and 75 to 100%.

      To specify custom boundaries, check the Manually Set Ranges radio button and select a specific percent for each zone.

    • Define a title using Map name or typing some text.

    • Choose to show the legend by checking the Show Legend box.

    • Set hyperlinks by clicking the Browse button and selecting a document from the InfoView list.

13. **Select all periods proposed in the Time Period section.**

    Choose this option because the default database doesn't have data for the current period.

    The map is now displayed, as shown in Figure 16-21.

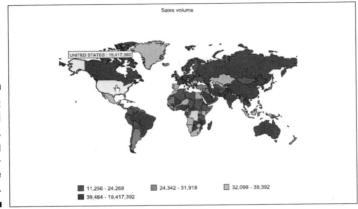

Figure 16-21:
A world map, showing sales-volume ranges.

The World map is colored according to sales volume ranges displayed in the legend. If you hover your mouse pointer over a country, a tooltip displays its long name and its total sales. Click the country and the analytic displays the map of the selected country, along with detail on a secondary level, as shown in Figure 16-22.

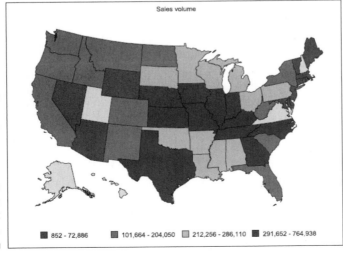

Figure 16-22:
A map of the United States, showing sales volume in different states.

TIP

Adding other maps

The maps delivered with BusinessObjects are not complete for all levels of every country, and they come with a predefined format.

If you want to add more detailed maps or add your own maps that you typically use in your company applications, you can do so.

Maps are stored at the following location:

```
$Tomcat_directory$\webapps\
    businessobjects\
    enterprise115\
    desktoplaunch\
    WEB-INF\classes\
    optimap\chart_root\
    maps
```

They are stored in an XML format, with the `.pcxml` extension.

The maps available in the map analytic are described at the following location:

```
$Business Objects_directory$\
    Performance Management 11.5\
    server\conf\map-properties.
    xml
```

Chapter 17

Using Performance Manager to Set Goals and Track Achievement

• •

In This Chapter

▶ Fitting metrics and goals into the big picture

▶ Creating your own metrics and goals

▶ Adding value through metrics, goals, and analytics

• •

*I*n the two previous chapters, we looked at how reports compare to dashboards, and how charts compare to analytics. In this chapter, we look at the differences between a universe measure and a metric.

Chapter 15 described how to create a dashboard containing a speedometer gauge based on a *metric* — that's business-speak for a named value used to evaluate performance — for example, *net sales by month* for a given time range. To get a handle on this metric, you can use a Speedometer gauge to compare current sales with the previous period's sales (or other such values) over the time range you specify, comparing the values you get when you run the analytic from time to time.

To get the sales history, we took three general steps:

✔ We defined a specific indicator as a metric: the one showing net sales (based on a universe measure).

✔ We defined as metadata the aggregation function over time, the time range, and the trend.

✔ We stored the values for the specified time range in system tables.

The Performance Management catalog comes with a series of analytics that compare metrics and goals, enabling you to monitor the value of data (both forecast and actual) over time. To access the Performance Management catalog, select the Performance Manager Analytics page from the Performance Manager Menu.

In this chapter, we show you how to set up your analytics to compare metrics with the goals of your company.

Configuring Your Environment to Build Metrics

A metric shows the measure obtained after you've run an analytic to examine some aspect of your company's performance. In BusinessObjects, you choose from three to five components for each metric you create: a measure, an aggregation function, a filter, a calendar, and a slicer.

A *measure* is a specific numerical value obtained at a specific time; its meaning is pretty limited unless placed in context. (The same is true when you create an analytic.) When you choose a measure, you must always choose a dimension — at the very least, the time axis. Simple measures with few dimensions can be adapted to just about any data context, but if you want the measure to serve as a *performance indicator,* it's better to freeze its definition: You must define your measure not only as a value, but also as belonging to a specific context — for example, *net sales by month* (value) *over the fourth quarter of fiscal 2008* (context).

When you accumulate instances of a BusinessObjects measure over a specified time period, what you get is a metric — a time-based aggregation of a

You got a license for that?

Dashboard Manager is the tool you use to create and measure your dashboards, analytics, and metrics. Using goals requires the specific license of the Performance Manager module. While Dashboard Manager is the basis of the Performance Management Business Objects Suite and can be used alone, Performance Manager is an additional part of this Suite that offers more advanced capabilities like use of goals and goals analytics.

Even if both modules are automatically installed at the same time, one more license key is required for Performance Manager. To make sure that you can use the goal-setting capabilities of Performance Manager, check your BusinessObjects installation to make sure that the appropriate product key has been added in the Central Management Console (CMC); this capability is not part of the standard installation.

From the CMC, open the license keys page and check that BusinessObjects Performance Manager is added. If your license allows you to use Performance Manager, the Performance Manager tab is visible to the right of the Dashboard Manager tab.

After you've ensured that you have the appropriate licenses in place, you can access metric tools from the Dashboard Manager tab and goal tools from the Performance Manager tab.

measure. You can also filter the measure to track it on a particular dimension (for more about dimensions, see Chapter 8), or slice the measure through a dimension to detect a trend — such as whether the metric is going up or down.

Typical metrics include some detailed specifications — for example, *average revenue per customer profile for each month over the last two years* or *net sales by region for the last four quarters*. Each metric comes with its own history, showing the value for each period over its associated time range.

A *slicer* is a dimension used to subdivide the values of a particular metric, or even of a particular measure. If you define (say) the Product Line dimension as a slicer, what you get is a *sliced metric* — in this case, a value for each product line. The user interface shows an individual value for each product line independently (say, *convertible sales* and *sedan sales* instead of the more general *car sales*).

You have to define four parameters for your metric — measure, filter, calendar, and slicer — before Dashboard Manager provides you with the needed aggregation functions. The following sections describe what you need to do to make the interface ready for creating metrics.

Setting up a universe to build metrics

Measures, filters, and the *fact table* (a table in which measures are stored) containing the fact date must be available before you can create metrics in specific universes. Each such universe has to be declared in the Setup application of Performance Management.

Your first step, then, is to open the `compuwarehouse metrics` universe, which is shown in Figure 17-1, that comes with BusinessObjects.

Here are some points to keep in mind about building metrics:

 ✔ In the Classes and Objects panel, you define one or more classes.

When you define dimensions and metrics in Performance Management, you see data displayed by classes and not by universe. This sample universe contains one `Metrics` class with measures, dimensions, and predefined filters. While you're creating and managing your metrics, you see the `Metrics` class — but not the `compuwarehouse metrics` universe name — on-screen.

Several universes have classes with the same name; in this case, the universe name is displayed between parentheses after the class name.

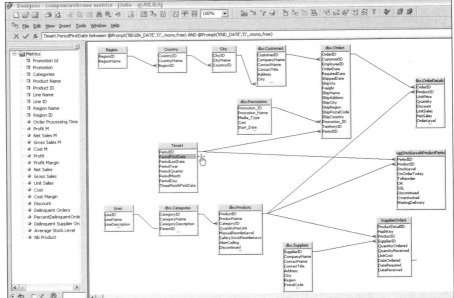

Figure 17-1:
Using the
demo
universe
to build
a metric.

✔ In your chosen universe, you define your dimensions, predefined filters, and measures in their relevant classes.

✔ To configure the time dimension, you must give every fact table (in this universe, the `OrderDetails` and `SupplierOrders` tables) the following auto-join on its date column. The metric engine uses this join; it has the following syntax:

```
between @Prompt('BEGIN_DATE','D',,mono,free) AND
        @Prompt('END_DATE','D',,mono,free)
```

`'BEGIN_DATE'` and `'END_DATE'` are variables used by the metric engine. Remember: They are case-sensitive.

Declaring a universe

When you have your main properties set up in your universe, you have to declare your universe in the Setup Application installed with Performance Management.

During this process, the metric engine reads and stores the metadata from the universe in its database — which is different from the CMC repository. The Performance Management repository has to be set in the System Setup tab of the Setup application.

To declare an object in a particular universe as a source for a metric, follow these steps:

1. **In Performance Manager, click the Setup button and then, in the Setup application that opens, click the System Setup tab.**

   The Repository page opens, which contains information about CMS and repository database connections.

2. **Click the Universes link on the System Setup tab.**

   The Universes page opens.

3. **Click the Add Universe button.**

   The Add a Universe dialog box opens.

4. **Select a universe from the Measure Universe drop-down list.**

5. **Click OK.**

   The dialog box closes.

6. **To upload the universe metadata in the Performance Management repository, select your universe from the Universe Definition box and click the Update button.**

   The universe content, measures, dimensions, and filters with their definitions appear in the lower area of the page, as shown in Figure 17-2.

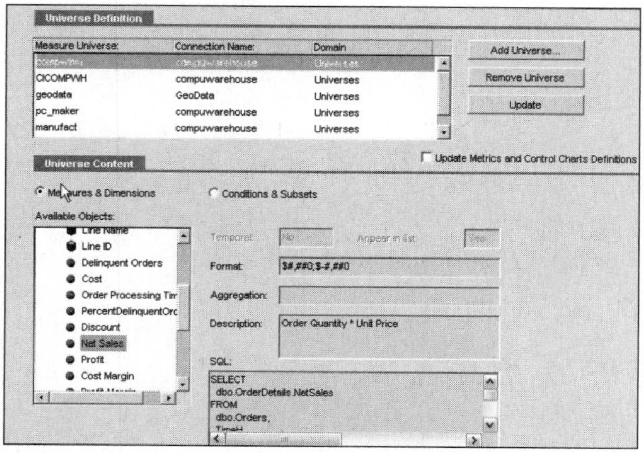

Figure 17-2:
The
Universes
page.

This area shows the SQL definition of each object.

If you want to build a metric over time, make sure its SQL statement contains a time filter on the fact table and the date in its WHERE clause. You can check it selecting your measure in the Available Objects list of the Universe Content section. The SQL of your measure must contain the following filter:

```
between @Prompt('BEGIN_DATE','D',,mono,free) AND
              @Prompt('END_DATE','D',,mono,free)
```

The metric engine stores metadata in its own repository. If you've changed the universe metadata and you want to update the existing metric definition automatically, check the Update Metric and Control Chart Definitions checkbox.

Declaring dimensions

After you update the universe you're using, your next step is to set up the dimensions of the metric. To do so, follow these steps:

1. **On the System Setup tab, click the Dimensions link.**

   The Dimensions page appears, as shown in Figure 17-3.

System Setup	Time Config	Parameters	Tools

Repository | System User | Universes | **Dimensions**

Dimensions can be used to personalize analytic content by defining associations between slices and users. They can also be

🗒️ Add...	🗙 Remove...	🖉 Edit Dimension...	
Name	Metric Creation?	Association	
Categories	Sliced Metrics	None	
cat_prod name 1	Sliced Metrics	None	
cat_prod name 2	Sliced Metrics	Manual	
Country Code	Sliced Metrics	Manual	
Country Code Name	Sliced Metrics	None	
Level1 code	Sliced Metrics	None	
Level1 Code Name	Sliced Metrics	None	

Click Edit Association to modify the dimension's association...

🖉 Edit Association...

User	Slice Name	Slice Code

Figure 17-3:
The
Dimensions
page.

2. **Click Add to add a new dimension.**

   The Create Dimension dialog box appears.

   A sliced dimension is made up of two main fields:

- *Slice Name* defines the slicer's purpose as a brief, functional name that shows up on the user interface.

- *Slice Code* is for query purposes. Taking the example of the geography dimension, viewing United States, for instance, is better than simply displaying its code.

3. **Enter an explicit name and place a check mark next to "Yes, I want to create sliced metrics on this dimension."**

   This process maps the chosen dimensions of the universe as names and codes, organized by class.

4. **Select the universe class from the Subject Area drop-down list, and then map the code and display fields with their universe counterpart.**

   - From the Object for Dimension Name list box, select the object to be displayed as dimension values.

   - From the Object for Dimension Code list box, select the object to query on (generally the code associated to the dimension display).

   - Fill the Global Sliced Name field to set the name you want displayed on-screen to identify the full dimension.

5. **Click the Next button.**

   The dimension values appear in the second panel.

6. **From this new panel, click the Refresh button to get the dimension values from the database.**

   The list box now contains two columns; each has a dimension name and code values.

7. **Click the Next button to define the level of security you want to set on this dimension.**

   In this area, you can add secured dimensions by user. If you don't want to do that yet, choose None for Now.

8. **Click End to exit the wizard.**

Your dimension is created and now appears in the list of dimensions on the Dimension page.

Creating a calendar

Calendars are the last part to configure in the System setup.

Calendars contain all the periods for which a metric can be computed. For example, the Speedometer analytic's time slider represents the periods of the calendar on which the metric has been defined.

You can create several kinds of calendars:

- ✔ A calendar based on a default interval (for Day to Year).

- ✔ A custom calendar where you define weekends or skip days. For example, if you have no business on weekends, you can skip them in your analytics. Monday will be the next day after Friday, and your chart will be continued without any discontinuity.

- ✔ An imported calendar (defined in a CSV file saved in InfoView).

To create a calendar, follow these steps:

1. **From the Setup application, click the Time Config tab.**

2. **Select the Calendar page.**

   For each calendar you want to set up, you need to define the different parameters.

3. **Click the Add button to create a new calendar.**

   The Add a Calendar dialog box appears. as shown in Figure 17-4.

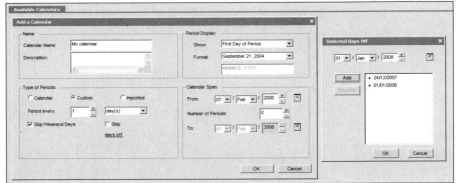

Figure 17-4:
The Add a
Calendar
dialog box.

4. **Give your calendar a name and a description in the Name section.**

5. **In the Type of Periods section, check one of the three radio buttons to define the calendar type: Calendar, Custom, or Imported.**

6. **Define your calendar depending on the type you chose in Step 5:**

   If you selected the Calendar option

   a) Select an interval from the Interval drop-down list. You select the period. In this case, a level of the Gregorian calendar: Day, Weekly, Monthly, Quarterly, or Yearly.

The interval you choose determines the date values for which the metric will be computed. For example, if you choose Quarterly, your calendar gets one value by quarter, so any metrics using this calendar get one value by quarter too.

b) In the Calendar Span section, set the first period with the From drop-down list. Set the last period of your calendar with the To drop-down list.

Notice that in each case, the calendar component to the right can help you to select a date.

If you select the Custom radio button

a) Specify the period frequency of your calendar from the Period Every drop-down list. You can define custom periods based on days, weeks, months, quarters, or years. For example, if you select 2 Months from the Period Every drop-down list, the calendar has one value every two months.

If you select the default selection — 1 Day(s) — you can skip weekends by checking the Skip Weekend Days box, and define your days off by checking the Skip checkbox and select the Days Off link. The Select Days Off dialog box opens. Select a date for the calendar components and click the Add button to add it as a day off. Your selected date is then added into the Days Off list.

b) In the Calendar Span section, set the first period with the From drop-down list. Specify the total number of periods you want for your calendar. The last period is then defined based on this number of periods.

If you select the Imported radio button

a) Click Browse to select it from the InfoView document or type the URL directly if the calendar is stored on the server file system. The imported file must contain one row per period, and this period must be a date.

b) Specify the format of the dates of the imported file, and specify whether the first row of this file contains a column header. In this case, no boundaries have to be set because the imported file contains all periods. So the Calendar Span section is empty.

c) Define the display of the calendar periods to be rendered in the analytic from the Period Display section. For the Gregorian or custom calendars, you can choose to display the first date of the end date of the period. For example, for a monthly period, the analytic shows the first date or the end date of the month.

d) Choose to show the period name (if the first row of the imported file contains a header).

e) To choose the display format of the date, select a format from the Format drop-down list.

7. **When you're done defining your calendar, click OK to build it.**

   Technically, each period of the calendar is being stored in the Performance Manager repository. If your calendar contains a high number of periods, computation can be long so this action may take some time.

   When the Add a Calendar dialog box closes and your new calendar is added into the calendar list, you've built your calendar properly.

 To define calendar properties for all calendars, click the Option button at the top right of the calendar list to set the first day of the week, the first day of the year, and weekends. Define those options at the beginning, before creating any calendars, because you won't be able to modify them later once calendars exist with the previous definition.

When you have the measures, filters, fact date, dimensions, and calendars set up, you're ready to build a metric.

Creating a Metric

You can define three types of metrics:

- ✔ **Metric without a filter,** such as the *sum of sales by month,* which has one value per month.
- ✔ **Metric filtered on a dimension,** such as the *sum of sales by month for European area.*
- ✔ **Sliced metric,** such as a *sum of sales by month for each product line* that has one value by month and product line.

You can create a metric in two ways:

- ✔ Building a metric from a computation of your detailed corporate data like `sales volume` or `salary average` stored in databases.
- ✔ Entering data manually to create an indicator from a macro and external data like `customer satisfaction`, which contains one value by month and doesn't come from corporate IT systems but external surveys.

Creating metrics automatically with the New Metric Wizard

To create a new metric using the New Metric Wizard, follow these steps:

1. **Click the Dashboard Manager tab of the Performance Management Application.**

   The Metric page opens. This is the page where you create your metric.

2. **From the Metric page, select a universe class from the Available Metrics drop-down list, click Add, and select new metric.**

   The three-step New Metric Wizard starts.

3. **On the first screen of the wizard, choose a measure in the Select a Measure drop-down list.**

   Selecting multiple measures creates multiple metrics based on those measures with same characteristics.

   When a measure in selected, the Select an Aggregation Function becomes active.

4. **Select an aggregation. If you want to create a sliced metric, select the dimension as slicer from the Select a Dimension drop-down list.**

   You choose a dimension declared in the dimension area of the System Setup application.

5. **Click Next to go to the next screen.**

   The Filter screen appears.

6. **Select a filter from the filter list. If you don't want to set a filter for the metric, choose None.**

   None is the default selected value.

   You cannot create two different metrics with the same measure and the same filter.

7. **Click Next to go to the next screen.**

   The Attributes screen appears.

8. **Fill in the metric name, description, and associate a calendar.**

   All calendars you defined in the setup application are available here.

9. **Set the parameters of your metric:**

   - *Refresh Type*: Select Independent to refresh the metric from the metric engine.

   - *Parameters:* Set a trend for the metric from the Trend Is Good When drop-down list to get predefined color-coding when you create analytics from it.

     For example, you probably want to see the sales trend when the value moves upward from one period to the next.

   - *Storage Options*: Choose whether to store the complete metric history or only its last value. If you check the Store All Metric Values radio button, define the metric history interval you want stored.

To change the default interval boundaries, change the start date (set by default as the first date of the calendar) and check the Stop Metric Calculation option and select an end date.

Check the Stop at Current Period checkbox to force the computation at the current period to avoid building empty periods until the end of the calendar.

10. **To populate your metric, click the Refresh button.**

When the refresh is being performed, a dialog box appears, showing the period being refreshed. When the metric refresh is done, the values of the start date and last date have a gray background in the metric's history (see Figure 17-5). (If the start and last date don't have a gray background in your metric, you haven't properly populated the metric. See the "Finding errors" sidebar if this happens to you.)

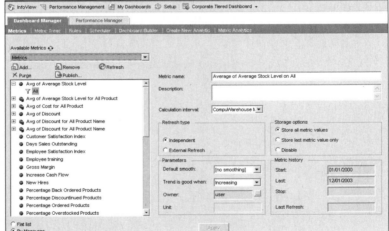

Figure 17-5:
A newly created metric, showing its properties.

Creating a metric manually

You can also create a metric by entering data manually. To do so, follow these steps:

1. **Click the Dashboard Manager tab of the Performance Management Application.**

The Metrics page opens. This is the page where you create your metric.

Finding errors

If a metric is not generated properly, it's usually because the SQL wasn't generated properly. This can happen as a result of incorrectly defined objects in the universe(s) providing the data, or incorrectly generated metadata in the Performance Management repository.

To localize errors, you need to look at the generated SQL in the logs file. To activate the trace, follow these steps:

1. **Click the Setup application.**

2. **Click the Parameters tab.**

3. **Open the Trace page.**

4. **Choose the log file location by checking Log to Folder and modifying the default path if you want.**

   To define which trace you want to activate, check whatever you want to trace in the

Select the Information to Log To and Enable Logs to These Modules sections.

In the case of a metric, check the SQL Queries and Metric Engine options.

In the Performance Management repository, which is the Repository page of the System Setup tab, the following tables are used most often to generate SQL:

✔ `ci_probe table` contains a list of metrics definitions

✔ `ci_probe_value` contains all values of all metrics

✔ `ci_probe_dim` contains a list of dimensions values

✔ `ci_probe_dim_value` contains the metric values by dimension.

2. **Click Add and then New Manual Entry Metric.**

   The Create Metric Wizard opens with different options.

3. **Fill in the name of your metric, a description, and a trend; then select a calendar and fix the boundaries of the metric's history.**

4. **Click Next.**

   The second screen displays the field to fill each period defined.

5. **For each period defined during the calendar selection, enter the metric value manually.**

   For instance, you can create a metric named My metric so that it shows one value every 10 days from Nov 1 for the next 20 weeks, after you define a custom calendar based on this time range. Figure 17-6 shows what that looks like in the user interface.

6. **Click Finish.**

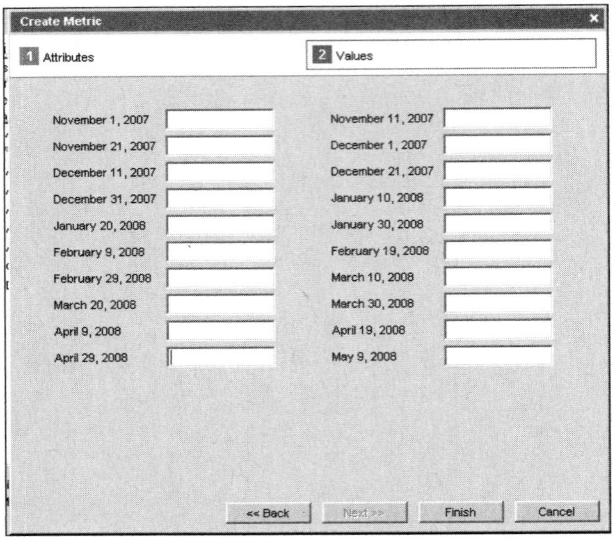

Figure 17-6:
Creating a
metric using
manual
entries.

Creating a Goal

Knowing where your company is at any given time is pretty meaningless if you don't know where you want your company to be. Accordingly, when you have your metric in place, your next step is to define a *goal* for the metric to be based on.

To create a goal, follow these steps:

1. **In the Performance Management application, from the Performance Manager tab, select the Goals Management page.**

   The Goal Management page displays a list of goals that already exist in the repository.

2. **Click the Add button.**

   The New Goal Wizard opens with the Name and Metric screen, as shown in Figure 17-7.

3. **Define a name and metric with which a goal is to be associated.**

   - *Goal Info:* Fill in the goal name. You can also give it a type to categorize your goal.

   - *Metric Info:* By definition, a goal must be associated to a metric. To set the associated metric, click the Select a Metric link to choose a metric from the list of all the metrics stored in the repository.

- *Goal Span:* Depending on the metric selected, adjust the goal boundaries using the metric-based calendar.

4. **Click Next.**

5. **On the Auto-fill and Tolerance screen (shown in Figure 17-8), define the way the goal values will be generated and a tolerance on which the metric status will be calculated.**

You can choose from four auto-fill methods:

- *Constant Value:* Use this method if your goal will always have the same value over time. In this case, you can set a constant or define this value from one of the metric values for a given period. Constant values are especially useful with an On-Target trend.

- *Period to Period Change*: This option increments the goal with a fixed value from one period to the next. You can either define the value for the first period and the last value of the goal — the increment is defined automatically, according to the number of periods you set — or you can define the value for the first period and set an explicit increment. You can fill in a constant or define your desired values from the metric's history. The goal of the period N is defined by $\texttt{Gn=G(n-1)+(constant)}$.

- *Period to Period % Change:* This option uses a fixed percentage of the goal value (in comparison with the previous goal value) as the increment. In this case, the line isn't straight but an exponential curve. The goal of the period N is defined by $\texttt{Gn=G(n-1)*(1+constant/100)}$.

- *Year to Year Change* and *Year to Year % Change:* These options use a fixed value or a fixed percent of the goal value (in comparison with the value of the same period from the previous year) as the increment. These methods are especially useful if you're monitoring indicators that follow seasonal trends.

You can also define tolerance in three zones (based on the goal value) if you overshoot the expectation, meet the expectation, or don't meet the expectation. Tolerance boundaries can be based, for each goal value, on constants or percentages of the goal value.

6. **Click Next.**

   The Edit Values screen (shown in Figure 17-9) shows goal values generated for all periods, according to the auto-fill rules you set up in Step 5.

7. **(Optional) If you want to modify some of the goals values for some specific periods, check the Manual Entry radio button.**

   Goal values of each period then become editable, so you can modify any one you want.

8. **Click Finish to compute your new goal and close the wizard.**

   The goal is created; you can visualize it in the analytic in the right panel of the page.

   Figure 17-10 shows an analytic with two curves: the regular one displaying the goal values and the second one displaying the metric values.

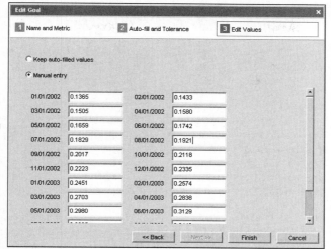

Figure 17-9:
Setting
values by
period in
the Goal
Creation or
Edit Wizard.

Goal Metric

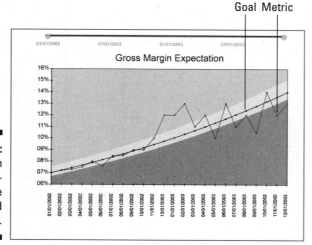

Figure 17-10:
On-screen
represent-
ation of the
metric and
its goal.

When you select a goal in the left list, the corresponding goal analytic is displayed on the right with this default rendering.

You can modify the analytic, save it in the repository, or add it to your personal or corporate dashboard.

Creating a Metric-Based Analytic

When you have a metric and a goal, you can now use them to create an analytic. In the following section, we show you how to create three of the more popular analytics: the Interactive Metric Trend, the Metric tree, and the Strategy Map.

Interactive Metric Trend

One of the most-used analytics is the Interactive Metric Trend. It offers powerful interactivity and visualization capabilities that allow you to analyze a metric over time.

To create an Interactive Metric Trend analytic and examine the result, follow these steps:

1. **In the Performance Management application, click the Dashboard Manager tab, and then, from the toolbar, select the Create New Analytic link.**

2. **From the metric template list, select the Interactive Metric Trend analytic.**

   The analytic template opens in Edit mode, as shown in Figure 17-11.

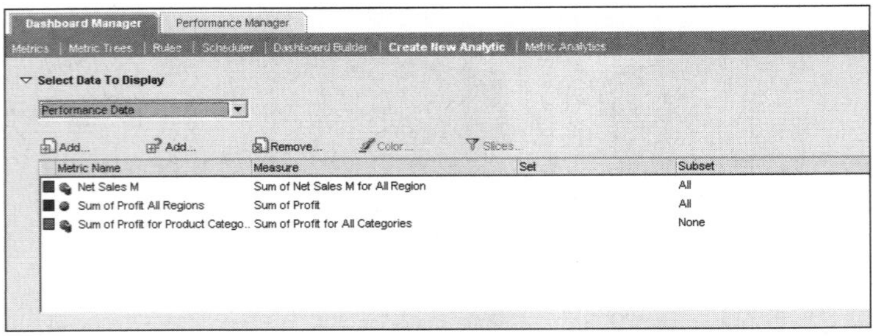

Figure 17-11:
Interactive
Metric Trend
properties,
shown in
Edit mode.

3. **Choose which data to display from the Select Data to Display drop-down list:**

   • *Performance Data:* Defines a list of metrics to display in the analytic. This is the default.

   • *Top Metric*: Sets a top of metrics to display according to their variation from the last period.

- *Set Data:* Relates to the Set Analysis module. The Set Analysis tool, which enables you to study population segmentation, requires a separate license and is beyond the scope of this book.

- *Goal Only:* Selects the goals to display.

- *Universe Query:* Defines data from a universe.

4. **From the empty list, click the Add button.**

    The Add a Metric dialog box displays a list of available metrics. They are listed according to the universe class on which the source measure is based.

    For example, the `Metric` class lists all metrics of this class, whether filtered or sliced.

5. **Select your metrics and click OK.**

    You can select several metrics by Shift+clicking.

    The metric you have selected is added.

6. **For each metric, set characteristics:**

    - *For a sliced metric,* you can specify slices to display in the analytic. Select a sliced metric, click the Slices button, and set values for the metric (as shown in Figure 17-12).

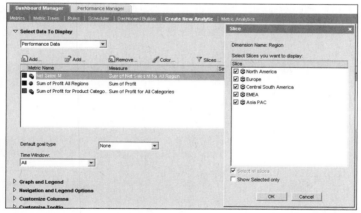

Figure 17-12: Slicer choice.

- *To define the color of each metric in the chart,* click the Color button.

- *To allow the user to select a metric directly from the analytic,* click the Add a Prompt button (the one with the ?).

7. **From the Time Window drop-down list, select a specific time range.**

   The default range is All Time Values for Which Metrics Are Computed.

8. **(Optional) In the Graph and Legend section, specify the rendering characteristics:**

   Metric Type: Here you can define how the data is displayed:

   - *Raw* shows the metric values for each period.

   - *% of Origin* and *% of Change of Origin* show, as a percentage, the comparison between the metric value and its initial value for each period.

   - *Change* and *% Change* show the variation in the value and as a percentage from one period to the next.

   - *Cumulative Sum* shows, for each period, the metric value added to the values of all values of previous periods.

   - *Month to Date, Quarter to Date,* and *Year to Date* show the variation from the beginning of the period.

   Compare To: Select From Previous Year to display a curve for the last year and a curve for the previous year, to compare data of both years for the same period (the same time axis is used for both curves in this case).

   Chart Type: Select the type of chart of the analytic. Stacked bars are useful to display sliced metrics.

   Specifying any rendering characteristics is optional because you can also let the user select the type of display dynamically according to the type of analysis being performed from within the analytic itself.

   When you're viewing the analytic, you can hide the comparison from the previous year by toggling the Show/Hide Comparison button.

9. **From the Navigation and Legend Options section, set links from the title, legend, and data point of a chart.**

   For example, you can define from the chart line a `sum of profit` metric, and link to a report that includes profit detailed data. If this report has a date prompt, you can set link a URL as a parameter on the date. The report displays data for this time range, according to the time period that the user selects on the graph.

   The sidebar "Linking to another document from an analytic" has more details on setting links.

10. **From the Customize Columns section, define the information to display in the analytic table.**

Linking to another document from an analytic

To include a link to another link from your analytic, click the Browse button and select a document from the list. To have something more dynamic, you can use some parameters. For example, in an interactive analytic that shows a metric's trend in terms of the date, the metric, and even the slice, you may want to open a different document.

The syntax that does this job looks like this:

```
"/apps/jsp/openAnalytic.jsp?
    RepositoryName=Document&
    RepositoryType=C&Document
    Ext=rep&DocumentName=The
    Doc&nbPrompts=x&Prompt1=
    value1&Prompt2=value2 "
```

where

✔ RepositoryName: The domain where you have saved the analytic

✔ RepositoryType: C for corporate and P for personal

✔ DocumentExt: Document suffix, REP for Full Client, WID for WEBI and AFD for analytic

✔ DocumentName: The document that you wish to display

To pass prompts you need to add the following extension syntax: -&nbPrompts=x&Prompt1=value1&Prompt2=value2 and so on

With this syntax, you can use the following variables: $METRIC_NAME$, $SLICE_CODE$, $SLICE_NAME$, $BEGIN_DATE$, END_DATE, $CURRENT_DATE$.

For more information, see http://www.forumtopics.com/busobj/viewtopic.php?t=41556.

11. **From the Customize Tooltip section, define any information to display in the tooltip,**

12. **Check the Display Mode option to define the level of the analytic interactivity.**

13. **Click OK to set those options and open the analytic.**

By default, you can visualize one line per metric for the entire time range. The table below the chart shows information about the metric: color coding, trend, first and end values, the previous-period value, and so on.

For example, Figure 17-13 shows an analytic that contains three metrics: sum of profit, net sales sliced by regions, and net sales sliced by product line.

For the two sliced metrics, the analytic displays by default the value for all the slices. The value of net sales by product line is not shown, because this is the same line as net sales by region.

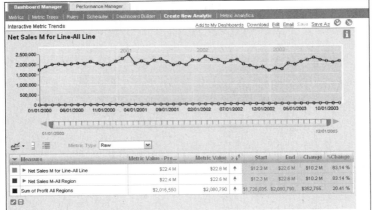

Figure 17-13:
The interactive metric trend: Net Sales M for Line.

When you have your analytic, you can change the way it's displayed:

- **Hide metrics:** To hide a metric, click the Color symbol of this metric in the table. To hide all metrics except one, select the metric you want to keep and click the Show Selected Metric Only button.

- **Remove metrics from the analytic:** Select them and click the Trash Bin button.

- **See values for each slice of a sliced metric:** Click the small arrow before the sliced metric name and you get one line per slice. You can also hide some selected slices.

  In Figure 17-14, the lines show the values of the Net Sales M by region: Asia-PAC, Central South America, EMEA, Europe, and North America.

- **Improve visibility:** Click the Legend button to display the legend.

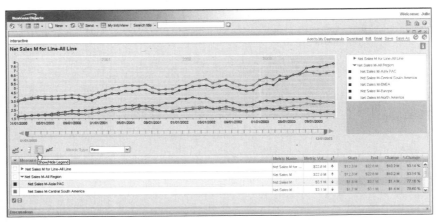

Figure 17-14:
The interactive metric trend with all slices displayed.

✔ **Reduce the time range:** By default the analytic shows the entire periods of the metric. To reduce the entire period from the beginning, move the slider from the first period to the period you want to set as the first period. To reduce the entire period from the end, move the slider, and repeat the step but from the last period of the slider.

✔ **Change the chart style:** Click the arrow in the Change Style button (the first button on the left behind the chart). From the pop-up menu, select one of the four styles: Line, Bar, Stacked Bar, and Stacked Bar Percentage.

✔ **Change the scale and the metric type:** Change the type from the Metric Type drop-down list. For example, if you select the Percent of Origin View, you can compare the trend of each metric (see Figure 17-15).

✔ **Visualize the trend quarter by quarter:** Select Quarter to Date from the Metric Type drop-down list. Figure 17-16 shows the Net sales trend for each region from periods of the same quarter.

Figure 17-15:
Zoom on a specific period.

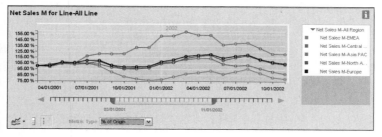

Figure 17-16:
Interactive metric trend analytic with a Quarter to Date trend.

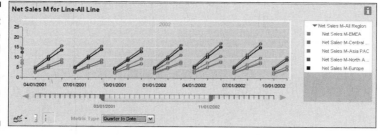

Metric Tree

Another interesting analytic that's based on a metric is the Metric Tree.

The Metric Tree analytic presents metrics — and relationships between metrics — as a tree view. The top levels of the tree represent high-level metrics — for instance, strategic metrics for the whole company. From the top, the Metric Tree can branch by domain; each domain can have several branches, and so on until you get to the *leaf* level that represents metrics for more detailed scope. This kind of visualization shows at a glance which lower-level data explains the results of a higher level. Causes and effects become clearer.

The Net Sales Metric Tree that comes with BusinessObjects (shown in Figure 17-17) has only two levels: The worldwide net sales at top level, which is then broken down for each world region. Displaying metrics information, this analytic shows the following:

- ✔ The yellow worldwide status, even if the trend is good, can be explained by the bad performance of Asia PAC, which is below objectives.

- ✔ The symbol representing status shows that the goals have been associated to metrics.

- ✔ The status color is the difference between the expected and the achieved values.

- ✔ To get details of each item, a link to a detailed report has been defined as a part of the Metric Tree's definition. The document symbol indicates a link is available; click the symbol to open the document.

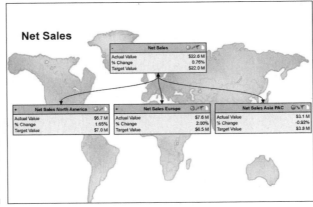

Figure 17-17:
The Net
Sales
Metric Tree.

To create a Metric Tree, follow these steps:

1. **From the Dashboard Manager application, click the Metric Tree link.**

2. **Click the Add button.**

   The Create Metric Tree dialog box opens.

3. **Drag and drop metrics from the left list into the right panel divided into several levels.**

4. **Define branches between each metric by clicking from a metric to the other one.**

5. **Add the Metric Tree to a dashboard, customize the dashboard, and select the Metric Tree template from the New Analytic drop-down list.**

   The template opens in edit mode.

6. **Select a Metric Tree, and define the rendering.**

   To define the rendering, you add a title, a background image, links to documents, the data you want to display in tooltips, the data you want to display in each metric container, the unfolded levels, and the number of levels per page.

Figure 17-18 shows a metric tree that represents the gross margin at the higher level that is divided into two branches: one for cost and one for gross sales. Each of them is divided by product lines.

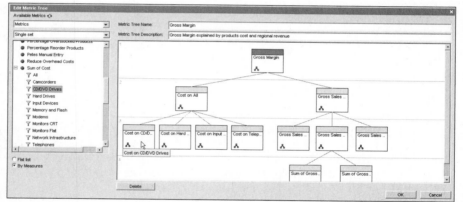

Figure 17-18:
The
Metric Tree.

Strategy Map

A Strategy Map has two axes: the high-level goals and the cause-and-effect relationships between them. Clicking an object on a Strategy Map allows you to analyze any causes and effects related to this object.

In contrast to the Metric Tree, the Strategy Map analytic is based on goals, and the ways of building links between goals are completely free. They don't require any tree view organization.

To look at the Strategy Map that comes with BusinessObjects (shown in Figure 17-19), choose the Performance Manager tab, open the Performance Manager Analytics page, and then open the Strategy Map analytic.

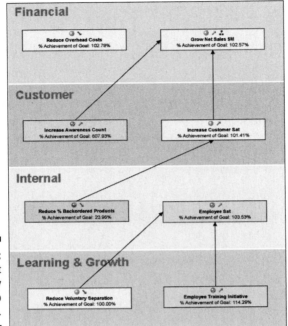

Figure 17-19:
The default
Strategy
Map
analytic.

This analytic gives an example of the implementation of a BI application based on the Balanced Scorecard method, which uses the Strategy Map analytic. Balanced Scorecard is a management system that enables an organization to clarify its vision and strategy and translate these relatively abstract things into action (for more information, go to www.balancedscorecard.org).

The balanced scorecard allows you to view the organization from four perspectives that shape corporate strategy: Financial, Customer, Internal, and Learning & Growth. Implementing the balanced scorecard requires the translation of the vision into operational goals, which means you define goals for each perspective indicators.

This Strategy Map provides a view of those four perspectives. For each of them, strategic goals based on metrics are defined; you can view them through a series of boxes — linked between them and linked in depth to more detailed information — similar to a Metric Tree, WebI documents, and analytics. In this way, the Strategy Map can support a cascading application that requires the Balanced Scorecard implementation.

To create a strategy map and include it in a dashboard, follow these steps:

 1. **In the Performance Management application, click the Dashboard Manager tab, and then, from the toolbar, select the Create New Analytic link.**

2. **Drag and drop the strategy map template into your dashboard.**

   The template is added into your dashboard, and you can now edit it to build your analytic.

3. **Drag and drop goals from the left list to the right panel to design your strategy map.**

4. To define relationship between goals, add arrows by selection from a goal to another one.

5. **Click the Add Item link and add text for your strategy map.**

6. **Click the Add Help Item link and to add help items.**

7. **Click on the Options link to customize the rendering.**

8. **Define the properties in the Graph Properties section:**

   - *To change the shape of a goal's boxes,* select a shape from the options available in the Box Outline list box.

   - *To modify the size of a goal's boxes,* set a value in the Box Width box.

   - *To add a background image from the server directory,* check the Show a Background Image check box and enter the path to where the image is stored in the field. Images must be set in the images directory of the application.

   - *To define the icons places,* select a value from the Display Icon on List box.

   - *To define links to metric trees or corporate documents,* click Attach an Analytic to Each Goal and click Browse or Multiple Links to add documents from InfoView's list of documents.

9. **From the Box Content section, define data to be displayed in the goal boxes:**

   - *To choose goals,* click the Add button to open the Customize View dialog box. Select the goals you want to display from the corporate list of goals and click OK. The selected goals are now displayed in the Box Content Section box.

   - *To order your goals,* click the Move Up and Move Down buttons on the top right of the List of Goals box to set their order in goal boxes.

10. **Define what you want to be displayed in the tooltip in the Box Tooltip section:**

    - *To customize the view,* click the Add button to open the Customize View dialog box. Select characteristics relative to the goals selected from the list and then click OK. The selected indicators are now displayed in the Box Tooltip Section list box.

    - *To change the order of the goals,* click the Move Up and Move Down buttons at the top right of the list of Goals Indicators list to set their order in the tooltips.

11. **To define the time period to display, use the Time Window section:**

   • *To display the last period,* check the radio button with the same name.

   • *To display another period,* check the Select Specific Period radio button and use the calendar to select a period. Don't forget that the metric goal is based on a calendar so select a period within the calendar.

Part VI

Getting the Best Possible Data with Data Marts

The 5th Wave — By Rich Tennant

"We're using just-in-time inventory and just-in-time material flows which have saved us from implementing our just-in-time bankruptcy plan."

In this part. . .

This part provides a brief introduction to the world of *data marts*, a specialized kind of data warehouse that allows you to ensure the data you use to build your reports is as accurate, up-to-date and auditable as possible.

Chapter 18 takes a look at Data Integrator, the Business-Objects tool that helps you prepare and integrate your data in a data mart or data warehouse for use with BusinessObjects.

In Chapter 19, we go on to examine where data warehouses (and data marts in particular) fit in to your BusinessObjects system.

Chapter 18

Putting Data Integrator to Work for You

*B*usinessObjects is a tool for more than just creating reports and sharing them among your work buddies. At the end of the data, BusinessObjects is all *about* data — how to access it, how to work with it, and how to make it count. Of course, it's not all glamour! Someone's got to get down and dirty so your "report in a couple of mouse clicks" is feasible!

To that end, BusinessObjects uses a data warehouse to store its data for you to access. It's literally the primary repository that your organization uses to store raw data. As discussed in earlier chapters, you can go *data mining*, which is just a fancy way of saying that you're going to dig in and perform some important analysis using BusinessObjects!

BusinessObjects uses the CMS repository to store its *metadata* (universe, security, documents); it doesn't use any data warehouse to store it. It can use a data warehouse or any production database to query data and make useful reports. The data you eventually use in your universes — all pulled from the data warehouse — has to get there somehow! It doesn't just happen overnight! Data can come from different sources; for example, HR data might come from PeopleSoft, while stock files may come from your production database.

BusinessObjects has a different tool, called Data Integrator, that is designed to help you prepare and integrate your data into any kind of data warehouse so it can be used in BusinessObjects.

You most likely don't need to worry about the Data Integrator if you're a beginning BusinessObjects user. Asking a novice BusinessObjects user to be responsible for preparing data is like asking a surgeon in residency to perform open-heart surgery in the first week!

Figuring Out Data Integrator

Admittedly, Data Integrator can be difficult to understand simply because it's several applications or components rolled into one! If you want to find out about each part of the Data Integrator application, we recommend consulting the Data Integrator Core Tutorial guide, which is available from BusinessObjects.

It's still important to understand what this helpful tool is — an essential part of the data-mart concept — and how it works. In this section, we discuss the three applications you're most likely to use: Repository Manager, Data Integrator Designer, and Data Integrator Web Administrator.

What is the Repository Manager?

The Repository Manager has but one purpose in life: to help you set up your Data Integrator repository.

The Data Integrator repository is different from your CMS repository.

There is some business to be dealt with before you can create your Data Integrator repository. For starters, you need a database account with some basic rights. Your organization's database administrator (DBA) can provide you with this information.

Do not use the MySQL database provided in the BusinessObjects XI Release 2 setup. If you used the default setup configuration, it would have been for naught as MySQL is not a supported repository in Data Integrator.

After you have your database account, as well as the database connection parameters, you can launch the Data Integrator Repository Manager. Flip ahead to the "Getting on to Designer and getting started" section, to find out how to do so.

What is the Data Integrator Designer?

The Data Integrator Designer — shown in Figure 18-1 — is probably the closest thing to an actual end-user Data Integrator application. The Designer is designed to work with jobs in the data warehouse. For example, you could envision creating and configuring objects or even data mappings (for example, workflows) for your application.

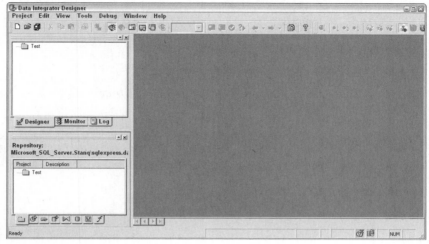

Figure 18-1:
The Data
Integrator
Designer
window.

Most frequently, you create flows that illustrate *ETL (Extraction, Transfor-mation, and Loading)* — the process of extracting raw data from its original source, transforming it into usable data, and then loading it into your data-base or data warehouse for use with BusinessObjects.

To get your flow to (ahem) *flow*, you create jobs and projects. We discuss both of these concepts, as well as how to create them in the "Getting the Hang of Data Integrator Designer" section later in this chapter.

What is the Data Integrator Web Administrator?

Like BusinessObjects itself, Data Integrator has a Web-based administrator panel that allows you to manage everything related to it. This panel is to Data Integrator what the Central Management Console (CMC) is to BusinessObjects Enterprise.

The Web Administrator application, as shown in Figure 18-2, is really for advanced users who are comfortable with Data Integrator and working with jobs, repositories, and such tasks as working with batch jobs, services, users, and adapters.

The Data Integrator Web Administrator is a completely separate application from Data Integrator!

Getting the Hang of Data Integrator Designer

Before you start working with the Data Integrator Designer, it's important to understand the two key concepts around which Data Integrator Designer evolves:

- ✔ **The project:** You can create objects, and one such object is a project. This entity is where you store your jobs for organizational purposes. Projects are single-user objects; you can't share them with any other user in your organization, and you can only work with a single project at a time. If you're the multitasking type, sorry, it's just not possible with projects.

- ✔ **The job:** A job is also an object; one which you can execute or run. Jobs can be as complex or as simple as you like, but it's best to try to keep them from becoming too complex. When creating a flow, you'll create several steps using *icons* (connected objects) to create a job diagram.

What we cover in this section won't make you an instant expert on Data Integrator Designer, but it does give you a good idea of how to get started using the application effectively.

Getting on to Designer and getting started

Getting on to Data Integrator Designer isn't as easy as clicking a menu item and digging right in. In fact, you have to perform a number of perfunctory steps before you can even launch Data Integrator Designer!

First, you set up your repository. And *then* you can log on to Designer.

Setting up your repository

Though you probably created a repository when you installed Data Integrator, you can always create another one. This repository is saved in your database account (see your database administrator). The Data Integrator repository is created in a database; for more information, see the "What is the Repository Manager?" section earlier in this chapter.

To create a repository, follow these steps:

1. **Choose Start➪All Programs➪BusinessObjects Data Integrator 11.5➪ Repository Manager.**

   The Repository Manager window opens, as shown in Figure 18-3.

2. **Enter the information for each field:**

   - *Database Type:* This drop-down list lets you set the type of database you are using, for example, Oracle, SQL Server, DB2.

   - *Database Server Name:* This is the name of the server that hosts your database.

   - *Database Name:* This is the name of the database being hosted by the database server.

   - *User Name:* This is the login for your database account.

   - *Password:* This is the password for your database account login.

   This information is found in your database account provided by your organization's database administrator.

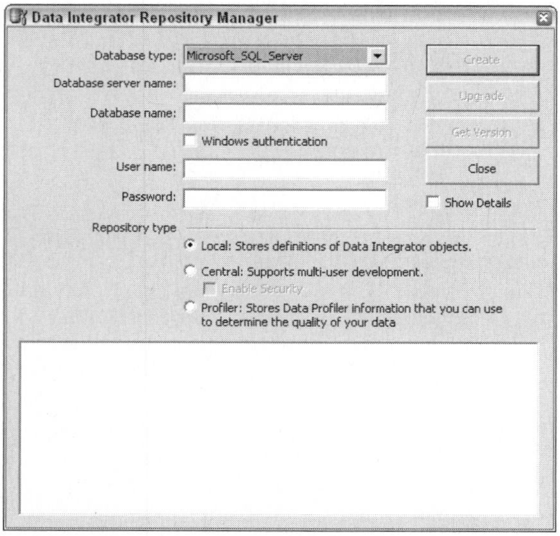

Figure 18-3:
The
Repository
Manager
window.

3. **Click Create.**

   The status of the repository is displayed at the bottom of the Repository Manager.

4. **Click Close.**

Logging in

After you create a local repository, you can log on to Data Integrator. Follow these steps:

1. **Choose Start⇨All Programs⇨BusinessObjects Data Integrator 11.5⇨ Data Integrator Designer.**

   The Data Integrator login window opens, as shown in Figure 18-4.

2. **Select the database type from the Database Type drop-down list; then enter the database server name and database name.**

3. **Identify yourself using the credentials you established creating your Data Integrator repository (database account) in the Repository Manager.**

4. **Click OK.**

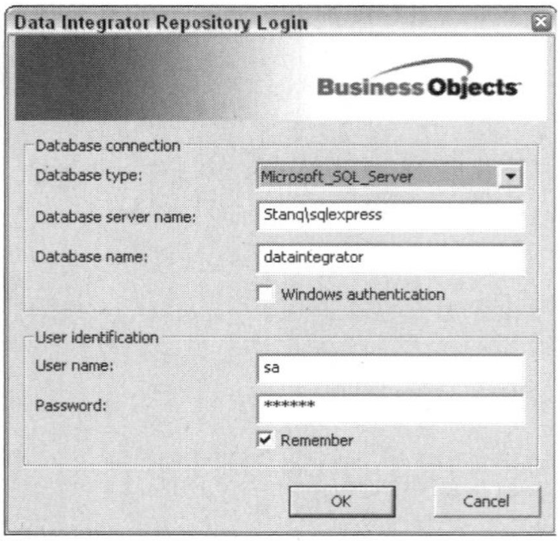

Figure 18-4: The Data Integrator Login window.

This, of course, presumes that your database is up and running! Simply creating the repository isn't enough. After you're logged on, you can use the Data Integrator Designer to start working with your objects, including projects and jobs.

The Data Integrator Designer can be broken into several different pieces. The left side is divided into two different windows or *panes*. The majority of the screen includes the work area. The top window contains three tabs: Designer, Monitor, and Log. The bottom window concerns the repository and its work-flow. This window contains a number of tabs, most of which you will not use. We discuss the more important ones in the following sections.

Creating jobs for your project

After you log onto your repository, it's now time to start working with your objects. Before you start creating jobs, you need a place to store them. Any ideas? How about in a new project? Actually, all objects are physically stored in the database to which you are connected!

Even if you can put a job in any project, you may want to use an existing project and add a new job to it, or start fresh and create your very own project.

To create a new project, follow these steps:

1. **Choose Project⇨New in Data Integrator Designer.**

   If you want to add a new job to an existing project, choose Project⇨Open.

2. **Choose whether you want to create a new job within the project area of Data Integration Designer or in the object library:**

   - If you want to create a new job in the project area, continue with Steps 3 and 4.

   - If you want to create a new job in the object library, skip to Steps 5–8.

3. **To create a new job in the project area, right-click and select the type of job you wish to create.**

4. **Enter a name for your new job.**

   Blank spaces and hyphens are not allowed. You can use numbers, letters, and underscores for naming jobs.

5. **To create a new job from the object library, click the Jobs tab.**

6. **Right-click either Batch Jobs or Real Time Jobs and select New to start creating a new job, as shown in Figure 18-5.**

7. **Edit the name.**

8. **(Optional) Drag your new job from the object library to the project area if you want to include it.**

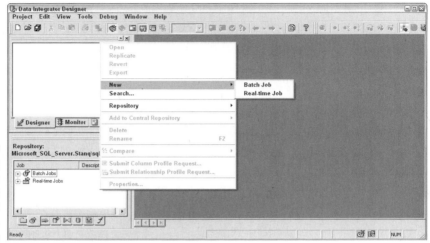

Figure 18-5:
Creating a
new job in
the object
library.

Creating workflows

With a basic knowledge of projects and jobs in your head, you can create a workflow. If you've ever worked with a diagramming application such as Microsoft Visio, then you're probably familiar with workflows.

If you're not familiar with workflows, here's the gist: They are roadmaps that detail the logic and thought process for executing your data. These are important documents because they allow you to study your system and make sure your planned executions are properly laid out. If necessary, you can always call another workflow into your current workflow — or even have it call itself for use in the same workflow (confusing but effective). There are very few limitations to workflow usage!

Workflows are graphic-oriented documents that use icons as part of the workflow diagram (see Figure 18-6). When reading a workflow, remember that everything is in its proper place for a reason. These should be read left-to-right because that's the way that workflows are executed. Each box has a single entry point and a single exit point. You can connect an exit point with only one entry point and one entry point is connected with only one exit point. To read the flow, follow the line.

You can create a workflow in Data Integrator Designer in two ways: either from the tool palette or the object library. Keep in mind that a workflow is an independent entity. You can create it from the object library but then it is only created — you need to insert it into a job by dragging it in the Job diagram.

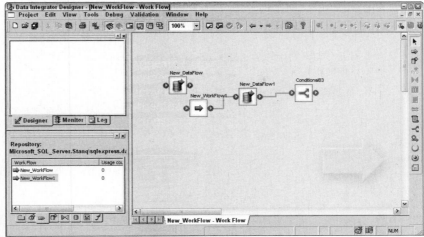

Figure 18-6:
A typical
workflow.

From the object library

To create a workflow from the object library, follow these steps:

1. **Click the Workflow tab at the bottom of the object library, as shown in Figure 18-7.**

Figure 18-7:
The
Workflow
tab in the
object
library.

Workflow

2. **Right-click anywhere in the tab and select New.**

   The job diagram opens.

3. **Drag your new workflow to the diagram.**

4. **Add any other information, such as data flows and conditionals.**

   See the nearby sidebar "Expanding your workflow" for more about data flows and conditionals.

From the tool palette

To create a new workflow from the tool palette, follow these steps.

1. **Click the Workflow tab at the bottom of the object library (refer to Figure 18-7).**

2. **Right-click anywhere in the tab and select New.**

   The job diagram opens.

3. **In the tool palette, select the Workflow icon, as shown in Figure 18-8.**

 — Workflow

Figure 18-8:
The tool palette.

4. **Click the area where you want to create your workflow.**

5. **Right-click anywhere in your workflow and choose Properties.**

   The Properties window opens, as shown in Figure 18-9.

6. **To allow your workflow to execute one time, check the Execute Only Once option. If you want your workflow to re-execute if the execution fails for any reason, leave the option unchecked.**

   However, should your workflow be successful, it won't re-execute.

   We don't recommend enabling the feature if the workflow is a recovery unit.

7. **Click OK.**

Jobs contain workflows, each workflow contains dataflows and conditionals. Each dataflow contains transformations. These require the knowledge of SQL, so if you're interested, we recommend picking up *SQL For Dummies*, 4th Edition, by Allen Taylor.

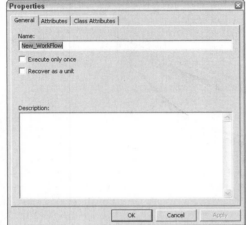

Figure 18-9:
The
Properties
dialog box
for your
workflow.

Playing Administrator with Data Integrator

As you probably guessed, the Data Integrator Web Administrator application is the brains of the operation. As with the Central Management Console, the Administrator is a Web-based application — you can use it on any computer connected to the Web, not just one that has Data Integrator installed.

Expanding your workflow

As we've mentioned in this chapter, you most likely won't need to master the creation of workflows. If you're curious, however, you can continue your research with workflows. For example, you may want to get a handle on these concepts:

✔ **Conditionals:** These are individual objects that use IF/THEN/ELSE statements in a workflow. To set up a conditional, you must designate a condition and two logical branches.

✔ **While loops:** This is used to repeat a series of steps within your workflow. The only requirement is that the condition is true.

✔ **TRY/CATCH blocks:** This is not an offered option, but rather a combination of objects (one is a try object, the other is a catch object) providing a backup workflow in case yours doesn't work.

✔ **Scripts:** These are individual objects that set values for variables or call functions within your workflow.

The Data Integrator Web Administrator is the central location where you can handle managerial tasks such as setting up users and roles, scheduling batch jobs to be executed, and working with Access Servers and Job Servers. Of course, this tool can handle plenty more tasks, but we just want to get you familiar with the application for now. (Expertise comes later.)

Logging on

Even though Data Integrator Web Administrator is a Web-based application, you can still access it from the Start menu. Before you try and log on, you should take a quick look and make sure that the Data Integrator Web Server service is on. If the service isn't on, turn it on — otherwise you'll never manage to get in. To do that, choose Start➪Control Panel➪Administrative Tools➪Services➪Data Integrator Web Server. If the entry is set to Stopped, right-click the service name and select Start.

Don't forget that as with any Web application, you can connect to it from any machine that is on your server. To log on to Data Integrator Web Administrator, follow these steps:

1. **Choose Start➪All Programs➪BusinessObjects Data Integrator➪ Web Administrator.**

2. **Enter the user name and password.**

   If you don't have a user name or password, you can use the default logon and password, which is pretty simple: admin/admin.

3. **Click Log In.**

   The Data Integrator Web Administrator appears, as shown in Figure 18-10.

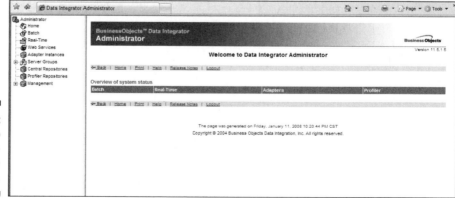

Figure 18-10:
The Web Administrator home page.

Adding repositories

Adding a repository to the Data Integrator Web Administrator is one of the first things you'll do once you're up and running. Sure, you may want to rush ahead and start scheduling jobs, but you need to add a repository connection in order to even see the jobs you have!

You can add a repository through the List of Repositories page in the Web Administrator. This applies to any kind of repository — local, central, or profiler.

To add a repository connection, follow these steps:

1. **In Data Integrator Web Administrator, use the navigation tree to locate Management⇨Repositories.**

2. **Click Add.**

   The page to enter your repository information appears, as shown in Figure 18-11.

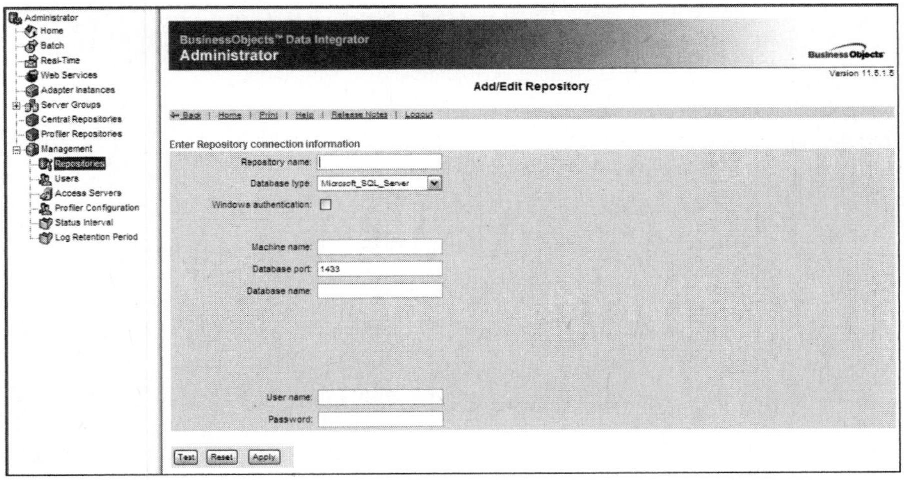

Figure 18-11:
The Add Repository Connection data.

3. **Add the necessary information:**

   - *Repository Name:* The name of the repository that you created.

   - *Database Type:* Select the type of database, for example, Oracle, DB2, SQL.

   - *Windows Authentication:* Check this box to apply Windows Authentication for validating your logon.

- *Machine Name:* This lets you enter the name of the machine hosting your repository.

- *Database Port:* This is the port number for the database on your machine.

- *Database Name:* This is the name of the database on your machine.

- *User Name:* This is the name of the login for your repository.

- *Password:* This is the password for your repository login.

4. **(Optional) Click Test to verify that your connection works.**

5. **Click Apply.**

   Your repository connection appears in the List of Repositories, as shown in Figure 18-12.

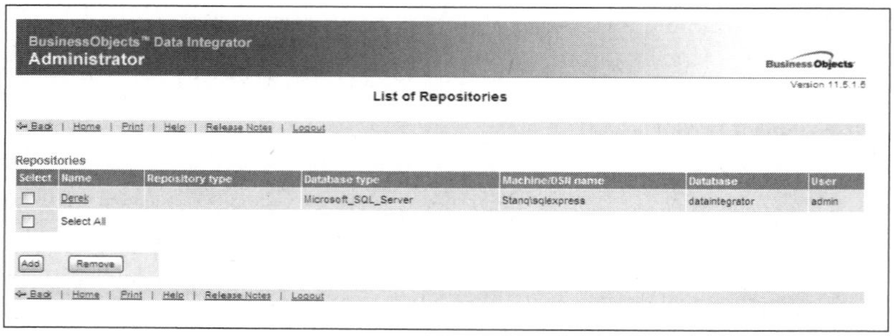

Figure 18-12:
The new
repository
connection
in the List of
Repositories.

Setting up a repository

Setting up a repository depends on how your database is set up, which goes beyond the scope of this book. This can be a pretty complicated procedure, especially if you're not used to working with databases.

For example, if you are using a SQL Server database, you need to know how to work with MS SQL Server Management Studio Express in order to create and set up your database. (See *Microsoft SQL Server 2008 For Dummies* for more help with SQL Server). We use MS SQL in this book as it is arguably the easiest type of database to work with, and the kind that you are most likely to use in a small to medium sized deployment. If you are using BusinessObjects in an enterprise setting, you likely all ready have the requisite database knowledge.

The central repository should be a secured central repository. When you're creating the repository with the Data Integrator Repository Manager, check the Enable Security checkbox. Users can connect to the central repository using the Data Integrator Designer. You must activate the repository before anyone can use it by filling in the user settings in the Central Repository Editor.

Accessing your repository

If you are using MS SQL Server, there are two different ways to access your repository. If you are using Windows Authentication, you can do it via ODBC DSN (Start⇨Administrative Tools⇨Data Sources (ODBC) and create your data-source connection). Enter your ODBC DSN name in the repository connection. If you are not using Windows Authentication, but rather Enterprise SQL Server Authentication, enter your database connection parameter in the interface and no ODBC DSN is required.

Managing your roles

Data Integrator Web Administrator allows you to create users and roles for use with Data Integrator. The process is similar to creating users and roles in the CMC with InfoView. Note that these users and roles are not used within Data Integrator Designer; they are used to log in the Administration console and in the report metadata tool, which is accessible using Data Integrator Designer.

Roles set boundaries and permissions for users so you can protect your system from inadvertent changes or other "accidents" caused by unauthorized access.

To create a user account and assign a role, follow these steps:

1. **In Data Integrator Web Administrator, choose Management⇨Users.**

   The User Management page appears, as shown in Figure 18-13.

2. **Click Add.**

3. **Enter a new user ID in the corresponding text box.**

4. **Enter a password for the user name.**

5. **Set a display name for the user.**

   This could be a full name or nickname that makes recognizing the log easier for you.

Figure 18-13:
The User
Manage-
ment page.

6. **Select a role from the Role drop-down menu (as shown in Figure 18-14).**

Figure 18-14:
The available
roles in Data
Integrator
Web Admin-
istrator.

7. **Set the current state of the new account, for example, active or suspended.**

8. **Go to the Profiler repository list and select the desired profiler repository for your users.**

9. **Click Apply.**

Working with users and groups

You can use Data Integrator Web Administrator to add groups and users through a central repository. To do that, first you add a central repository. (We discuss adding a repository connection earlier in this chapter, in the "Adding repositories" section.)

When you have a central repository, follow these steps to add a group:

1. **In Data Integrator Web Administrator, expand the Central Repositories menu in the hierarchical tree.**

2. **Click Users and Groups; make sure you're on the Groups tab.**

3. **Click Add.**

4. **Enter a name for your new group.**

   Choose a name that will be largely self-evident to all users who work with your groups.

5. **Add a brief description of your group name in the Description text box.**

6. **Click Apply.**

   Your group now appears in the list of Groups in the Groups tab.

To add a user account, follow these steps:

1. **In Data Integrator Web Administrator, expand the Central Repositories menu in the hierarchical tree.**

2. **Click Users and Groups; make sure you're on the Users tab.**

3. **Click Add.**

4. **Enter the requested information, such as a user name, password, display name, default groups, status, and so on (as shown Figure 18-15).**

   The user name is the name of the user to be used with Web Administrator, while its display name is the name that you will actually see when logged in. The password is for logging in. Default groups are the initial groups that the user is affiliated with by default. The status shows the current state of the user.

   Even though it is optional, be sure to add a password for the user account, otherwise the user cannot connect through the Data Integrator Designer application to the central repository. Even though the interface allows you to keep an empty password, the system really doesn't like that too much.

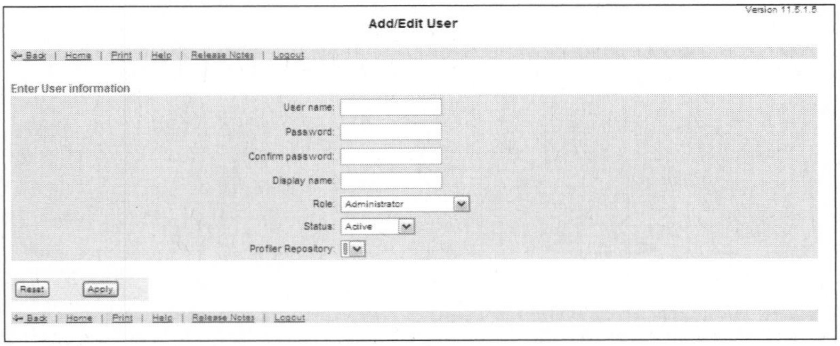

Figure 18-15:
The New
User
Information
window.

Version 11.5.1.5

Add/Edit User

Back | Home | Print | Help | Release Notes | Logout

Enter User information

User name:	
Password:	
Confirm password:	
Display name:	
Role:	Administrator
Status:	Active
Profiler Repository:	

Reset   Apply

Back | Home | Print | Help | Release Notes | Logout

5. **Click Apply.**

   The new user account appears in the Data Integrator Web Administrator, showing the new user as a member of the list, as shown in Figure 18-16.

Figure 18-16:
The new
user
account
appears.

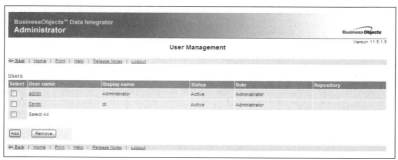

Scheduling batch jobs

When you create a scheduled event, you're actually using the Job Server (another component of Data Integrator). Therefore, in this section, we cover the easiest way to schedule an event. In addition, if you need to schedule a batch job, you can do so using third-party schedules and the Data Integrator job launcher.

To create a scheduled batch job in the Web Administrator, follow these steps:

1. **Choose Data Integrator⇨Batch and then select the repository.**

2. **Open the Configuration tab.**

3. **Select the job that you want to schedule and choose Action⇨Add Schedule.**

4. **Configure your job schedule.**

5. **Click Schedule.**

Chapter 19

Working with Data Marts

In This Chapter

▶ Getting smart about data marts

▶ Speeding up with BusinessObjects Rapid Marts

*B*ack in the good old days, the first data warehouses (the ancestors of today's data marts) were heralded as a wonder solution, set to usher in a glorious new age in which everyone in an enterprise would have all the data they could ever need right at their fingertips — and all at exactly the same time, thus ensuring that a company's whole workforce would all be on the same page . . . and all would be well in the world.

Well, as we know, it didn't quite work out like that!

A *data mart* is a specialized kind of data warehouse that's been around since at least the 1980s. However, in the current business environment — where having credible and trustworthy data has moved beyond being an operational advantage to become a legislative requirement for many — the improved data quality that data marts help provide is more relevant today than ever before.

This chapter takes a brief look at how data marts fit into your BusinessObjects system — and how they enable you to ensure that you always have the most accurate, up-to-date and auditable information available.

Choosing Between a Data Warehouse and a Data Mart

In truth, data warehouses are good to have: Everyone having access to the same data — all of it as accurate and up-to-date as possible — can only be a good thing, right?

In practice, data warehouses had a tendency to become somewhat unwieldy behemoths, packed so full of data — everything you ever wanted to know about absolutely anything to do with your company (but were afraid to ask) — that they quickly proved impossible to manage. Indeed, if you've ever had the misfortune of having to search for information stored away in the dark, dingy corners of a data warehouse, *needles* and *haystacks* are two words that may well spring to mind when you're describing the experience.

A data mart, in its contemporary form, provides a snapshot of the data in a database at any given time. Where data marts differ from the larger, more unwieldy data warehouses is that they focus solely on meeting a previously identified need for a specific subset of data.

It soon became apparent to the creators and administrators of enormous data warehouses that — much to their surprise — not everyone *needed* to know everything about everything. Most users, as it turns out, only need access to specific subsets of data. The sales team doesn't always need to keep track of company head count, for instance; a Human Resources manager may not be interested in the current levels of stock at the production plant.

So why not just tell people what they need to know? That, in theory, is the job of the data mart.

If extracting information from a data warehouse is like scanning over the aisles of an entire supermarket with a security camera, imagine a data mart as being like a camera trained on a single aisle — or even a single shelf — and sending you time-stamped photographs of that aisle at regular intervals. Which of these two methods do you think would be more effective as a means of stock control?

Although its narrow focus gives a data mart a big advantage — namely, that you can be sure the information it contains is relevant to the subject at hand — this information (say, the time-stamped photograph in our example) may not be completely up to date. After all, it's a snapshot rather than a live stream of data. Performance issues dictate how, and how often, your data is updated.

Figure 19-1 shows the relationship of a typical data warehouse and data mart.

The data warehouse versus data mart debate has two main schools of thought. One proposes that data marts should be created first and then joined together to create a data warehouse; the other thinks that the data warehouse should come first and then be broken down into smaller units.

We take a look at each approach in the following sections. Both have advantages and disadvantages; your company's circumstances dictate which is most appropriate for you.

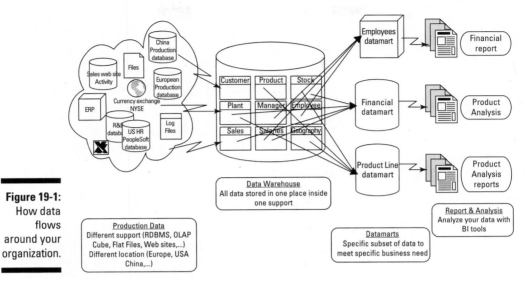

Figure 19-1: How data flows around your organization.

Starting with data marts

The so-called Kimball School proposes a *bottom-up approach:* A data warehouse is nothing more than a series of small data marts grouped together into one larger whole.

The advantage of this bottom-up approach is that it is much quicker to implement in the first instance because it allows you to start small and grow incrementally.

The disadvantage of stringing together data marts is that you have to take care of *metadata consistency* (making sure that each department calls a spade a spade and all have consistent terminology) or it can lead to integration problems further down the line.

This approach works best when you want to focus on individual business processes or business groups as separate entities.

Starting with a warehouse

The Inmon School believes that a *top-down approach* is best: Deal with metadata consistency problems first by conceiving the data warehouse as a single repository that feeds the separate data marts.

The advantages of a top-down approach are

- ✔ It makes it easier to handle data that is common across different business groups.
- ✔ Taking care of metadata consistency up front helps prevent unexpected integration issues later on.

However, breaking down a data warehouse into data marts is not without its disadvantages:

- ✔ Doing *everything* from the start obviously requires a much greater financial investment.
- ✔ The time it takes to implement may not be acceptable to many enterprises in today's fast-moving business world.

If you can afford the time and cost involved, a top-down approach to managing data is best if you want to focus on the bigger picture, and if there is a sizeable amount of data that is common across different business groups.

BusinessObjects Rapid Marts

Clearly, any tool or system that deals with data cannot exist in a vacuum: The data has to come from somewhere — preferably fast.

The data you want to query, report on, and analyze most likely already exists *somewhere* in your company, be it stored in an Enterprise Resource Planning (ERP) system or Customer Relationship Management (CRM) system such as the SAP R/3 and SAP BW, PeopleSoft, and J.D. Edwards applications commonly used in many organizations.

Enterprise Resource Planning (ERP) systems are designed to unify an organization's data and processes into a single, integrated system. An example of such a system could be a software package that combines accounting, payroll, and other human resource management functions. *Customer Relationship Management (CRM)* is a business strategy that aims to increase profitability and customer satisfaction, and is supported by a range of tools and technologies that enable you to capture and store information about your organization's customers, suppliers and partners.

Typically, in order to work with such data, you (or your Database Administrator) are obliged to jump through a series of hoops. Here's an equally typical short list of them:

✔ Ask yourself and/or your colleagues exactly what (type of) data you need to access.

✔ Create the new target database in which you're going to store the data you need.

✔ Study the ERM/CRP system and decide from which tables and columns you can take the data you're going to use to populate your new database.

✔ Map the contents of your source database to your target database — and then either write some custom code or use a commercial tool to actually *perform* those mappings.

✔ Write some more code to tidy it all up in the target database afterward.

Sound like fun? We thought not. Fortunately, help is at hand: BusinessObjects Rapid Marts.

Built principally with the BusinessObjects Data Integrator (which has a starring role in Chapter 18), Rapid Marts provide an off-the-shelf data-integration package for a whole range of enterprise applications, making it quicker and easier for you to get your hands on the data they contain.

Rapid Marts help kick-start your Business Intelligence projects by providing you with some very handy features:

✔ A prebuilt BusinessObjects universe and reports to go with it

✔ Ready-to-run extract, transform, and load (ETL) jobs

✔ Source-to-target mappings

✔ An extensible data model

Rapid Marts free you from having to slog through the lengthy data-mart development cycle or — worse still — having to wait around until your database administrators can do that slogging for you.

Part VII
The Part of Tens

In this part. . .

Hopefully, this information doesn't come too late in the game, but this part includes information that is good to know before you start implementing Business-Objects XI Release 2 at your place of work. Preparing a migration or installation of a new enterprise software package takes some preparation. Just as Rome wasn't built in a day, neither will your BusinessObjects environment be complete right out of the box.

Chapter 20 provides important tips and other helpful information about preparing your IT environment for welcoming BusinessObjects XI Release 2. Chapter 21 features some helpful online resources that help make installation and integration easier!

Chapter 20

Ten Ways to Prepare for BusinessObjects Integration

● ●

Getting ready for BusinessObjects XI Release 2 is no easy task. It's a lot like preparing for the holidays. It involves a lot of thankless work ensuring that everything is exactly where it should be and as it should be. Of course, your job is a lot easier than that of the poor guy or girl who actually has to *install* BusinessObjects for your company. Those poor folks have to think about server configurations, processors, and Web servers.

However, that doesn't leave you off the hook. You need to take into account a number of considerations before you start using BusinessObjects — or even installing it on your own machine. By laying the groundwork and doing your homework ahead of time, you can (potentially) save yourself a lot of time and avoid a lot of headaches.

Now, don't get us wrong. BusinessObjects XI Release 2 isn't some sort of scary monster. Still, large applications can often require a rather time-consuming installation; you'll definitely want to make sure your computer is up to speed — and that you're actually ready to *use* BusinessObjects — before launching headlong into the installation (ahem) adventure. This chapter helps you prepare both mentally and physically for integrating BusinessObjects XI Release 2 to make it a positive experience.

Do Your Research!

We're sorry to have to give you work to do, but what did you expect? Would you go out and buy a new car or a new flat-screen TV without doing a little research into what you're buying? (We thought not.)

Software is the same way. Even if it's a corporate decision to go with Business-Objects XI Release 2, you still need to do some research to find out what you're using — and if you're reading this book, you're on the right track. Still, your research needs to go a little further than that.

Business intelligence is a hot topic these days; in fact, it's bandied around quite a bit by marketing types who might not fully understand everything the term really means. That's why the glossary in this book helps you get familiare with frequently used jargon; some entries might actually ring a bell from the office if your administrator has already installed BusinessObjects XI Release 2.

Check Out businessobjects.com

As obvious as it might seem, we recommend visiting the Business Objects Web site to find out more about the application. While the documentation line is quite robust (and may be confusing to a number of readers), they definitely have a few manuals that are worth checking out if you're new to BusinessObjects.

Also, if you're preparing to do your own local installation, consult the installation or deployment documentation as a roadmap. These guides have more detailed information concerning installation — especially in terms of minimum requirements for both your computer and network.

The Business Objects Web site also has valuable information such as forums and a knowledge base that can provide quick answers to some of your more frequently asked questions. The forum, which is available to any registered user, is at `http://technicalsupport.businessobjects.com/cs/forums/default.aspx`.

Pick the Right Computer

This section applies to anyone who is planning to install BusinessObjects locally or who isn't planning on running the installation on a dedicated computer.

Ideally, we recommend hosting BusinessObjects XI Release 2 *only* on a dedicated server. BusinessObjects should run on a powerful computer whose *sole mission* is to run BusinessObjects for your organization.

Some situations may warrant installing BusinessObjects XI Release 2 in "less than ideal" hardware situations, but that doesn't mean that you have to shortchange the software. For example, if you're looking to test the software in a live environment before buying a brand-new computer to host it or putting it on an enterprise-wide server, it's totally plausible that you install it on a test machine.

If that's the case — or if you're a small to mid-size company looking to install BusinessObjects on a spare PC — you can do so, but you'll want to stack the computer in your favor.

Okay, you've heard this before, but take the necessary precautions to guarantee that your installation will work. Here's a quick checklist:

✔ **Make sure that you're using a powerful processor that is in line with BusinessObjects' minimum requirements.** See Chapter 2 to find out what the minimum requirements are.

✔ **Keep extra RAM on board to ensure better performance. If you're buying a new computer these days, the standard seems to be 2GB.** We recommend having that amount available if you're installing Business-Objects, even if the minimum requirements are significantly lower. You can never have too much memory.

✔ **Keep a significant amount of hard-drive space free for your installation.** For example, when we install large applications or need to serve, we keep an entire hard drive available for that application. For example, if we were installing BusinessObjects XI Release 2 on a spare PC, we'd buy an extra disk (even an external USB drive works) and dedicate it to BusinessObjects.

You'll have to store all of the documents that your users create, too!

✔ **Make sure that you have the proper malware applications, as well as an active firewall.** To cover your malware protection, we recommend an antivirus and anti-spyware combination for complete coverage. Our standard approach is to use several different anti-spyware applications to cover all our bases.

✔ **Use a computer that you can leave turned on continually.** Business-Objects XI Release 2 requires continual uptime so others can access applications — such as InfoView — so you'll want to use a computer that not only can be left on continually but also has a continual broadband Internet connection. Otherwise, when your host computer is off, your colleagues can't use BusinessObjects.

Are You Upgrading?

Are you an existing BusinessObjects user that is simply new to XI Release 2? If so, you'll have some extra concerns that you should think about prior to integrating BusinessObjects XI Release 2. Here's our short list:

✔ **Everyone in your organization who runs Desktop Intelligence locally must upgrade to BO XI R2.** Migration is an all-or-nothing deal — either everyone upgrades or things get ugly fast.

✔ **If you've saved any BusinessObjects or Web Intelligence documents, you need to upgrade them (in DeskI or WebI) to BO XI R2.** You can do this using the Import Wizard tool.

After you upgrade a document, it cannot be used retroactively with any earlier version of BusinessObjects.

✔ **If you're administrating the upgrade, think about upgrading everyone's personal documents and InfoView Inbox documents.** Neither of those groups migrates automatically; each requires your guidance in order to happen correctly.

If InfoView, WebI, and DeskI are similar to previous versions, there are no similarities with XI Release 2. You go from a BusinessObjects 6.0 repository, which is located in different relational databases, to a CMS structure. If you are coming from BusinessObjects 6.0 environment, the security management changes completely as well. The Import Wizard helps you with this; however, if you are coming from Crystal Reports 9, use the Repository Migration tool.

Though there are many similarities between this release of BusinessObjects and earlier releases, throw out your preconceived notions of how the upgrade should occur. To make the most out of BusinessObjects XI Release 2, remain flexible and be prepared to adapt with the application.

Back Up Your System

Before you attempt to install BusinessObjects XI Release 2 on any computer, be sure to perform a full backup of your entire computer. Even if you're performing a full installation on a new hard drive on your computer, perform a backup of all other media drives and their files.

You certainly don't want to take any unnecessary risks of data loss; computer backups are relatively quick and easy to perform. In fact, we'll go one step further and urge you to perform a full backup *even before* adding another hard drive or more memory to your machine.

Any type of "operation" on your computer is sufficient reason for backing up your data. If you've been a conscientious PC user, you're likely already performing regularly scheduled backups to be safe. Don't worry — we're not impugning the reliability or stability of BusinessObjects XI Release 2, but rather offering a universal piece of advice that's appropriate to any sort of software installation.

Organize Your Computer

As you get ready for your first steps using BusinessObjects XI Release 2, you can make your life easier by organizing your computer accordingly. As mentioned earlier, we recommend installing BusinessObjects on a new partition — or disk — to keep things clean and organized.

You can take that concept a step further by organizing your My Documents folder in Windows XP with the specific purpose of storing your BusinessObjects documents or queries. While this might not prove instantly valuable, you will see the benefits as you save more reports and your repository increases in size.

Organize Your Organization

In the previous section, we suggested organizing your computer for ease of use with BusinessObjects XI Release 2 — especially when working with large numbers of documents or queries. You can also apply that bit of advice to your organization.

Before your organization gets busy creating document after document, organize your folders in InfoView so all users can easily and clearly understand where they should be storing documents.

How you choose to organize your folder structures is entirely up to you or the administrator, but keep in mind that the structure should make sense to your organization. For example, you might want to separate documents by universe — or perhaps create folders for each user and have each user store documents in their respective organizations.

The important thing here is to clearly communicate the naming structure and make sure that all BusinessObjects users are certain where to save documents and where they can find others.

Verify Troop Readiness!

A good friend once said that if you want to make sure something is done right, you should do it yourself. A little cynical perhaps, but also sage advice, especially when working with lots of people who are frequently under the gun and might not always have time to cross every *t* and dot every *i*.

If you're responsible for BusinessObjects integration, take a few minutes to make sure your colleagues are ready for installation. If your office is running relatively new computers, the minimum requirements shouldn't be an issue — but you might want to verify that everyone is running a compatible Web browser. Because every Web browser renders HTML slightly differently, it's important to make sure that you're using Internet Explorer or Firefox.

If you plan to install BusinessObjects XI Release 2 manually on multiple computers in your office, you may want to consider a checklist of compliance requirements — and be sure you can verify them one by one. This checklist might include (for example) adequate memory and disk space.

If any of your colleagues are working from home, you might want to send a memo on compatibility so they can check whether they can use InfoView. Most users probably won't have DeskI access on home computers, so hardware requirements per se aren't a pressing concern. If users do need to access DeskI from home, make sure your company has Virtual Private Network (VPN) access so remote users can connect securely to their office computers over a high-speed Internet connection.

As you check each computer, have each colleague sign off on compliance or provide some sort of written acknowledgment that the computer is ready for BusinessObjects integration.

Check for Any Service Packs or Hot Fixes

BusinessObjects is no different from any other software application in its need to be regularly maintained and updated. As is often the case with most large software companies, larger clients tend to find important bugs or software glitches — and the developer quickly issues a fix or patch to resolve the issue.

Before you install BusinessObjects XI Release 2 either on a sever or locally for DeskI use, we recommend that you or your administrator consult the Business Objects support Web site and verify that no service packs were released since your software CDs were released.

It's very important to check for updates whenever you install new software; the actual installation CDs or executables are not regularly updated with bug fixes. When you're installing BusinessObjects XI Release 2, it's safe to assume that some updates are available for your application.

A number of release-specific hot fixes and patches are publicly available for download on the Business Objects Web site. Some service packs are also available via download; others may require a valid support plan in order to access the downloadable file. For information on your support plan, check with your administrator, whoever purchases the software from Business Objects in your company, or your Business Objects account representative.

After you complete the BusinessObjects installation, you can install any service packs or product updates manually, one at a time. These updates must be performed manually for each local installation of BusinessObjects. Once the hosted edition is updated, any authorized users who log on to the server to use InfoView can be sure they're using the updated version.

Be Patient!

Finally, the last tip for preparing for BusinessObjects integration is to be patient. There's certainly a lot of ground to cover as you get ready for using BusinessObjects. You may not be surprised to learn that there's still a lot of ground to cover even after you're actually up and running.

BusinessObjects XI Release 2 greatly simplifies data mining and report creation to help you get easy-to-understand answers to often complicated business questions. It will take some time before you finally understand all the ins and outs of the software. That shouldn't dissuade you from enjoying the many benefits that it can offer your organization.

Hopefully this book has taught you enough to feel confident in your first steps — and has whetted your appetite for learning and using some advanced features in BusinessObjects XI Release 2.

Chapter 21

Ten Resources to Help You

• •

Although this book aims to be a handy reference for you to have by your side as you start to delve into the BusinessObjects XI Release 2 Enterprise suite, we're modest enough to recognize that we can't claim to be the *only* source of information on such a vast topic.

With this in mind, this chapter points you in the direction of a few useful Web sites that you should bookmark and consult regularly.

The Business Objects Web Site

`www.businessobjects.com/`

When you're looking to learn more about any product, be it a piece of software or a car or a washing machine, one of your first ports of call should undoubtedly be the manufacturer's Web site.

From the Business Objects Web site you can download official product documentation (`http://support.businessobjects.com/documentation/default.asp`), find out how other people are using Business Objects products, discover more about the different aspects of business intelligence, and (if all else fails) even contact customer support (`http://technical support.businessobjects.com/cs/forums/default`).

Needless to say, the main aim of the site is to sell Business Objects products, but it also contains some useful information underneath the marketing sheen.

Diamond Community

`http://diamond.businessobjects.com/`

One particularly useful section of the Business Objects Web site is the Diamond Community, which is the official Business Objects "community" site. It features forums, developer resources, product news, tips and tricks, together with a series of specific portals for some of the company's main products (including Web Intelligence).

When you sign up for the Diamond Community, you also have the opportunity to participate in Beta programs that give you early access to new versions of the products.

Insight Blog

```
http://insight.businessobjects.com/bi-blog/
```

Despite the fact that two of the three authors on this collaborative blog are Business Objects employees and it's hosted on the Business Objects Web site, it still manages to provide some good . . . insight (sorry) into why Business Intelligence matters — beyond simply trotting out the company line.

BOB: BusinessObjects Board

```
http://www.forumtopics.com/busobj/
```

If you don't want the official word, but would rather ask questions and share information with other users of the BusinessObjects suite who aren't afraid to point out when (and why) things are going wrong, and who can often provide ways around even the thorniest of problems, then the BusinessObjects Board is the place for you.

As it says on its home page, the lively BOB forum is "a community of people with a common interest: getting the most out of their investment in Business Objects products." This is a great place to learn from other, more experienced Business Objects users.

GBS — Business Objects Admin and Security Solutions

```
http://www.gbandsmith.com/
```

Dealing with the complexities of the Business Objects security model, as in Part II, is no easy task. GBS provides a handy, Web-based tool enabling you to implement, manage, and document your BusinessObjects XI Release 2 security more effectively.

Business Intelligence.com

```
http://www.businessintelligence.com/
```

The Business Intelligence.com Web site provides a host of material covering the many facets of business intelligence as a whole, rather than focusing solely on the products in the BusinessObjects suite.

The site features numerous short articles, opinion pieces, and news stories, and also offers more in-depth white papers for download (although to access these you have to register with the site).

ITtoolbox Business Intelligence Knowledge Base

```
http://businessintelligence.ittoolbox.com/
```

Like Business Intelligence.com, the BI corner of the ITtoolbox Knowledge Base (one of the Web's most successful IT knowledge-sharing sites) is a gold mine of information on every aspect of the field of Business Intelligence. One of its strengths lies in the way it breaks down its information by topic, and the fact that it includes a specific BusinessObjects section, making it much easier to find stuff that is of direct relevance to BusinessObjects.

Business Intelligence Network

```
http://www.b-eye-network.com/
```

If you can get past the packed home page, and the cutesy URL, the Business Intelligence Network is one of our favorite sites on the Web for Business Intelligence news, thanks to the sheer mass of information it provides about the world of BI.

The Interop Vendor Alliance — Business Objects

```
http://interopvendoralliance.org/blogs/Business_Objects/
          Default.aspx
```

Hidden away on the Web site of the Interop Vendor Alliance — which describes itself as "a community of software and hardware vendors working together to enhance interoperability with Microsoft systems on behalf of our mutual customers" — is this Weblog that contains a series of links to case studies, data sheets, news stories, presentations, and even podcasts on Business Objects and its products.

Admittedly, this is all information that can be found on the Business Objects Web site — which is where most (if not all) of the links point — but we find that the blog format makes it easier to keep up to date with the freshest content.

Crystal Reports Links

http://www.kenhamady.com/bookmarks.html

This page contains a list, breathlessly described by its creator as "unique on the Web," of what he claims is "virtually every" third-party Crystal Reports–related software product on the market. Certainly, the list is impressively long. Now, if only something similar existed for the rest of the Business Objects product range . . . .

BusinessObjects XI Release 2 For Dummies Companion Web Site

http://bofordummies.com/

We couldn't provide a list of Web sites without mentioning our own — the companion site to this book, where we provide tips and tricks for using BusinessObjects XI Release 2 more effectively.

Part VIII
Appendixes

The 5th Wave   By Rich Tennant

"They can predict earthquakes and seizures, why _not_ server failures?"

In this part. . .

As we finished writing this book, we thought hard to see whether we might have forgotten something. After all, BusinessObjects XI Release 2 is a pretty robust piece of software; there's a lot to learn! In fact, we've really just scraped the tip of the iceberg of what you can do with the application. So, is there any parting advice or wisdom that we should impart to you?

You bet there is! This part includes two appendixes.

Appendix A features an overview of Crystal Reports and some of its key features. Though it is the subject of its own *For Dummies* book, we provide you with some information to help get you started.

Appendix B is a glossary of commonly used terminology in this book and in business intelligence in general. It's not a complete list, but it can get you started with words that you'll encounter more than once as you explore the application.

Appendix A

Reporting on Crystal Reports

In This Appendix

▶ Getting a clear look at Crystal Reports

▶ Comparing Crystal Reports and Webl

*I*n case you missed it, the title of this book is *BusinessObjects XI Release 2 For Dummies*. (Hey, we're just staying focused here.) However, Business-Objects XI is not the only query-and-reporting tool on the market — and not even the only such tool that Business Objects offers. And thereby hangs a tale: Back in December 2003, Business Objects acquired Canadian company Crystal Decisions, and with that acquisition, the company added Crystal Reports to its range of business-intelligence software.

This appendix provides a brief overview of Crystal Reports, especially with regard to how the software compares to and complements Web Intelligence. For a more detailed guide to the workings of Crystal Reports, we recommend *Crystal Reports 2008 For Dummies*, by Allen Taylor, also published by Wiley.

What Is Crystal Reports?

Crystal Reports is a software tool that allows users to obtain rows and columns of data from compatible data sources — including most common databases, spreadsheets such as Microsoft Excel, XML files, and even text files — and then arrange and format that data in the manner most appropriate to creating a report.

Sound familiar?

The people who build Crystal Reports reports (is there an echo in here?) are called *report designers*. These stalwarts share the fruits of their labor with others, who can then look at the finished result using a range of report-viewing tools. Some of those viewers are produced by Business Objects itself, others are third-party tools.

A quick Web search for "Crystal Reports viewer" gives you an idea of the range of viewers available. (*Plethora* wouldn't be overstating matters.)

Crystal Reports is often the first name that springs to mind when people are asked to name a report-writing tool. The product has gained considerable market share by being bundled in with many other applications, including Microsoft Visual Studio.

Crystal Reports versus WebI

We wanted to set up this comparison as a heavyweight bout: "In the red corner, we have the mighty Web Intelligence; and in the blue corner, that young pretender to the throne, Crystal Reports. Who will win this clash of the titans as they both bid to become heavyweight champion of the enterprise reporting world?"

The truth, however, is that WebI and Crystal Reports — although they are both report-creation tools — are not really in competition with each other. They each address different markets; which one is right for the job at hand depends largely on what you want to do and how you want to work, and to a certain extent on the size of your business as well.

Building the report

One of the first — and major — differences between Crystal Reports and Web Intelligence lies in who actually builds the report. Whereas WebI is designed to make it easy for ordinary business users to generate ad-hoc reports in a jiffy, using common business terms instead of arcane database/IT terminology, report creators in Crystal Reports still need a certain level of special knowledge (and, okay, some arcane language) — as a result, they're mostly IT staff (or business power-users at the very least).

Put plainly, if you want to use Crystal Reports for anything other than simply viewing reports created by others, you have to know your way around a database in far more detail than you do if you're using WebI.

Crystal Reports is much more of a top-down tool in its conception, built around the idea that one expert creates pixel-perfect reports that are then to be viewed and admired by many.

Making your report pretty

Our use of the term "pixel-perfect" in the previous section was deliberate. One area where Crystal Reports arguably has an advantage over Web Intelligence concerns the level of control that report creators have over how the finished output looks. Formatting is far more important in Crystal Reports. Specialist users can take the time to create perfect-looking reports (see Figure A-1).

WebI, on the other hand, is all about empowering business users to create their own reports with minimum fuss (see Figure A-2). The fact that you can build your reports yourself, rather than having to rely on the IT department to take care of it for you, means greater independence and flexibility. If you're working with Crystal Reports and your needs change or you want to analyze a specific problem that crops up, you have to ask IT to do it for you, which takes time — and because business users and IT don't always speak the same language, you may not even get exactly what you're looking for when it finally does arrive. With WebI, on the other hand, you can be sure that the document matches your specific needs — because you will have created it yourself!

Use Crystal Reports if you want canned reports built by IT and distributed to a large user base, or if you need your reports to be pixel-perfect in their presentation. Use WebI (or DeskI, of course) for creating your own ad-hoc reports, and for better analysis.

Figure A-1: Crystal Reports lets you create "pixel-perfect" reports.

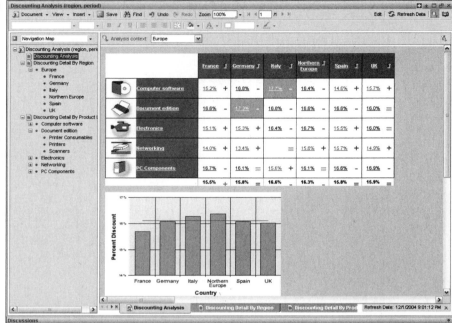

Figure A-2:
WebI lets
business
users build
their own
reports,
without
having to
go through
IT for
every little
change.

Mass reporting

Another strength of Crystal Reports over WebI lies in the area of mass reporting. By tweaking the parameters of the different reporting elements, you can
send out a single report to a large audience, but users can view a tailored
subset of the overall data — and, best of all, they'll get it more quickly than
they would using WebI.

Appendix B

Glossary

● ●

Ad-hoc report: A report you create on your own, using either Desktop Intelligence (DeskI) or Web Intelligence (WebI). An ad-hoc report is the opposite of a *canned report*.

Administrator: The person responsible for your BusinessObjects XI Release 2 system. This person creates user accounts, sets permissions, and manages servers. Effectively, this person is the boss of the BusinessObjects environment.

AF: *See* Application Foundation (AF).

API: *See* Application Programming Interface (API).

Application Foundation (AF): This is the old name for the Performance Management tool for BusinessObjects version 6.0.

Application Programming Interface (API): This is an interface that a computer program uses to respond to requests from the computer program.

Blocks: In the report, this is a generic word for the table, crosstab, and charts.

BO: An acronym for Business Objects; *see* Business Objects (BO).

Business intelligence (BI): A somewhat generic term used for computer programs that store, analyze, and broadcast data to users to answer business questions. Frequently abbreviated as *BI*.

Business Objects (BO): The name of the company that provides the Business-Objects XI Release 2 suite. This is the former name of DeskIntelligence.

BusinessObjects: The business-intelligence (BI) suite of applications from Business Objects (note the space).

Cache: A small area of your computer's hard drive used for temporary storage of frequently or recently used data. A prime example is the Internet Explorer cache. For performance and security reasons, caches should be regularly emptied.

Canned reports: An informal term for pre-packaged Web Intelligence documents or reports. When you create your BusinessObjects environment, you can provide a number of canned reports that are made available automatically to other users so they don't have to create them.

Cardinality: The minimum and maximum number of times an event or occurrence can take place between two distinct entities. The cardinality between Country and City tables is 1,n; a city belongs to only one country, and a country owns many cities.

CCM: *See* Central Configuration Manager (CCM).

Central Configuration Manager (CCM): The console where all BusinessObjects services are managed, where you can start, stop, enable, and disable services.

Central Management Console (CMC): The Web application where the administrator defines users, groups, security, right management, and other tasks.

Central Management Server (CMS): The server and its associated service where all objects are stored (document, universes, dashboards, connections).

Class: A group of objects within a BusinessObjects universe. You can create a class to better organize a set of objects.

CMC: *See* Central Management Console (CMC).

CMS: *See* Central Management Server (CMS).

Common Warehouse Metamodel (CWM): This specification describes metadata interchange among data warehousing, business intelligence, knowledge management, and portal technologies. This XML model is used by Universe Builder to automatically create universes and by Data Integrator to export its model.

Conditions: These are also known as *query filters*; they are used to restrict the number of fetched rows from the database server. It is composed of an object, an operator, and operands.

Cookie: A text file that a Web site gives your Web browser when you first visit the Web site. This text file is updated with information about you and your computer during your visit. For security and performance reasons, you should regularly clear your list of cookies. This is especially true if you're using a public or shared computer.

Corporate documents: These are Web Intelligence documents or reports that are made available to other users in your BusinessObjects environment.

Corporate hierarchy: These are document categories or hierarchies that are expressed in InfoView as collapsible menus/categories.

Crosstab: A table displaying data as columns and rows as well as their corresponding intersection.

Cube: This is where data is stored in OLAP. In BusinessObjects, however, it is part of the document where query results are stored before being displayed in the document.

CWM: *See* Common Warehouse Metamodel (CWM).

Dashboard: This is a business application that gives users a macro and summarized view of the activity trends for their company.

Data Integrator (DI): This is an ETL tool provided by Business Objects. Its primary applications are the DI Designer, DI Repository Manager, and DI Web Administrator.

Data mart: A specialized type of data warehouse that works with a specific set of data to answer a specific need. A data mart is designed to provide quick, easy access to crucial data.

Data provider: A system that brings data from data sources to documents in BusinessObjects. This can include, for example, SQL scripts or universe queries.

Data Source Name (DSN): A data structure (containing the name and structure of a database being used as a data source) that enables a standard ODBC driver to connect to the database.

Data warehouse: A logical warehouse of data that gathers production and operational information from various departments of a corporation into a single data entity. This information is loaded regularly, which allows for careful analysis over a period of time.

Designer: *a)* An application used to create and edit universes in BusinessObjects. *b)* An application used in Data Integrator to access repositories.

DeskI: *See* Desktop Intelligence (DeskI).

Desktop Intelligence (DeskI): A full-client (desktop) application, installed with the BusinessObjects suite of applications, that allows reporting and analysis. *See also* Web Intelligence.

Detail: An element associated with a dimension that provides additional information on the dimension within an object.

Detail object: An object associated with a dimension object.

DHTML: *See* Dynamic Hypertext Markup Language (DHTML).

DI: *See* Data Integrator (DI).

Dimension: In data analysis, a specific perspective based on a business concept (such as product line, sales period, and so on).

Dimension object: An object that corresponds to a specific business concept, used to retrieve the data to be used in analysis and included in a document created after a query.

Document: A file in BusinessObjects that can contain several reports.

Drill: To analyze query results by clicking a link to access a closer, more detailed view of performance data. For example, you could drill from a State level to a City level in a query.

Dynamic filters: These filters allow you to satisfy conditions using formulas so specific data is displayed. For example, you can create a formula that tells the filter to display only stores that had over 1,500 transactions per month.

Dynamic Hypertext Markup Language (DHTML): These HTML pages provide content, using Javascript and style sheets (such as CSS).

ETL: *See* Extraction, Transformation, and Loading (ETL).

eXtensible Markup Language (XML): A markup language (a more advanced descendant of HTML) that uses tags for organizing content.

Extraction, Transformation, and Loading (ETL): The very essence of business intelligence, this is the process of removing raw data from a data system, processing and cleaning it, and then making it available in a business-intelligence database.

Formulas: A BusinessObjects language that allows users to manipulate and transform data. A formula can be used inside a variable. Note that syntax between DeskI and WebI is different.

Full-client document: A document created in BusinessObjects using the Desktop Intelligence application.

Function: A predefined formula in Web Intelligence that is used on document values.

Hierarchy: A ranking of dimensions in multidimensional analysis or in a universe, an object organization defining a path used during drilling operation.

HTML: *See* Hypertext Markup Language (HTML).

HTTP: *See* Hypertext Transfer Protocol (HTTP).

Hypertext Markup Language (HTML): A generic language for publishing content online, using hypertext.

Hypertext Transfer Protocol (HTTP): This standard is used for publishing hypertext documents over the Internet.

InfoView: A portal that allows you to navigate within your documents, create, organize, and manage them.

Internet: The worldwide system of interconnected computers, accessible to millions of people around the world and containing, but not limited to, the World Wide Web.

Intranet: A private internal network for a company. An intranet is Web-based and provides content that is available only to authorized users on the company's network.

Internet Protocol (IP): Part of the TCP/IP protocol, the IP portion moves data from node to node.

Java: A multi-platform language created by Sun Microsystems, used to create an applet.

Javascript: A script language used to create interactive content that is embedded in HTML files.

Join: *a)* In a universe, an operation that combines two distinct tables with a common domain. For example, two tables that both feature a `user_id` column can be joined. *b)* In Desktop Intelligence or Web Intelligence, a way to combine data when a data provider executes more than one query (multiple measure, context in the data provider). This method occurs when all queries have the same dimension. *See also* Synchronization.

LDAP: *See* Lightweight Directory Access Protocol (LDAP).

Lightweight Directory Access Protocol (LDAP): A protocol used to find organizations, people, or devices online.

Linked universes: BusinessObjects universes that feature shared objects, classes, contexts, and so on.

List of Values (LOV): A list of specific data values associated with an object in Web Intelligence or in Desktop Intelligence documents.

Load balancing: A way of redirecting incoming requests to machines with less traffic in order to accommodate more users in the BusinessObjects environment.

Measure: A name for objects and report variables that use the aggregate function, which performs calculations on data.

Measure object: An object that gets numeric data (or also date info) that comes from calculations performed in the database.

Microcube: A small cube embedded in BusinessObject's document. *See also* Cube.

Multi-level dimension: A dimension with multiple levels of detail.

Nesting: Placing a logical item within another logical item — for example, a List of Values within another List of Values.

Object: An element in a BusinessObjects universe that corresponds to an item of data in a relational or OLAP database, mapped by using terms that are meaningful to business users. Objects can be grouped together in classes.

ODBC: *See* Open Database Connectivity (ODBC).

Offline mode: Working only with BusinessObjects items stored directly on your local computer (such as DeskI documents, local universes, and imported universes) without any connection to your CMS. You can still access the remote database but you can't import/export universe, or publish and retrieve document from your CMS.

OLAP: *See* Online Analytical Processing (OLAP).

Online Analytical Processing (OLAP): A category of software tools used to analyze data stored in a database by looking at multiple dimensions of consolidated data.

Online mode: In BusinessObjects, the default way of working by connecting to the repository and use all the repository content; the repository need not be stored on your local computer.

Open Database Connectivity (ODBC): A standard database-access method that acts as a middle layer (called a *database driver*) between any application and any database-management system.

Operand: In a query filter or condition, an operand explains with what the object will be compared. For example, perhaps a constant, a constant coming from a LOV, or a prompt.

Operator: An item in a filter query, a condition, or in the formula language that describes how the object relates to the operand. Examples include Equal To, Less Than, Between, Matches Pattern, Both, and Except.

Outer join: While a join combines records from two tables in a database into a temporary, "joined" table, the peculiarity of an outer join is that it does not require matching records in *both* joined tables.

Parse: In the processing of a SQL statement, the checking of syntax and object validation before retrieving the relevant information. In BusinessObjects, this operation is used to check the validity of your SQL from Query Panels, universe objects, and universe joins.

PDF: *See* Portable Document Format (PDF).

Performance Management: A suite of tools that is used in BusinessObjects to create and edit dashboards, metrics, analytics, goals, and so on.

Personal document: A document you save in your personal document-storage area on the server, to be used only by you.

Portable Document Format (PDF): A file format that enables you to read a document on any computer platform using Adobe Acrobat.

Portal: A Web site that typically aggregates information from a range of sites and other sources. The BusinessObjects portal is InfoView.

Portlet: A user-interface component that includes markup code from an external source (often another Web page) in a Web portal.

Prompt: The point in a query condition or filter at which you enter or select a value in order to advance the query. A prompt can be filled at every document refresh.

Proxy: A server that handles requests from its clients by forwarding them to other servers.

Publish: Saving a document to make it available to other users.

Purge: Deleting the data returned by a List of Values or a query, without deleting the List of Values or query itself.

Query: A type of data provider used to obtain information from a database. You build queries containing objects from a universe, and then run them to create a document. A term used in Web Intelligence, this is the same as a condition.

Query result: The data returned by a query. *See also* Result object.

RDBMS: *See* Relational Data Base Management System.

Refresh: Updating the data returned by a document's query.

Relational Data Base Management System: This is the most-known database system where the main vendors are Oracle, MySQL, SQL server, Teradata, and Sybase.

Report: A graphical and textual rendering of data from one or multiple sources, produced and distributed for viewing, analysis, and formatting.

Report Panel: Java applet or ActiveX control that you use to build your queries and format your documents.

Repository: A central place where metadata (such as universe and security information) is stored and maintained.

Resource: Any data that can be accessed over the Web, including text, images, and executable files.

Result object: The object included in a query. *See also* Query result.

Schema: A collection of tables, indexes, views, and so on in a database.

Semantic layer: Patented by Business Objects in 1990, this networking layer shields you from the complexity inherent in many database structures by letting you come up with names for tables and columns that are meaningful to you — which are then superimposed on the real structure of the database.

Shortcut join: Used in a schema with redundant joins that lead to the same result.

Skin: A predefined look and feel for software features. You can choose skins for InfoView, Web Intelligence, and Dashboards and change how your reports appear.

Slice and Dice mode: A way of working by changing the structure of each block inside your report so you can examine the data from different viewpoints to understand it better. You cannot move, add, or remove a block from the slice and dice; you can transform a table to a crosstab, but not remove it.

Sort: Forcing the data obtained from objects in queries and in different report blocks to appear in ascending or descending order, or ordering documents by name, author, date, or size.

SQL: *See* Structured Query Language (SQL).

Standalone setup: An installation of BusinessObjects that requires no network connections, enabling you to work in offline mode if you choose.

Structured Query Language (SQL): The syntax that lets you define and manipulate data from a relational database.

Subquery: A query nested inside a main query.

Synchronization: A way of combining data when a data provider executes more than one query (multiple measures or context in the same data provider). This method occurs when all queries don't have the same dimension. *See also* Join.

Table: A type of block that displays data in columns and rows.

Thin-client document: A document created when you generate reports in Web Intelligence, called *thin-client* because it requires less software installed on your local machine. *See also* Full-client document.

Time dimension: Time considered as a business dimension, broken down into standard subdivisions such as Year, Quarter, Month, or Day or monitoring time data in EPM modules.

Timeout: The length of time a user has to connect, read, or write to a network before the attempt to complete the transaction is stopped.

Uniform Resource Locator (URL): An address that specifies where to find a resource, such as an Web page or an image, on a network. Often, this may simply be the address of a Web page, such as `http://www.dummies.com`.

UNION: In SQL, an operator that combines the results of two queries into a single result.

Universe: In BusinessObjects, the semantic layer between a user and a database, made up of classes and objects. Objects in a universe correspond to items of data in the database and are used by users to build their queries.

Universe designer: The user responsible for creating and maintaining universes.

URL: *See* Uniform Resource Locator (URL).

User account: An individual account created within the repository that dictates what each unique user is authorized to do.

User group: A group of users who have access to a specified document domain in the repository, as defined by the Supervisor.

Variable: A document element that corresponds to a formula based on objects returned by a data provider, as well as other variables and functions.

Web Intelligence (WebI): The Business Objects tool that lets you perform ad-hoc queries, reporting, and analysis over an intranet, extranet, or the Internet. A Web-based application in BusinessObjects that allows you to perform reporting and analysis using your universes. You can create, refresh, edit, send, or distribute documents and reports with InfoView.

Web server: A computer that hosts Web pages, scripts, programs, and other files, making them available over an intranet, extranet, or the Internet to client software that runs on other computers.

WebI: *See* Web Intelligence (WebI).

XML: *See* eXtensible Markup Language (XML).

Index